THE POETRY OF THE POSSIBLE

THE POETRY OF THE POSSIBLE

Spontaneity, Modernism, and the Multitude

JOEL NICKELS

 University of Minnesota Press
Minneapolis
London

Portions of chapter 2 were previously published as "Anti-Egoism and Collective Life: Allegories of Agency in Wyndham Lewis' *Enemy of the Stars*," *Criticism* 48, no. 3 (Summer 2006): 347–73. Portions of chapter 4 were previously published as "Wallace Stevens' *Owl's Clover* and the Dialectic of Deceit," *Arizona Quarterly* 64, no. 4 (2008): 103–28; reprinted with permission of the Regents of the University of Arizona. Portions of the Conclusion were previously published as "The Art of Interruption: William Carlos Williams and New Materialist Poetics," *Paideuma* 35, no. 3 (Spring 2009): 35–52; originally published and reprinted with permission of the National Poetry Foundation.

Poetry by William Carlos Williams copyright 2012 by the Estates of Paul H. Williams and William Eric Williams. Copyright 1946, 1948, 1949, 1959 by William Carlos Williams. Reprinted by permission of New Directions Publishing Corporation.

Poetry by Laura Riding from *The Poems of Laura Riding* by Laura (Riding) Jackson. Copyright 1938, 1980 by Laura (Riding) Jackson. Reprinted by permission of Persea Books, Inc., New York, and the Board of Literary Management of the late Laura (Riding) Jackson. In conformity with the wishes of the late Laura (Riding) Jackson, her Board of Literary Management asks us to record that, in 1941, Laura (Riding) Jackson renounced, on the grounds of linguistic principle, the writing of poetry: she had come to hold that "poetry obstructs general attainment to something better in our linguistic way-of-life than we have."

Poetry by Wallace Stevens from *The Collected Poems of Wallace Stevens* by Wallace Stevens. Copyright 1954 by Wallace Stevens and renewed 1982 by Holly Stevens. Reprinted by permission of Alfred A. Knopf, a division of Random House, Inc. "Owl's Clover" from *Opus Posthumous* by Wallace Stevens, edited by Milton J. Bates, copyright 1989 by Holly Stevens. Copyright 1957 by Elsie Stevens and Holly Stevens. Copyright renewed 1985 by Holly Stevens. Reprinted by permission of Vintage Books, a division of Random House, Inc.

Copyright 2012 by the Regents of the University of Minnesota

All rights reserved. No part of this publication may be reproduced, stored in a retrieval system, or transmitted, in any form or by any means, electronic, mechanical, photocopying, recording, or otherwise, without the prior written permission of the publisher.

Published by the University of Minnesota Press
111 Third Avenue South, Suite 290
Minneapolis, MN 55401-2520
http://www.upress.umn.edu

Library of Congress Cataloging-in-Publication Data
Nickels, Joel.
  Poetry of the possible : spontaneity, modernism, and the multitude / Joel Nickels.
  ISBN 978-0-8166-7608-8 (hardback) ISBN 978-0-8166-7609-5 (pb)
  1. American poetry—20th century—History and criticism. 2. English poetry—20th century—History and criticism 3. Spontaneity (Philosophy) in literature. 4. Modernism (Literature)—United States. 5. Modernism (Literature)—England. I. Title.
  PS323.5N53   2012
  811'.509—dc23   2011049427

The University of Minnesota is an equal-opportunity educator and employer.

FOR CARRIE

AND FOR ALL THE WORKERS AND STUDENTS
FIGHTING TO SAVE PUBLIC EDUCATION

CONTENTS

Acknowledgments ix

Introduction: Modernism and Spontaneous Organization   1

1 Rising from Nowhere
   Self-Valorization in William Carlos Williams's Poetry   47

2 Wyndham Lewis, Constituent Power, and Collective Life   91

3 "An Instantaneous Sympathy of Communication"
   Laura Riding and the Politics of Spontaneity   133

4 Rhapsodies of Change
   The Location of the Multitude in Wallace Stevens's Poetry   181

   Conclusion: Beginning Again   219

   Notes   227
   Index   265

ACKNOWLEDGMENTS

Behind every page of this book is a human relationship that made the writing possible, intellectually, practically, and spiritually. At the University of California at Berkeley, Kaja Silverman's tireless aid and mentorship helped make me the scholar I am today; I'm lucky to be able to call her a friend. Charles Altieri supported my development in countless ways, and I'm grateful for his attention and feedback. Barrett Watten, Anthony Cascardi, and Joseph Jeon have my thanks for engaging helpfully with my work. My associates at *Qui Parle* and the many diehards who attended meetings of Phenomenology Now also have my thanks, along with the Doreen B. Townsend Center for the Humanities, which supported these forms of intellectual community.

This project was supported by fellowships from the University of California at Berkeley English Department, the Andrew W. Mellon Foundation, the University of California Regents, Phi Beta Kappa, the University of Miami Office of the Provost, and the University of Miami Center for the Humanities.

I am grateful to Jennifer Scappettone, Michelle Neely, Liz Young, Ted Martin, Annie McClanahan, Charles Sumner, Monika Gehlawat, and Jasper Bernes for the sustaining dialectic of friendship; to Joshua Clover, Trane Devore, and Jen Neuber for being there; and to Chris Chen and Chris Daniels for nights of Scriabin and Sonny Chiba. My new Miami community has helped me thrive in this city of dragon fruit and plate glass; thanks to everyone who has dropped by for French toast and bocce, come to an opening, sat through *Zardoz*, or convened at Fritz and Franz. I'm especially grateful to Frank Palmeri, Mihoko Suzuki, Ranen Omer-Sherman, Joe Alkana, Pat McCarthy, and Walter Lew for their mentorship roles; to Tim Watson and David Luis-Brown, my go-to men; to Brenna

Munro, a true friend; and to John Funchion, the guy who will read your introduction and then rescue you when your car breaks down in the Everglades.

Above all, I owe my happiness and creative optimism to Carrie Sieh, my heart's desire and the center of my world. My love, you make everything possible.

INTRODUCTION
Modernism and Spontaneous Organization

"SPONTANEITY" MIGHT NOT BE THE FIRST WORD that comes to mind in relation to modernist literature. After all, the term "spontaneity" brings to mind aeolian harps and sentimental raptures of various kinds— models of literary agency that had lost much of their credibility with authors we tend to describe as "modernist." In fact, the very idea that it is possible, let alone desirable, to act spontaneously in any conventional sense is treated with suspicion by many modernist authors. Spontaneous actions are typically defined as those that proceed from a "natural feeling, temperament," or "native internal proneness"[1] "without external stimulus or constraint."[2] Such an idea of spontaneity implies an unmediated, natural inwardness that lies outside the external constraints of shared social meaning systems. The modernists I examine in this book all question this idea of spontaneity, because they suspect that ultimately it may be impossible to separate "spontaneous" internal thought patterns from external social mediations.

I focus on William Carlos Williams, Wyndham Lewis, Laura Riding, and Wallace Stevens in this book, because each is especially sensitive to the ways socially conditioned responses can shape even one's deepest, most private cognitive and affective orientations, making them seem like natural, spontaneous dispositions. Williams describes this deep conditioning in terms of one's being "pretwisted in the underlying depths of [one's] brain";[3] Riding describes it in terms of "prearranged responses" that masquerade as "a general spontaneity of response."[4] In other words, these authors believe that acting in a natural-seeming, unpremeditated fashion may provide for no real spontaneity, only pretwisted affective outpourings.

Images of this kind of pseudospontaneity are everywhere to be found in the modernists I examine. Wyndham Lewis, in particular, produces a host of pseudospontaneous characters and types. The "contemporary man" of Western democracy, for example, who is always invited to express his "inalienable, mysterious 'personality,'" does not realize that what he is expressing is largely "a pattern imposed on [him] by means of education and the hypnotism of cinema, wireless, and press."[5] In a totally administered social environment, then, expressing oneself "spontaneously," without forethought, means consenting to become a "disinterested machine, ecstatically obedient" to the "principle of authority."[6]

And yet, modernist models of artistic production seem to demand some account of spontaneous creation, some way of describing how creative impulses take shape and become publicly intelligible. Laura Riding refers to a "spontaneous essence of humanness" that artists seek to express;[7] Lewis describes the creative will as something that "pretend[s] to rise spontaneously in the body of the world or of the crowd";[8] William Carlos Williams describes himself as a "rudderless nonentity" in dialogue with unconscious pulsions;[9] and Wallace Stevens describes poetry as a music that comes to the poet "in sounds not chosen, / Or chosen quickly... eked out / By the spontaneous particulars of sound."[10] Indeed, as Daniel Belgrad points out, "the spontaneous gesture, understood as an act of freedom originating in the unconscious," is central to modernist aesthetics, as well as to postwar literary, musical, and painterly avant-gardes.[11] So what did modernists have in mind when they invoked the idea of spontaneity? If the idea of natural inward tendencies, cordoned off from the corrupting mediations of the social world, no longer furnishes a credible model of spontaneity, what does?

In this book, I argue that Williams, Lewis, Riding, and Stevens locate spontaneity less in isolated, individual minds than in sites where individual mental impulses overlap with modernity's large-scale mechanisms of public contestation and collective life. In other words, they tend to identify spontaneous creation less with private internal processes than with public spaces where collective powers of judgment and mediation can be exercised. Parks, workplaces, and city streets often furnish the physical locations for these collective processes, but in the works I consider, it is less the physical geographies of collective life that are at issue than the partly real, partly imaginary networks of human faculties, energies, and affects that subtend these geographies.

Sometimes this collective potentiality is imagined as the metabolism of an abstract social body, as in Williams's *Paterson;* sometimes it is imagined as a "subman" existing beneath the surface of existing social institutions, as in Stevens's "Owl's Clover." But in each of the works I consider, some *virtual public* exists beneath or between the lines of modernity's crowds and standardized cityscapes.[12] This alternate public and its alternate social sphere constitute this book's object of analysis—an unstable object, to be sure, since in the modernist works I examine, it often exists only as a spectral presence. But at the same time, this other public—this host of faculties and creative potencies that can find no expression in the institutional cultures of modernity—tends to be invested with exceptional power by modernist authors. It is most often represented as a vast reservoir of untapped energy—a wellspring of creative spontaneity from which the modernist must continually derive impetus and direction.

Making this claim means reassessing modernism's highly ambivalent attitudes toward individuality, mass politics, and creative production. Wyndham Lewis, for example, is most well-known for his claims that the multitude embodies nothing more than a "passive . . . rhythmic, mechanical life" and that artists must cultivate a principle of individuality that will allow them to resist its life patterns.[13] In a 1925 essay titled "The Foxes' Case," however, Lewis asserts that great artistic personalities are spawned by "the consciousness of the crowd"—that "if a thousand people could have a child, as two people can have a child, he would be rather like Shakespeare or Newton, or some other great 'personality,' according to the quality of the crowd."[14] In his 1925 "Physics of the Not-Self," Lewis describes a "disintegrated *not-self* principle" that allows individuals to participate in the collective life of their society, acting as dissolvents of social barriers and helping to awaken the critical powers of the multitude.[15] For this less well-known Lewis, it is only broad and sustained contact with their fellows that allows individuals to express their "untaught, spontaneous" faculties.[16] Spontaneity in this context is synonymous with an "eccentric play of the 'personality'" in which one may "pass from place to place and man to man at will (which would be the dispensation most favourable to elasticity and life)."[17] Lewis's idea of spontaneity is thus intertwined with forms of social mediation, critique, and interpersonal contact. It is a public, political form of spontaneity more than a private, internal one.[18]

The other modernists I consider also redefine spontaneity in some surprising ways, approaching it as a collective phenomenon in which the artist can participate only by venturing outside the habitual thought patterns of his or her individual ego. William Carlos Williams, for example, refers to himself as an "interpreter" whose "aspirations... arise from the people," not from a purely individual enclave of feeling.[19] In fact, Williams suggests that spontaneous creation requires a subjective death on the part of the artist, that the artist "keeps alive by losing his life, in a brutal sense, and losing it by making 'plays,' objects, realities which he has to abandon to make another, and another."[20]

Similarly, Laura Riding imagines a social utopia in which political order would be "spontaneously generated within the social substance" of "civically located" groups.[21] One of the new roles of artists in this society would be to serve as guarantors of this collective spontaneity, fostering an "instantaneous sympathy of communication" between different social elements.[22] But in order to serve this role, the artist must liquidate his or her sense of being a "personality-coloring... a lone peculiarity among others" and "a private sanctuary."[23] What must occur instead is a subjective death similar to what Williams imagines—what Riding describes as a "final, irrevocable, ridding of the self of all with which it is substanced as a center of social identity."[24]

Wallace Stevens, too, uses the word "spontaneity" to describe transpersonal processes. In "Owl's Clover," for example, "spontaneities of rain or snow" represent a process of social dissolution that destroys "an age" equipped only "with appropriate, largely English, furniture" and "barbers with charts of the only possible modes."[25] In this context, spontaneity is attributed to whatever *intrudes upon* the privacies of the individual ego and the stable social affirmations that undergird it.

In all of these cases, spontaneity is no longer defined as an uncensored outpouring of individual feeling. Instead, it is a strangely violent process that begins with an act of self-extinction and is sustained by the deliberate liquidation of everything in one's disposition that is habitual and natural seeming.

This wrenching act of self-extinction provides access to something that I will spend the majority of this book trying to define. Stevens describes it as "the gibberish of the vulgate... the peculiar potency of the general";[26] Lewis describes it as the "common life";[27] Williams describes it as "the collective world";[28] and Riding describes it as "the collective manifestation of Spirit in the total human substance of the time."[29] These phrases all have different emphases, reflecting these authors' often quite divergent philosophical orientations, but they all describe something that is complex, preindividual, nonnatural, and transpersonal. Some origin of artistic spontaneity is being gestured toward in these quotations—one that lies not in the isolated unconscious mind of the artist but in a transpersonal complex of affects, actions, and capacities. In their creative works, these modernists frame themselves as the spokespeople of this transpersonal complex. The more rigorous the artists' acts of self-extinction, the more fully are their own creative capacities imagined to be in the service of this interhuman matrix.

But how, one might ask, does the language of spokesmanship fit in here? Such language suggests that these artists imagine themselves in a political or quasi-political role with respect to the collective world they posit. And yet, this collective world is so loosely defined—as a "gibberish," a "potency," or a "human substance"—that it is difficult to imagine *what* these artists believe themselves to be speaking *for* or how to measure the success of their exponency. Furthermore, it is unclear why these artists believe they must extinguish their selves in order to serve this advocating function. Even if it were possible to imagine what a self-extinguishing self would look like, it would still be unclear why such a process of depersonalization would be regarded as an exemplary process for a spokesperson of any kind to undergo.[30]

In *A Singular Modernity*, Fredric Jameson approaches the idea of depersonalization in a way that promises to help answer some of these questions. Jameson places the concept of depersonalization at the center of his more recent arguments about modernism, claiming that modernism might best be understood as "a programmatic movement away from the psychological and from personal identity itself."[31] This is a surprising claim, given the emphasis that many theories of modernism have placed on "some 'inward turn' of the modern or on its increasing subjectivization of reality" (135).[32] Jameson counters that "the great modernist evocations of subjectivity" are "so much longing for depersonalization, and very precisely for some new existence outside the self, in a world radically transformed and worthy of ecstasy" (136). In other words, modernist evocations of subjectivity are in the service of "a momentum that cannot find resolution within the self, but that must be completed by a Utopian and revolutionary transmutation of the world of actuality itself" (136). In this context, depersonalization is a "psychic allegory": imagining the liquidation of their own thought habits and defense mechanisms allows modernists to evoke a much larger process of social transformation— one that involves "immense new social forces" such as "political suffrage and the growth of labour unions and the various socialist and anarchist movements" that "seem to menace the stifling closure of high bourgeois culture, and to announce some impending enlargement of social space itself" (134). In other words, the depersonalization that modernists continually stage is a way to imagine the demise of an immense network of social regulations, prohibitions, and estrangements that isolate the individual from the transpersonal political pulsions that are coming on the scene of modernity.

This helps explain why modernist ideas of spontaneity so often involve a process of depersonalization. Only by unlearning the thought habits of individualist society will modernists be fit to channel the transformative collective energies to which Jameson makes reference. What is still unclear, however, is how exactly modernists conceived of these collective energies, which social groups they located them in, and what kinds of political agency their own acts of depersonalization were supposed to make imaginable. When Jameson refers to political suffrage, labor unions, and socialist and anarchist movements, he is describing the impact on modernism of social groups that stood at the margins of political representation, but that were beginning to develop organizational logics of their own: working people, women, and the large number of unemployed and disenfranchised inhabiting modernity's cities. But this leaves us with a matrix of political forces that is highly various and differentially organized. How to imagine the transformative thrust of this differential political matrix without reducing it to any of its constituent parts?

In this book I use the term "the multitude" to describe this differential complex of political forces. The term is useful because it does not refer simply to the numerical human populations who were mobilized by the forces of industrial modernity. It also refers to the unrealized powers of association, counsel, and social recombination that exist *potentially* within this collective body. Thus Michael Hardt and Antonio Negri define the multitude both as "all those who work under the rule of capital" and as a "living social flesh," a "pure potential... an elemental power that continuously expands social being, producing in excess of every traditional political-economic measure of value."[33] They describe the multitude in these terms to emphasize the fact that the multitude does not simply produce goods and services but also "produces cooperation, communication, forms of life, and social relationships."[34] That is, the multitude produces a "common" that is defined not simply by static social conventions but also by capacities for creative interaction and social arrangement that vastly exceed what is concretely realizable in modernity's bureaucratized social institutions.

When it comes to modernist fantasies about the collective world and the artist's capacity to act as its spokesperson, the multitude is thus a very fruitful concept. On one hand, "the multitude" refers to specific populations created and dispersed by the forces of industrial modernity, populations set adrift from the land, with nothing to sell but their labor power and no material investment in the social order that governs their everyday lives.[35] On the other hand, the multitude is a philosophical concept as much as a sociological one. It describes not so much any concrete associational tendency or movement as what Paolo Virno calls the "generic, undetermined potential" of the social body.[36] In *A Grammar of the Multitude*, Virno defines this *potenza* of the multitude as a "general intellect": not simply the "know-how on which social productivity relies" but "the totality of poietic, 'political,' cognitive, emotional forces" that compose the "objective, external intellect" of the multitude.[37] In this context, "the multitude" refers not simply to the empirical existence of social beings but to their combined, preindividual capacity for sensual, linguistic, and material recombination. In Virno's terms, the multitude thus embodies a collective "virtuosity" that invisibly subtends the much more rigid, policed social bodies of modernity.

This virtuosity, however, is a fairly abstract phenomenon; it exists primarily as an "apotropaic resource,"[38] which sometimes seems to be semimythic or even theological in character. Indeed, Alex Callinicos sees the entire concept of the multitude as a way to replace "straightforward class analysis" with a form of vitalism that "absolutize[s] the subjectivity of the masses" while approaching "the physical and social world in its entirety as expressions of some underlying life force."[39] In another vein, Ernesto Laclau argues that the concept of the multitude is falsely universalizing—that it ignores "the present proliferation of a plurality of identities" in favor of "a set of unconnected struggles" that, as if by magic, "*spontaneously* converge[ ] in their assault on a systemic center."[40] Timothy Brennan argues that the very idea of a new, global, postindustrial economy, fueled by the "immaterial labor" of the multitude, is a theoretical fiction that bizarrely ignores the "vast manual system of interlocking, armed work farms in the clothing industry, the prison-labor system, massive new infrastructural projects (in the laying of fiber optic cable, for example) ... new arctic drilling ventures ... a *bracero* economy of controlled 'illegal' immigration and the reinstitution of slavery (in the Chinese tenement halls of the United States as well as in rural Sudan and Myanmar)."[41]

In the sphere of political theory, these critiques are on the whole well placed; the idea, for example, that "industrial production is no longer expanding its dominance over other economic forms and social phenomena"[42] is simply unsustainable, given the massive industrialization projects currently occurring across the world; equally problematic is the idea that scientific innovation is somehow more hegemonic in today's economy than it was in the period when electricity, steel construction, and the internal combustion engine revolutionized the production processes and lifeworlds of industrial societies. Such ideas reflect, more than anything, the highly specific mixture of ecstasy and anxiety that accompanied Italy's belated economic restructuring of the mid-1970s and the crisis confronted by groups such as Autonomia Operaia during this period, when their relative isolation from the traditional working class often prompted them to discover "another proletariat" composed of student groups, professional workers, and activists.[43] Nevertheless, within the sphere of modernist aesthetics, the idea of the multitude has an especially strong theoretical purchase, precisely because modernists were facing crises of political leadership and class composition that paralleled those Negri faced in the 1970s.

For these modernists, the idea of the "masses," with its connotations of passivity, irrationality, and manipulability, is indissociably linked to the social figure in which it supposedly finds its fulfillment and directive force: the vanguard party. And like the Negri of the mid-1970s, these modernists were sharply attuned to the authoritarian and bureaucratized quality of many of Europe's and America's vanguard parties. The image of a collective force possessed of latent organizational powers and capable of spontaneous, decentralized decision making—that is, the idea of a multitude, rather than the "masses"—therefore had enormous appeal among many early twentieth-century authors. And since Negri's idea of the multitude is not distinct from that of the proletariat, but is rather an identification of this social figure with the self-organizing potentialities of manual and intellectual workers, his idea of the multitude gives expression to one of modernism's most central visions of collective life: that of a large-scale, mobile, and deracinated productive force, animated by industrial relations of production, but not identical to them, and existing somewhere beyond the univocity of "the people" or "the masses." Unlike these social figures, which achieve coherence only as functions of the nation-state and the vanguard party, respectively, modernism's agents of self-organization are often imagined as a network of manual and intellectual workers, existing outside transcendent apparatuses of power and improvising ever-new configurations of counterpower: social figures best expressed by the idea of an immanently self-ordering *multitude*.

The specific value of the multitude concept to modernist studies can perhaps be most clearly discerned in Negri's differentiation of the idea of the multitude from that of these related social figures. As Negri points out, "*The concept of the people appears in modernity as a production of the state*—'people' understood as the ensemble of property-owning citizens... who have abdicated their freedom in return for a guarantee of their property."[44] "The people" is thus defined by its relationship to the representational apparatus of the state, whereas "the multitude" denotes a potentially self-organizing network of capacities and powers that exists beyond state-sanctioned distributions of rights and duties. Similarly, the concept of "the masses" evokes a sheerly quantitative aggregation of labor power, incapable of self-organization and achieving direction only in the mechanisms of the party, the demagogue, the charismatic genius. Modernist authors struggled to conceptualize human networks that existed beneath such familiar images of collective life—human networks that were not demographically distinct from the proletariat, broadly conceived as the ensemble of social producers, but that express the dynamic and self-organizing creative powers of these producers. Modernists thus seek out the multitude that is hidden within the peoples, masses, and proletariats of the modern world.

The idea of "the multitude" is thus useful to modernist studies because it describes networks of association that came to maturity during the historical period in which modernist authors were writing. Though Negri often suggests that the multitude is a specifically "post-Fordist" phenomenon, in works that predate *Empire* he defines the multitude as "an infinite multiplicity of free and creative singularities" whose "creative force" is "constituent power": the ability to create and undo constituted power structures, which "modern capitalism brings to maturity... by constructing it as the pervasive force of the entire society, as the continuity of a social power that absorbs and configures all other power."[45] In other words, modern capitalism brings the constituent power of the multitude to maturity since it increases "the force of associative productive labor... at such a rate that it begins to become indistinguishable from social activity itself."[46] This observation opens up some fascinating lines of inquiry, for it means that the central phenomena Negri associates with the "post-Fordist" multitude—abstract labor, self-valorization, the general intellect, the socialization of labor, and the real subsumption of social relations by capital—have their origins in social developments with which early twentieth-century authors were particularly obsessed.

Take, for example, the "socialized worker" of the 1960s and 1970s, which according to Negri displaces the "mass worker" of the early and mid-twentieth century. This new proletarian figure, which is a conceptual precursor to Negri's "multitude," contains within itself "invention-power freed from capital and completely subject to the collective human individual." This, we are told, is in marked contrast to the "mass worker" of earlier decades, which "objectively demanded external political mediation" in the form of the Leninist party, which "projected itself as an alternative schema of social management."[47]

Though Negri makes a schematic distinction between the socialized worker, who is capable of self-organization, and the mass worker, who apparently needed the bureaucratic-authoritarian party as an organizational node, Negri derives his idea of the socialized worker from a source that significantly predates the 1960s—namely, Marx's *Grundrisse*, where "socialization" refers to the process whereby labor is revealed in its generality: "labour separated from all means and objects of labour... existing as an *abstraction* from these moments of its actual reality... existing without mediation... the *general possibility* of wealth as subject and as activity."[48] In this context, "socialization" refers to the way that capitalist industry transformed labor from a particularistic, craft-oriented activity into a general social force, and in doing so created "the material elements for the development of the rich individuality which is as all-sided in its production as in its consumption... because a historically created need has taken the place of the natural one."[49] In his lessons on the *Grundrisse*, Negri admits that this "development of labour's creativity" becomes fully active in the period of capitalist industrialization—the period of urbanization, factory labor, and, ultimately, literary modernism.

In his political pamphlets from the 1970s, however, Negri reserves the term "socialized worker," and the image of the spontaneously self-valorizing, immanently creative collectivity, for workers of his own generation. He does this, in part, because in the mid-1970s, Italy's radical movements, including *operaismo*, had difficulty reaching members of the industrial working class, despite the importance the movements accorded to them on a theoretical level; the idea of a postindustrial multitude thus provided hope for a struggle that would be conducted beyond the very palpable divide that separated Italy's student activists and militants from the traditional working class. In a complementary way, the idea of the multitude helps gloss over the differences in expectations and means of intellectual and manual workers—resolving them into a self-creating network without the hierarchy of leadership and led that Negri claims early twentieth-century movements needed.

A closer look at much early twentieth-century literature, however, reveals an ambivalence about hierarchically structured parties at least as profound as Negri's, and an eagerness to imagine exactly the kinds of networks of intellectual and manual labors Negri describes. In "Owl's Clover," for example, Stevens describes a group of politically evolving workers in a park as "sleepless sleepers moved / By the torture of things that will be realized"; then he adds, "but how and all of them asking how / And sighing" (92). In describing these workers as "sleepless sleepers," Stevens attributes to them robust powers of intuitive recalibration; they appear as a *multitude* capable of exercising spontaneous powers of intuition and reflection. But when Stevens reminds himself of the "pay-roll water-falls" (93) that supposedly limit these workers' imaginative horizons, he despairs of their ability to realize their collective intuitions and shifts his focus to the imaginative journey of the poet himself—to the individual, synthetic will that must supplement the spontaneity of the multitude.

At moments like these, it is not clear whether the term "multitude" should be applied simply to the workers Stevens represents, to the workers as focalized through the imagination of the modernist, or to some imaginary fraternity in which workers and modernists both participate. At different times in the texts I examine in this book, it seems appropriate to apply the term "the multitude" to each of these things, since modernists sometimes imaginatively merge with the multitude they represent and sometimes stand apart from it, posing as its directive will. This ambiguity is precisely what Ellen Minkins Wood and Michael Rustin critique Negri for: conflating intellectual and manual workers into the continuum of the multitude, all the while ignoring the very real differences in their conditions of existence.[50] I have adopted the term "multitude," therefore, as a way to explore both the blind spots and the immense speculative power of modernism's own models of intellectual and material recombination.

"The multitude" is my name for a *problem* that modernists confronted as they situated themselves with respect to collective existence in the early twentieth century. This problem has to do with who the imaginary agent of society's creative *potenza* is. At some point or another, all of the modernists I consider imaginatively identify themselves with the collective power of large groups of people. Imagining themselves as disruptive and recombinative social forces, acting outside established social institutions, these modernists tend to align their creative powers with the multitude's capacity to undo current power structures and search for new ways of ordering social life. At the same time, however, they often see themselves as autonomous agents within the multitude—as only partially or experimentally identified with it. In this context, the spontaneity of the individual artist is framed as a way to walk abroad in the multitude's midst, intuit its deep pulsions, and then "oversee" the expression of these impulses in the work of art. Such a model of agency allows modernists to position themselves as conduits of the multitude's collective energy without sacrificing their artistic autonomy in any irreversible way. But it also places the artist in a delicate position vis-à-vis the multitude.

Such partial, tenuous identifications with the spontaneity of the multitude resemble all too clearly the early twentieth century's various forms of authoritarian governance, which similarly attempted to pass themselves off as collectivist manifestations. The ambition of modernists to serve as spokespeople of the multitude, while developing only an experimental, strategic relationship to them, thus resembles the populist pretensions of pseudodemocratic leaders—the complex ruses that allow ruling elites to pass off their decisions as the *volonté de tous*.

That their artistic orientations toward the multitude possessed this potentially damning political association was not lost on modernists such as Williams, Lewis, Riding, and Stevens. To varying degrees, therefore, each was attracted to one of the classic modernist solutions to this problem, namely, reintensified depersonalization on the part of artist—the attempt to strip oneself *absolutely* of individualistic colorings, so as to serve as a "pure" vessel of the multitude. However, when contemplating the subjective zero point of this evacuating process, all of the modernists I consider experience moments of social panic. In this mode, they are less afraid of the authoritarian implications of their own models of agency than the chaos they imagine would result if their autonomous intellectual powers were drowned in the collective body of the multitude. Imagining a complete merger with the multitude, a complete absorption in its pulsions, tends to transform the image of the multitude as a potential ordering force into the image of a terrifying, suffocating mass, unable to achieve direction without the artist as a subjective focal point. The *multitude*, in other words, often becomes a *mob* the moment the artist ceases to imagine him- or herself as its centralized, directive will.

What is fascinating about this ambivalent dialectic between the modernist and the multitude is that it perfectly rescripts the dialectic between centralized leadership and collective initiative that dominated debates about political spontaneity in the early twentieth century. At the center of these debates is a double image of the social body very similar to the one we find in modernist texts. In essays such as Lenin's "The Spontaneity of the Masses and the Consciousness of the Social-Democrats" and Georg Lukács's "The Spontaneity of the Masses and the Activity of the Party," the masses appear as a powerful but fundamentally disorganized force, capable of "once-and-for-all, sudden and unmediated" actions but unable to "accelerate and provoke development" in the way the vanguard party can.[51] "Spontaneity" is typically used with a pejorative inflection in this context, synonymous with "mechanically and automatically conducted struggles" that "cease spontaneously when their immediate objectives appear to be realized or unattainable."[52] In these texts, the term "the masses" is used to represent a social figure from whose reflexlike reactions the vanguard party must retain a degree of autonomy. The party must not fully identify itself with the spontaneous pulsions of the masses, or the masses will be left without a centralized will to provide them direction.

In works such as Rosa Luxemburg's "Was Weiter" and *The Russian Revolution*, however, the "spontaneous, so to speak improvised capacity for action" of the "unorganized popular masses" is imagined as a primary force of social change that is capable of self-direction.[53] Such spontaneity is not incommensurable with political discipline, according to Luxemburg. On the contrary, "the most important and fruitful changes in ... tactical policy during the last ten years have not been the inventions of several leaders and even less so of any central organizational organs. They have always been the spontaneous product of the movement in ferment," an expression of the "spontaneous coordination of the conscious, political acts of a body of men."[54] Here, Luxemburg allies the idea of spontaneity to a social agent fundamentally different from Lenin's and Lukács's masses, a collective figure quite proximate to what will later be described as the multitude—an immanent ordering force that, even at the level of "tactical policy," should direct the revolutionary movement as a whole.

What is at issue in this debate, then, is whether the masses can in fact function as a *multitude*, that is, as a network of singularities capable of sustained self-organization. The idea of spontaneity is central to this debate; whether it is employed in a derogatory or a celebratory way, it describes political action undertaken by human networks outside established political institutions. Indeed, the question here is whether the multitude can *organize* its political activity *spontaneously*—whether its political manifestations must remain spontaneous in the sense of being spasmodic and superficial, or whether they might be spontaneous in the sense of being part of a sustained creative evolution.

Contemporary multitude theorists have inherited this early twentieth-century problematic concerning spontaneity—a problematic that is visible in the conceptual seesawing they display in using the term. In Negri's political pamphlets from the 1970s, this ambivalence about the category of spontaneity is directly tied to the importance he accords to the vanguard party. In "Workers' Party against Work," for example, Negri celebrates the "spontaneous forms of behavior of [the] unified and associated working class," in which the "refusal to accept the rules of training for abstract labor" is visible.[55] But in an earlier pamphlet he had already cautioned that "action by the mass organisms alone is blind" and that "subjective initiative" therefore "needs to be pressed toward centralization and the organizational formalization of the vanguard; even—in certain cases—toward the liberation of the subjective vanguards from preconstituted levels of autonomy and class spontaneity which, having been fundamental in the struggle over the wage, now run the risk of becoming suffocating."[56]

This line of argument repeatedly steers Negri into the Leninist antinomy between "blind" proletarian spontaneity, which is supposedly focused exclusively on short-term gains, and the tactical savoir faire of the party, which, according to Negri, "has to prove capable of interpreting and directing the mass will to appropriation."[57] With the collapse of Autonomia Operaia in 1977 and 1978, however, Negri begins to rethink this stark antinomy between spontaneity and organization, and in works like *The Politics of Subversion*, he will place more emphasis on forms of organization that are implicit in "the spontaneity of creation, innovation ... and of communicative and productive activity"—in short, in the "cooperative potentialities of social labour."[58] This revaluation of the category of spontaneity reaches a high point in *Insurgencies*, where

Negri magnifies the workers' councils of the Russian Revolution for "their spontaneous capability as organizers of struggle" (278), explicitly contrasting this "socialist self-administration of the masses" (281) to Lenin's "bureaucratic dictatorship of the party" (294). In other words, the Leninist party, which in 1971 seemed like the only organ that could organize the masses, now comes to appear as the principal obstacle to "the creative spontaneity of living labor" (33).

If this political about-face is surprising, it is nevertheless continuous with a long history of similar political reversals performed by twentieth-century artists and thinkers. Autonomia's inability to establish itself as a large-scale directive organ and its corollary isolation for the traditional working class as a whole are in many ways afterimages of the early twentieth century's great revolutionary upsurges and defeats, which often centered on the difficulties parties faced in establishing themselves as integral directive forces of the multitude. Negri's turn to the idea of a spontaneously self-organizing multitude is therefore not unique to the post-Fordist world; it echoes everything from Kropotkin's idea of workers' self-organization to Trotsky's early celebration of the workers' council as "an organization which . . . could immediately involve a scattered mass of hundreds of thousands of people while having virtually no organizational machinery [and] which was capable of initiative and spontaneous self-control."[59] No doubt, many of Negri's ideas about globalization and informatization are specific to the contemporary world, but the core idea of a multitude that is composed of abstract, socialized labor and is capable of spontaneous self-organization forms a broad arc that unites contemporary ontologies of the multitude with the modernist authors who first sought to chronicle its creative potential.

For these modernist authors, the concept of spontaneity formed a crucial bridge between the models of creative agency they hoped to elaborate and the early twentieth-century theories of political organization their work engaged. Indeed, the concept of spontaneity could be said to demarcate a conceptual zone in which modernist ideas about artistic production *are at the same time* modes of speculation about social order and the extent to which it must rely on central mechanisms of power. I have chosen to focus on the problem of spontaneity in modernist literature for precisely this reason. Almost any time modernist authors use the word "spontaneity" or reflect on the status of involuntary pulsions in their work, they begin mobilizing a vocabulary that belongs to the realm of political organization at least as much as to the realm of creative phenomenology. Indeed, what I hope to demonstrate in this book is that the experiential logic of much creative production in the early twentieth century is impossible to disentangle from the social logic that wedded the multitude and the vanguard in a complex and often violent dance.

Williams, Lewis, Riding, and Stevens are particularly useful to this argument because they describe the creative process in more detail than do many other poets and dramatists of the multitude. In doing so, they show that even modernists for whom the multitude often seems little more than an equivocal background presence can hardly broach the topic of creative production without simultaneously broaching the topic of collective life and its modes of organization. Indeed, it sometimes seems as if the very ambivalence of these authors about collective spontaneity causes them to rediscover it in another form in their creative phenomenologies, where it can be made the object of obsessively textured speculation. However this may be, the category of spontaneity has a particularly robust political life in the modernists I consider, to the extent that when they describe and narrativize their own creative processes they should always be suspected of describing and narrativizing powers of recombination that lie well beyond their own inward lives.

To be sure, these narratives are rarely consistent, and they are never wholly sanguine about the creative powers of the multitude. At one moment, Williams will imagine the multitude as a potentially self-regulating organism, and at the next he will claim that only strong individuals can keep political order on behalf of constitutionally irresponsible crowds. At one moment, Lewis will represent the multitude as a "wild body" spontaneously evolving its own rituals and orders, and at the next he will vilify the idiocy of the masses and depict the artist as their inveterate enemy. Similarly, Riding writes in *The World and Ourselves* that "the multitudes cannot experience truth, cannot 'know'" (500). But in *Anarchism Is Not Enough*, she writes of "the co-operative unanimity of the many"—the possibility that "the mob might develop a social regularity, an automatic geometricity" that even a figure such as Wyndham Lewis "might share in without disturbance to his individuality."[60] Such statements indicate that modernist ideas about creative spontaneity are imaginative interventions into a larger political debate about the relationship between centralized direction and collective life in the early twentieth century. Sometimes the multitude appears to modernists as an enormous infant whose spontaneity is in the nature of a reflex reaction: sudden, powerful, but without intelligent direction or staying power. But sometimes the multitude appears capable of generating a cooperative "geometricity," that is, a set of norms and interactive processes that is collectively binding but plastic enough to allow for the expression of highly idiosyncratic creative faculties, even those of an artist such as Lewis.

The point to make here, then, is that the fundamental modes of spontaneous self-organization that Negri attributes to the postmodern multitude are present, in a strong form, in the early twentieth century, as are the dilemmas involving leadership with which Negri wrestles. In modernism, as in contemporary multitude theory, the term "spontaneity" demarcates a complex speculative field in which dilemmas about organization, self-valorization, constituent power, affect, and negativity are continuously in play.

Anxious Utopias

That modernists' ideas about spontaneity would carry these political connotations is not at all surprising, given the importance of the term "spontaneity" in early twentieth-century political discourse. Journals in the cultural orbit of the modernists I analyze repeatedly use the term "spontaneity" to describe political action occurring outside established institutional channels. In 1917, for example, an article in *The Masses* states, "It was wise direction as much as spontaneity that has characterized the Butte strike."[61] And in 1934, Jack Conroy writes in the *Partisan Review* of a fictional labor struggle in California: "When they find during the next day that they have been double-crossed... the men spontaneously vote a strike."[62] These references to political spontaneity are essentially casual and descriptive, but just beneath their surface lies an impassioned debate about leadership and collective initiative that gripped the minds of twentieth-century artists and political thinkers alike.

Often these debates about political spontaneity revolved around the question of how leadership apparatuses could serve as exponents of the multitude while remaining formally distinct from them. In other words, the central modernist question about how artists can express and develop the spontaneity of the multitude while retaining a critical distance from them is taken up, in almost identical terms, by political theorists of the period. Antonio Gramsci is just one of many radical political thinkers to write extensively on the problem of political spontaneity in precisely this way. In *The Prison Notebooks*, he writes, "Can modern theory be in opposition to the 'spontaneous' feelings of the masses?"[63] He answers himself: "A reciprocal 'reduction' so to speak, a passage from one to the other and vice versa, must be possible" (199). According to Gramsci, this reciprocal reduction would occur through "a continual adaptation of the organisation to the real movement, a matching of thrusts from below with orders from above, a continuous insertion of elements thrown up from the depths of the rank and file into the solid framework of the leadership apparatus" (188–89). In other words, spontaneity—the vital, passionate, but unorganized self-assertion of the multitude—requires the directive will of the party lest it "scatter into an impotent diaspora" (152).

Gramsci thus strikes a compromise on the question of spontaneity that we encounter in different forms in many modernist writers. Like Williams, Lewis, Riding, and Stevens, Gramsci worries that in posing as exponents of the multitude, leadership apparatuses could degenerate into bureaucratized, unresponsive entities detached from collective interests. To combat this tendency, Gramsci recommends the political equivalent of modernist depersonalization. He indicates that the philosophy of praxis, like the political party it informs, must "purify itself of intellectualistic elements of an individual character and become 'life'" (330). In other words, the party must merge with the spontaneity of the multitude to such an extent that it can present itself as nothing more than an "auto-reflection on the part of the people—an inner reasoning worked out in the popular consciousness" (126–27).

Gramsci recognizes the dangers of such a political maneuver. It deteriorates all too easily into the empty reassurances of the "totalitarian party," which seeks "by various means to give the impression that it is working actively and effectively as an 'impartial force'" (148). But because large groups of people cannot spontaneously organize themselves, because "there is no organisation without intellectuals" (334), the best remedy for this political malady is constantly renewed acts of self-purification on the part of the leadership apparatus—constant attempts to rid the party of personalistic motives and interests.

The modernists I consider often experiment with such a model of self-liquidation in the aesthetic sphere. Indeed, as Jameson suggests, the impulse toward depersonalization could be viewed as an originary moment of much modernist art practice. But what distinguishes these modernists from so many early twentieth-century theorists of political spontaneity is that they refuse to accept the self-liquidating operations of artists, intellectuals, and leadership apparatuses as the ultimate solution to the problem of political spontaneity and directive agency. Each of the modernists I consider suspects centralized political control far more deeply than Gramsci does, and each attempts to imagine a multitude capable of organizing and directing itself much more energetically than Gramsci does.

What we see in the work of these modernists, then, is a palimpsest of social postures. The idea of a self-liquidating imagination is often tried on as a way to imagine a directive agency that would be free of personalistic distortions. When this posture seems bankrupt, some collective organizational complex often appears on the horizon to take its place. When this collective complex, in turn, threatens to disperse into an impotent diaspora, new directive principles are experimentally advanced. These are then tested for their structural integrity and staying power, and so on, in a process that is almost never linear or internally consistent, and that often falls back paranoiacally on positions it has already rejected.

Williams, for example, can imagine a self-organizing social body only by likening it to a constellation of Freudian component drives—a body not yet centralized around the image of the phallus, and maintaining an androgynetic balance between receptive and productive functions. Lewis ultimately imagines the multitude as organizing itself around the negative space opened up by the missing or dethroned leader. It is as if by stripping the leader naked, the multitude realizes that *it* is the complex of faculties the leader mobilized to ensure his or her rule. An intricate transformation is therefore made possible, which Lewis likens to the metamorphoses of insect life, but which he suspects may be capable of intelligent self-direction in human society.

What these images of a self-transforming multitude make visible is something rarely glimpsed in modernism's landscapes of suffering and alienation. One might call it an anxious utopianism, one that consists less in concrete recommendations than in complex testing operations—measuring the potentiality of the multitude as a function of faculties it is currently prevented from developing. Under these circumstances, it is less a question of whether the multitude is capable of self-direction than of how this potentiality can be made visible despite the fragmentariness and alienation of everyday life. It is a question of how to *figure* something quite resistant to concrete figuration of any kind: a collective recombinative activity that, strictly speaking, does not yet exist.

The Literature of the Multitude

The works I analyze in this book all share this figural ambition, the desire to make visible spontaneous patterns of collective existence that contain the elements of social and artistic order. Williams's epic poem *Paterson*, Lewis's closet drama *Enemy of the Stars*, Riding's lyric poems "Disclaimer of the Person" and "I Am," and Stevens's long poem "Owl's Clover" all represent these virtual orders as implicit in the multitude. As such, these works belong to a subtradition of modernism that might be called the literature of the multitude. One of the prime characteristics of this subtradition is its ambivalence about collective action of all kinds. Too nervous about the power of the multitude to heroize any of its concrete political manifestations, it nevertheless tracks the movements of the multitude with obsessive care, and often with undisguised utopian optimism.

This subtradition is thus distinct in some ways from the magnificent array of committed, overtly revolutionary modernisms that scholars such as Daniel Aaron, Charlotte Nekola, Paula Rabinowitz, Barbara Foley, and Carey Nelson have helped to rediscover.[64] At hardly any point in any of the works I analyze does an obvious political message, or even an obvious political *orientation*, announce itself. The political status of the Social Credit tracts in *Paterson*, the protofascist protagonist of *Enemy of the Stars*, and the authoritarian speaker of "I Am" continue to baffle critics in ways that committed artworks usually try to avoid. Does Williams have a satirizing intent when he inserts in *Paterson* a leaflet—like a poetic "readymade"—that claims: "To win the cold war we must reform our finance system. The Russians understand only force. We must be stronger than they and build more airplanes"?[65] How seriously are we supposed to take the socialist organizer in "Owl's Clover," who says: "The workers do not rise, as Venus rose, / Out of a violet sea. They rise a bit / On summer Sundays in the park, a duck / To a million"?[66] It is extremely difficult to say. Indeed, Williams and Stevens seem to be trying on these political propositions in real time, in a way that seriously detracts from any immediate effect of political suasion they might be striving for.

And yet, the literature of the multitude I analyze is much closer, in its figural ambitions and social attitudes, to what Alan Wald calls "the revolutionary imagination" than to the authoritarian modernisms of figures such as Ezra Pound and F. T. Marinetti.[67] The overt hostility of these figures to multitudes and collectives of all kinds distinguishes them clearly from the authors I analyze. Even Lewis, whose endorsements of fascism place him in the greatest proximity to Pound, advances a prototype of aesthetic cognition for which Pound has unmitigated contempt, a prototype in which the artist moves amid the multitude as a self-abnegating force, attempting to awaken its capacity for critical judgment and collective action. Lewis's description of himself in *Blasting and Bombardiering* as "mix[ing] with the crowd... *to act its mood*" so that he "could persuade its emotion to enter him properly,"[68] along with similar self-descriptions in the work of Williams, Riding, and Stevens, simply has no place in the kind of authority-centered political imagination that sees in collective life nothing more than "multitudes in the ooze, / newts, water-slugs, water-maggots."[69] At the same time, however, the work of Williams, Lewis, Riding, and Stevens is also distinct from committed leftist literature in that it highlights an aesthetic subjectivity determined to act as a "free agent" within the multitude, attempting to deal with its collective energetics directly and plastically, not as part of a political apparatus whose dictates it must observe.[70]

This fantasy of the artist as an *autonomous force* immersed in the multitude is the central link between the works I examine. It is the fiction that permits Williams, Lewis, Riding, and Stevens to imagine the artist's faculties as powers that could provisionally *stand in for* the mechanisms of political rule without ever becoming identical to their concrete functions. Of course, Williams, Lewis, Riding, and Stevens did not invent this fantasy. Indeed, it is one that modernism is difficult to imagine without. Charles Baudelaire's "The Little Old Women," Hugo Ball's "The Sun," Aimé Césaire's *Notebook of a Return to the Native Land*, and André Breton's *Nadja* all participate in this fantasy, which has taken on the stature of a major modernist literary trope. According to the conventions of this trope, the author represents him- or herself as stepping into the street, the arcade, the park, or some other public place in order to establish contact with the multitude and symbolically elaborate its potentialities, usually with reference to the person of the artist him- or herself.

Paterson, Enemy of the Stars, "I Am," "Disclaimer of the Person," and "Owl's Clover" are some of Anglo-American modernism's most important enactments of this trope; this is precisely why they are grouped together in this book. But unlike works such as Arthur Rimbaud's "Parisian Orgy" and Jules Romains's "To the Multitude Which Is Here," there is nothing *ecstatic* about Williams's, Lewis's, Riding's, and Stevens's encounters with scenes of collective life. Instead, these encounters mobilize an array of highly self-critical analytic operations, which are continued in theoretical works connected to the literary works in question: "Owl's Clover" and

Enemy of the Stars are both supplemented by companion essays, *Paterson*'s models of spontaneity are restaged in prose works such as "Against the Weather" and "The Basis of Faith in Art," and from 1941 onward, Riding abandoned poetry altogether, viewing it as merely the first phase of an "autochthonous sponsoring of words" that she would henceforth continue in various forms of theoretical prose.[71]

In this way, the authors I examine announce their critical distance from the models of spontaneity and exponency advanced by the continental avant-gardes. Romains's unanimist exclamation, "Oh multitude! Thy whole soul stands in me,"[72] or the Russian Futurists' vanguardist proclamation, "*We* alone are the *face* of *our* time,"[73] has no equivalent in the works I analyze, whose moments of cosmic rhetoric are so tenuous and awkward that they immediately mobilize forms of self-consciousness and critique. No doubt this signals Anglo-American modernism's distance from the continental vanguard parties of both the right and the left, whose rhetorical forms and modes of organization saturated experimental writing in much of Europe. Radical mass parties of the size and power of the Parti communiste français, the Partito Comunista Italiano, or the Bolshevik Party simply never established themselves in the political universes of Williams, Lewis, Riding, or Stevens, despite the fact that mass actions such as the Seattle General Strike, the Paterson Silk Strike, and the British General Strike of 1926 loomed large in their political imaginations. It is as if the immense power of such networks of resistance, and their lack of a single, centralized party to exercise hegemony over them, helped promote an alternative range of literary fantasies in the Anglo-American world, fantasies that positioned the artist directly in the multitude's midst, as the internal reflection of its latent critical powers, rather than as a charismatic demagogue backed by a small cadre of faithfuls.

This decentralized literary imagination thus allows for highly plastic and internally self-correcting discursive modes, but it also gives rise to a body of literature that feels incomplete, socially and aesthetically. The modernist subtradition I track is composed of decanonized works by major modernist authors and of decanonized authors' major modernist works—a subtradition whose virtuosities are marred by stylistic gaffes and incompletions, and whose fragmentariness often seems unintentional or the result of fatigue. In this book, I explain that the decentered, incomplete feel of this subtradition and its works is part and parcel of their political ontology. When an author such as Stevens writes a long poem about communism, art, and social ferment, or when Williams abandons the terse, antisymbolic style for which he is best known and writes an epic filled with gods, historical deeds, and symbolic presences, he is approaching the multitude in a way that strains his sensibilities and figural resources to the utmost.

The boldness and political clarity of many of the poets of *The Masses* or *The Liberator* are simply not at the disposal of Stevens and Williams, both of whom suspect the centralism and hierarchy of institutional leftism. And yet, unlike modernism's right wing, Stevens and Williams are drawn even closer to *the multitude itself* because of these political suspicions. "Owl's Clover" and *Paterson* approach the multitude as the political dynamo that parties, leadership figures, and revolutionary bureaucracies continually betray and domesticate. They therefore attempt to approach the multitude in the raw, so to speak, not through the tropological filter of what Williams calls "our revolutionary literature."[74] In doing so, however, they sometimes seem to lack any coherent vision of the multitude at all, resorting instead to the nervous layering of political propositions and perspectives we find in "Owl's Clover" and *Paterson*.

Lewis and Riding confront the same problems in *Enemy of the Stars*, "I Am," and "Disclaimer of the Person." In these works, the multitude appears neither as a heroized political unity nor as a corrupting, hysterical mob. Instead, it appears as a human matrix that is fundamentally indeterminate and potential. One of its most salient positive characteristics is that it is *imperiled*—threatened with co-optation by leadership figures of both the left and the right, and needing to educate itself in the mechanisms of self-rule. Accordingly, these works imagine the author as a possible catalyst of this self-educative process. Neither the hortatory bard of much committed literature nor the Nietzschean genius of right-wing modernism, the author in these works is represented as an uncertain, deracinated force, wandering among the multitude in an attempt to awaken its political faculties. But in Lewis's and Riding's work, this kind of improvised political tutelage is impossible to distinguish from the manipulations of dressed-down agents of political power. Indeed, the message of these works, if they have one, is that benevolent, "personal" excursions into the multitude should always be regarded as the work of disguised political bureaucracies. This means that the governing image of the literature of the multitude—the author as an autonomous agent within the multitude—cannot be sustained, and *Enemy of the Stars*, "I Am," and "Disclaimer of the Person" all implode as a consequence, even to the point of losing stylistic coherence and thematic integrity.

The works I examine, then, occupy no comfortable place in the history of twentieth-century literature. They do not share the cyclical, Spenglerian time sense with which Anglo-American modernism is often identified, nor do they evolve cults of inwardness to separate themselves from the vulgarities of the multitude. The premium they place on spontaneity is a way of signaling their imaginary distance from party-aligned rhetorical modes and political tropes. And yet the spontaneity on display in these works has nothing to do with modernism's most well-known examples of disruptive, "irrationalist" spontaneity: works such as André Breton and Philippe Soupault's *The Magnetic Fields*, Robert Desnos's *Deuil pour deuil*, and Gertrude Stein's *Stanzas in Meditation*. With the exception of Williams's *Kora in Hell*, none of the works I consider offers itself as an automatic transcription of mental impulse. Instead, these works represent, evoke, and allegorize forms of spontaneity that are collective and self-mediating in nature, usually by depicting the artist as a dynamic figure amid the multitude.

The literature of the multitude that I analyze thus critiques and modifies the idea of aesthetic spontaneity at least as much as it dramatizes that idea. In doing so, it intervenes in a philosophical tradition that treats spontaneity both as an aesthetic category and as a tool of critical self-consciousness. In the twentieth century, Theodor Adorno and Herbert Marcuse are the most nuanced representatives of this tradition, and it is with their models of spontaneity that the literature of the multitude is most profoundly in dialogue—and, ultimately, in disagreement.

Mediated Spontaneity

Theodor Adorno is probably the twentieth century's most complex and fruitful theorist of aesthetic spontaneity. From his early essays to his unfinished masterwork, *Aesthetic Theory*, Adorno continually revisits the problem of involuntariness in art. But like the modernists I study, Adorno defines spontaneity not as a condition of pure involuntariness but as a peculiar mixture of voluntariness and involuntariness, which places the artist in contact with collective potentialities.

Take, for example, Adorno's analysis of automatic writing, probably the best-known form of modernist spontaneity. Adorno acknowledges the sense of "utopia" that automatic writing affords. It seems to promise a complete merger of the individual mind with transindividual currents that announce themselves spontaneously in the work of art.[75] And in paying homage to automatic writing in *Aesthetic Theory*, Adorno even goes so far as to claim that art's "immanent process has the quality of following a divining rod"; its mandate is "to follow where the hand is drawn" (115).

Adorno, however, also senses a danger in completely surrendering the artistic will to the "art-alien," and his mixture of optimism and trepidation in the face of this kind of aesthetic spontaneity mirrors many of Williams's, Lewis's, Riding's, and Stevens's ambivalences about the multitude and its forms of political initiative. Continuing his analysis of automatic writing, Adorno argues, "When untamed by taste or artistic understanding the need for expression converges with the bluntness of rational objectivity" (115). Expanding this observation to include several other models of artistic spontaneity, Adorno writes:

> *Action painting, l'art informelle*, and aleatorical works may have carried the element of resignation to its extreme: The aesthetic subject exempts itself of the burden of giving form to the contingent material it encounters, despairing of the possibility of undergirding it, and instead shifts the responsibility for its organization back to the contingent material itself. (221)

In both of these passages, Adorno describes a "pure relinquishment to the material" (220) that masquerades as artistic spontaneity but in fact degenerates into a merely "statistical" recording of data. Such statistical, automatic art offers itself as a pure, unmediated expression of objectivity. But in its wholesale abandonment of technique and its pretenses to scientific neutrality, this art adopts the logic of instrumental rationality. It becomes an inert object among the other inert objects of everyday life: an undifferentiated part of the art-alien world to which it at first so ecstatically surrendered itself.[76]

Such automaticity is not the same thing as spontaneity for Adorno. In fact, spontaneity is the very category Adorno deploys in order to critique the aesthetic and political consequences of automatic art. Unlike automaticity, spontaneity exists only as a tension between artists' self-relinquishment and their active, constructive faculties. In *Aesthetic Theory*, Adorno describes spontaneity as a productive dialectic that "theorists take for a strictly logical contradiction" but that "is familiar to artists and unfolds in their work as that control over the mimetic element that summons up, destroys and redeems its spontaneity" (114). Artistic spontaneity, then, is the capacity to summon up, destroy, and redeem . . . spontaneity itself. Or, put another way, the spontaneity of artists consists in their surrendering themselves to some deeper principle of spontaneity in order to redeem it—a deeper spontaneity that belongs to "a collective subject that has yet to be realized" (231).

There is an aporia at the heart of Adorno's writings on artistic spontaneity, then, that we recognize in modernist writings on spontaneity as well. It is an aporia that centers on this "collective subject that has yet to be realized"—a collective subject defined primarily by its virtual powers and capacities, and that I have been describing as "the multitude." This collective ensemble—more a "physiologically primordial form of spirit" (113) than a concrete movement or tendency—haunts Adorno's writings on spontaneity, sometimes appearing as a complex, intersubjective sensorium that guides the artist's formal decisions and sometimes appearing as a welter of involuntary pulsions that must be ordered "from above" by the artist. But in whatever guise this collective ensemble appears, it is always presented as the mimetic element of art: the social processes *that art imitates.*

The location of spontaneity is therefore in the interchange between artists and this collective mimetic element, and there is a complex politics to this interchange. In this respect, the work of art—as an expression of "mimetic preindividual elements" (42)—obeys the same logic as Gramsci's philosophy of praxis, which must incorporate collective "thrusts from below" within the "solid framework" of the leadership apparatus. And just as Gramsci worries that any political representation of the multitude contains the threat of betrayal and domination, Adorno worries that any aesthetic representation of the multitude contains the threat of betrayal and domination. Indeed, Adorno argues: "Even in the greatest works of aesthetic unity the echo of social violence is to be heard. . . . The aesthetic unity of the multiplicitous appears as though it had done no violence but had been chosen by the multiplicitous itself" (134). For this reason, nominalistic artworks—those that renounce technique and present themselves as having been organized spontaneously out of presubjective impulses and currents—are the most politically suspect to Adorno. In such works,

> the illusion is created that there is no illusion; that the diffuse and ego-alien harmonize with the posited totality, whereas the harmony itself is organized; that the process is presented from below to above, even though the traditional determination from above to below, without which the spiritual determination of the artwork cannot be conceived, persists. (108)

In other words, the "spontaneity" of automatic writing or anti-art makes it seem as if "life" itself had organized its own structures of representation, as if artistic structure is an unmediated expression of the multitude's own capacities and forms of life. For Adorno, this is akin to the totalitarian party's reassurances that the apparatuses of the party-state are the immediate expression of the multitude's will. Spontaneity under these auspices is little more than the empty claim that there are no mediations separating the multitude from the institutions of social power.

Genuine spontaneity, for Adorno, is the opposite of this feigned immediacy. It refers to the play of tensions that testifies to a work's uneasy, incomplete figuration of the multitude. Indeed, a work's spontaneity is the index of its inability to contain and domesticate the multitude's collective potentiality while striving to *imitate* it nevertheless. This kind of spontaneity becomes legible in an artwork through the dissonance between its figural resources and a collective element that can never express itself within the realm of individualized construction. In this context, spontaneity is not the feigned absence of mediation but the sensed presence of a collective "emancipated subjectivity" that the artwork can evoke only in the modality of "the *yet to be*" (172).

In the modernist works I consider, it is this kind of spontaneity that is at issue, not the "spontaneity" of automatic writing and anti-art. The works on which I focus do not abdicate technique in an attempt to become a part of the art-alien world. Instead, they function more like diagrams of the claims spontaneous intuition makes for itself. These claims are tested in various ways in these works, often by representing the artist's own spontaneity as a *character* who attempts to merge with scenes of collective life. In representing the results of these excursions into collective life, these works reveal spontaneity to be the aesthetic correlative of a wide range of political attitudes and processes, which are tried on, evaluated, and revised in the work of art itself.

The twentieth century's other great theorist of aesthetic spontaneity, Herbert Marcuse, refers to this dynamic as "mediated spontaneity." In explaining this concept, Marcuse draws connections between aesthetic and political spontaneity even more forcefully than Adorno does. In describing the feigned immediacy of anti-art in *The Aesthetic Dimension*, Marcuse writes:

> The desublimation of art is supposed to release spontaneity—of both the artist and the recipient. But just as, in radical praxis, spontaneity can

advance the movement of liberation only as *mediated spontaneity,* that is, resulting from the transformation of consciousness—so also in art.... In this sense, renunciation of the aesthetic form is abdication of responsibility. It deprives art of the very form in which it can create that other reality within the established one—the cosmos of hope.[77]

Marcuse's verdict on anti-art here is clear. Its attempt to create an immediate unity between art and life results only in a false obviousness that is deprived of critical content. Anti-art's renunciation of form is the renunciation of the "cognitive and cutting power" that allows humanity to transform reality, not just reflect it.[78] As in Adorno, then, for Marcuse "form" represents the possibility of introducing transformative mediations into the raw material of everyday life—mediations that reflect humanity's ability to organize social relations otherwise. And, like Adorno, Marcuse does not claim that artists should in any way provide concrete, politically educational content in their works. At the very most, it is the artist's job to educate the sensorium of the viewer, to reacquaint the viewer with the form sense present in all humans—that is, their capacity to assume a mediative distance with respect to the prepackaged responses that announce themselves from the surface of consciousness.

But notice how Marcuse establishes an unambiguous connection between the mediated spontaneity of art and that of radical praxis. He seems to be claiming that, on a formal level, political spontaneity and artistic spontaneity have, or should have, the same internal structure. Take, for example, Marcuse's reference to "organized spontaneity" in the realm of politics.[79] In Marcuse's meditations on the New Left, "spontaneity" refers to unofficial political manifestations on the part of the multitude—spontaneous actions that take place outside established leadership structures. And, according to Marcuse, such "decentralized forms of organization" of a "largely 'spontaneous' character" are capable of a high degree of "self-imposed discipline and authority."[80] In these formulations, Marcuse is clearly echoing Luxemburg's ideas of "spontaneous coordination." But Marcuse also insists that *pure* spontaneity—in "radical praxis" as in art—would only end in cognitive regression. To counteract this tendency, mediations must be introduced into the spontaneous manifestations of the multitude.

But introduced by whom? In *Counterrevolution and Revolt,* Marcuse clearly signals his opposition to the "bureaucratic-authoritarian mass party" that promises to shape collective spontaneity from above, but neither does he trust the multitude to mediate their social activity independently. Why not? Marcuse explains: "The *immediate* expression of the opinion and will of the workers, farmers, neighbors—in brief, of the people—is not, per se, progressive" (45). Accordingly, the primary liberation of people from their own administered consciousnesses "cannot be 'spontaneous' because such spontaneity would only express the values and goals derived from the established system" (47). Instead, an educated leadership is necessary whose function is to "'translate' spontaneous protest into organized action which has the chance to develop and to transcend immediate needs and aspirations toward the radical reconstruction of society: *transformation of immediate into organized spontaneity*" (47).

In other words, a leadership apparatus must translate spontaneous impulses into conscious, organized activity. In doing so, this leadership apparatus relates to spontaneity in a way that is similar to the ways in which artists relate to spontaneity. It works with the half-formed social intuitions of the multitude in the same way that artists work with collective undercurrents of experience: social "raw materials" are redeemed from their immediate, unselfconscious condition through an organizing, mediating process. This results in a condition of mediated spontaneity— a condition in which social impulses are set in relation to one another and are transformed in the process. What occurs, then, is a "dual transformation (of the subjects and their world)" that can lead to a "democratizing and generalizing [of] creativity."[81]

Of course, Marcuse never makes it clear how this democratizing process is to occur or how the organized spontaneity brought about by his educated elite would differ from the "superimposed, administered unification" of the bureaucratic party.[82] The creative process is supposed to offer a suggestion of how a socially spontaneous process could, at the same time, be self-mediating. But the mediated spontaneity displayed in the work of art is superintended by a central artistic will, as indeed it must be, since artworks are typically produced by individuals, or at most by small groups. For this reason, the stain of subjectivity can never truly be removed from them—unless, of course, the artistic "materials" were somehow capable of "organizing themselves."

But this fantasy of the self-organizing artwork is precisely what Marcuse and Adorno both condemn in their critiques of anti-art. As Adorno argues in *Aesthetic Theory*, such artworks pretend to come into existence "by being organized from below to above, not by having principles of organization foisted on [them]" (220). However, "no artwork left blindly to itself possesses the power of organization that would set up binding boundaries for itself: Investing the work with such a power would in fact be fetishistic" (220). Indeed, the idea that an artwork could *organize itself* is more than fetishistic; it is thoroughly bizarre. Nevertheless, in Adorno's meditations on artistic spontaneity, the idea of the self-organizing artwork is always on the horizon, usually as some dimly glimpsed capacity for collective automimesis that the individual artist must continually betray.

In their aesthetic writings, then, Marcuse and Adorno oscillate between the image of a multitude that possesses the elements of artistic order but is incapable of self-organization and the image of an artist who possesses rich organizational capacities but always betrays the collective elements out of which his or her artwork is constructed. The result of this anxious dialectic is a conception of the artist as an eternally guilty subject, pretending to allow the artwork to organize itself from below, while in fact covertly "preforming all individual [artistic] elements backstage."[83] Under these circumstances, Adorno states in *Aesthetic Theory*, "art is complicitous with ideology in that it feigns the factual existence of reconciliation" (134). This "imposture" (108) can never be eradicated from the artwork and terminates in the image of artists as perpetually attempting, and failing, to rid themselves of the subjective determinations that alone qualify them as organizational centers.

It is no surprise, therefore, that Hardt and Negri criticize Adorno for locking himself within an antinomial conceptual structure that "leav[es] humanity doomed to the eternal play of opposites."[84] Rather than recognizing the multitude's capacity for spontaneous self-organization, such a conceptual system reduces this *potenza* to "a tame dialectical play of opposite identities,"[85] in which individual and collective, semblance and expression, mediation and immediacy are maintained in a nervous counterpoint without any genuine rupture or liberatory potential. For Negri, this reflects the intellectual legacy of Hegelian dialectics, which, according to his analysis, continually inscribes the immediacy of the multitude within a system of transcendental mediation, falsely viewing the administrative functions of the state as the consummation of the multitude's self-organizing power. To escape from this model of transcendental mediation and the forms of aesthetic spontaneity to which it gives rise, Negri turns to an entirely different intellectual tradition, one whose roots lie in Spinoza's conception of the multitude as "the constitution of collectivity as praxis."[86]

This alternative model of spontaneity and collective life will be crucial to my analysis of modernist literature, because the modernists I consider were also searching for a way to imagine processes of social transformation that would not be overseen by parties, states, or any other figure of transcendental mediation. No doubt Williams, Lewis, Riding, and Stevens often view artists themselves as agents of dialectical mediation, as guilty, self-expurgating souls, attempting to access some spontaneous, collective existence that lies just beyond their figural resources. But each of them explicitly critiques this image of the artist as well. Riding is particularly forceful in her critique, identifying this image of the self-expurgating artist with what she views as one of the most central political fictions of modernity—that of the socially disconnected, "unlocatable" spokesperson, who makes a great show of merging with the multitude, all the while ensuring that the collective voice of the multitude will be muffled by his or her own rhetorical virtuosities.

Williams, Lewis, and Stevens also critique this image of the self-expurgating artist, sometimes by renarrating the encounter of the artist and the multitude in complex, ambivalent ways, and sometimes by leveling much more overt political polemics against it. They therefore deviate from both Adornian and Marcusean aesthetic models, in which the multitude comes to presence only as a tortured by-product of the artist's subjectivity. The modernists I consider therefore call out for some new way of imagining modernism's relationship to the spontaneity of the multitude, some new aesthetic paradigm that would move beyond the image of the self-evacuating artist whose displays of subjective destitution are always complicit with social domination.

Multitude theory provides some useful tools in this critical project, because it shares with modernists such as Williams, Lewis, Riding, and Stevens a distrust for the entire dialectic of self-loss and merger that is at the center of Adorno's aesthetic theory. Negri's turn to Spinoza thus encodes a fundamentally *modernist* desire to describe forms of social organization that lie outside the party/class dialectic so central to twentieth-century political vanguards. It is a project that turns on a question at the heart of modernist aesthetics: how could a collectivity be simultaneously spontaneous and self-organizing? In short, how could a collectivity become a *multitude*?

Immanence and Transcendence

One of the most urgent intellectual and political challenges faced by Negri and the entire Autonomia tendency in the 1970s was to define a radical politics separate from the Partito Comunista Italiano, the hegemonic electoral Communist party in Italy, which had overseen the Historic Compromise with Italian Christian Democracy and a restructuring of the Italian economy that saw large-scale layoffs, work speedups, and the criminalization of workplace radicalism.[87] Where the PCI advocated reformist stabilization of the economy and top-down command, autonomists advocated a militant deepening of capitalist crisis and fluid, horizontal networks of resistance. In short, to autonomists, the PCI came to represent an external political force, communist only in name, and allied with the state in its attempts to quell workplace struggle and bridge over capitalist crisis.

Because of its role in helping to absorb the negativity of capitalist crisis and effecting a "synthesis" of socialism and capitalism in the social welfare state, the PCI came to be associated more and more with the Hegelian dialectic by Negri, to the extent that in Negri's work, Hegelian thought as a whole often becomes nothing more than a stand-in for the feints and ruses of electoral-bureaucratic communism. This is clear in Negri's description of Hegelian mediation as "the continual attempt to organize power functionally," whose legacy is a "hegemony of the relations of production over the productive forces" that ultimately "dons the garb of reformist teleology."[88] Hegelian sublation—once imagined as the dynamic merger of the associated producers and society's productive forces—is now reimagined as a phony "capitalist *Aufhebung*," which sees the PCI participating in a new, reformist "social State" and its "patriotism of common well-being in social production."[89] "Sublation," in other words, is Negri's name for a political fantasy: that the separation between the workers and the state has been overcome, with the PCI as the principal agent of this dialectical deceit.

If Hegel thus becomes the emblem of Italy's historic compromise of the 1970s, Spinoza emblematizes the associative potential of social networks that operate outside of bureaucratic parties and the dialectical deceptions they perpetrate. Refusing the abstraction of power in transcendental apparatuses of rule, Spinoza's "*multitudo* is... nothing but the interconnection of subjects that has made itself an ontological project of collective power."[90] Spinoza's multitude is thus a figure of the "free and open flux of the self-organization of reality," expressing Spinoza's cosmogenic ideal of "spontaneity in organization."[91]

Of course, Negri admits that Spinoza falters when he tries to imagine democratic institutions of the multitude. Indeed, Spinoza cannot imagine them in the absence of the state, which, according to his *Theological-Political Treatise*, "must be preserved and governed solely by the policy of the sovereign power"—to the extent that "if anyone embarks on some undertaking of public concern on his own initiative and without the knowledge of the supreme council, he has violated the right of the sovereign power and is guilty of treason and is rightly and properly condemned."[92]

Balibar is thus at least partially correct to see in Spinoza's multitude "an analysis of institutional mediation," with the multitude expressing itself through "functional relations... between the leaders and the led, between executive power, deliberative power, and power of oversight."[93] In other words, at the level of concrete politics, Spinoza's multitude functions much like that of Machiavelli: as a limit to the *potentia* of the sovereign.[94] Negri's innovation, then, is to see in Spinoza's multitude something more than this functional operator within the realpolitik of the Dutch mercantile state. Reimagined as the social vessel of Spinoza's entire theodicy, the multitude becomes a highly speculative figure, pregnant with a robust capacity for spontaneous self-organization.

In this way, Negri abstracts the Spinozan multitude from its historical roots in the carefully balanced administrative spheres of the Low Territories and reimagines it as an autonomous ontological ensemble of powers and capacities, mobilized whenever horizontal human networks oppose constituted regimes of power. This is why the language of spontaneous organization Negri uses in his analysis of Spinoza reappears in his description of the "spontaneity of the constituent process" in the Russian Revolution[95] and in his description of the socialized workers' "collective corporeality," whose "unity is spontaneous."[96] The multitude, in other words, is not a philologically self-identical concept, but rather a term Negri appropriates strategically in order to break with the entrenched dualisms of Italian vanguard party politics and to describe systems of spontaneous self-government that could exist outside transcendent systems of rule. And this is precisely what links Negri's appropriation of Spinoza to the modernists I consider, who so often find themselves in opposition to the vanguards of their own political universes while at the same time trying to imagine forms of spontaneous coordination that could exist in the absence of parties, governments, and spokespeople of all kinds.

Of course, the modernists I consider never dispatch with dialectics, mediation, and transcendence with the finality and confidence Negri evinces in his turn to Spinoza's philosophy of immanence. On the contrary, the figure of the multitude, as an immanent, self-organizing network, typically emerges in the works of these authors only through a prolonged struggle, in which artists variously substitute *themselves* for the vanguard party, attempt to radicalize the moment of Adornian depersonalization— as if it could become identical to the immanence it confronts—or simply insist, through a dialectical *fiat*, that the artist's subjective reactions contain and express the immanence of the multitude. Williams's essay "The Basis of Faith in Art," for example, flirts with all of these possibilities, registering his attraction to the idea of the artist as a figure of dialectical mediation as well as his profound reservations about it.

The essay records an imaginary conversation between Williams and his brother in which Williams describes the modernist imagination, in Adornian terms, as a medium of the multitude's vitality. But when Williams describes "humanity as whole" as the "life-giving artery" of the artist, his brother attempts to rebut him with the observation, "I notice you're not too anxious to be classed among them."[97] The conversation continues as follows, with Williams speaking first, offering his counterrebuttal:

> He must maintain his independence—
> Which amounts to a divorce from society.
> —in order to be able to perceive their needs and to act upon the imperative necessities of his perceptions.
> Independent and dependent! you make me laugh.
> Independent of opinion, dependent of body. The artist had better be a poor man.
> A sort of sleuth, eh? who goes smelling about to unearth social requirements.
> Ridiculous, eh?
> Absurd. Shouldn't we rather say a rudderless nonentity furiously laboring away at random whims, from among whose works, with time, a public takes the initiative to select its equally haphazard choices?
> Quite.[98]

If it is impossible to decide who is *right* in the conversation, it is because the exchange testifies to a conceptual impasse confronted by modernist artists—an impasse documented, but not really resolved, in Adorno's and Marcuse's theories of artistic spontaneity. In the passage above, Williams wants to claim that his body is dependent upon the multitude, as if the metabolic rhythms that pace his metrics and shape his sensorium are derived from the multitude, inextricable from their collective body. But another side of Williams, represented here by his brother, keeps stubbornly insisting that "you wish to retain the government"[99]—that is, Williams merely pretends to surrender his organizational capacities to the multitude, pretends to allow them to speak through him. This is only an elaborate masquerade, akin to the political deceit practiced by pseudo-democratic leaders upon the multitude.

Williams's epic poem *Paterson* documents this political anxiety, as do all of the works on which I focus in this book. Lewis's *Enemy of the Stars* represents the multitude as the victim of a protofascist artist figure's experiments; Riding's "Disclaimer of the Person" and "I Am" represent the multitude as mesmerized by the political hypnosis artists perform; and Stevens's "Owl's Clover" represents the multitude as a social reality that the artist has difficulty perceiving, let alone representing adequately. Crucially, however, these works are not content to invoke the political betrayals and frauds practiced upon the multitude in the mode of aesthetic guilt alone, by registering the multitude—in Adornian fashion—as a disembodied, anguished cry, audible in the artwork's formal dissonances and incongruities. Instead, they accord the multitude a clear thematic presence in their narrative and symbolic structures. They figure the multitude concretely in various scenes of collective life, even as they evoke it as a more abstract matrix of powers and faculties. Most important of all, these works recount narratives of political agency in which the multitude becomes an actor in its own right. Not simply an ineffable, unrepresentable presence, continually betrayed by the artist, the multitude in the works of Williams, Lewis, Riding, and Stevens has a variable relationship to the central individuals who seek to represent it, sometimes threatening these individuals from without, sometimes incorporating them within its own processes, sometimes becoming like them, assassinating them, or expropriating their directive will as its own.

Images of spontaneity in these texts, then, function as robust political diagnostics. What they demonstrate is that the twentieth-century fantasy of creative production as an upwelling of spontaneous energy contains, hidden within it, a political narrative in which artists are recast as spokespeople of the collective energies of the multitude. But rather than approaching the work of art as the scene where this collective mandate is inevitably betrayed, the modernists I examine ceaselessly dramatize the encounter between the artist and the multitude, testing and retesting the adequacy of the artistic imagination to the collective subject whose potentialities it hopes to express. Often this encounter does end in a betrayal of some kind; the artist's promises to represent the multitude are exposed as the prototype of pseudodemocratic political representation. But in restaging the conflict between the multitude and its presumptive spokespeople in abstract aesthetic ensembles, where a great deal of intersubjective dynamism is imaginable, Williams, Lewis, Riding, and Stevens are able to evolve models of social exponency far more nuanced than what Adorno's individual/collective dyad or Gramsci's party/class dialectic allow for.

The forms of spontaneous organization these works represent are therefore contributions to the intellectual history of the multitude as much as to the aesthetic history of modernism. They ask us to view the multitude as a complex of faculties capable of sustained, horizontal self-organization, and they reimagine the work of art as an *imitation* of the relational processes of which this human complex is capable. Moreover, each of the modernists I examine explores the multitude's capacity for self-organization within concrete political contexts that act as staging grounds for the particular forms of spontaneity he or she takes up for consideration. In this way each demonstrates that abstractions such as "spontaneity" and "the multitude" have stakes that extend well beyond the refinements of aesthetic theory. They are, at their heart, attempts to organize forms of social practice for which institutional politics as yet has few conceptual categories or practical venues.

Modernism's Speculative Politics

In each chapter of this book, I examine the complex mixture of concrete political ideology and speculative abstraction that helps to shape the models of spontaneity deployed by the modernist on whom I focus. In each case, I identify specific political discourses that the modernist takes up, as well as conceptual excesses that cannot be accounted for according to any of these concrete political ideologies. These moments of conceptual excess are typically the place where the multitude's spontaneous potencies are explored—in images and narratives that are inevitably inflected by the concrete political ideologies that intellectually engaged each modernist author, but that are irreducible to them. At these points, it is usually necessary to synthesize hybrid conceptual languages, from the theoretical texts the authors were reading and from more recent exercises in political ontology, in order to account for the models of spontaneity these modernists are trying out.

For example, in chapter 1, I explain the centrality of Social Credit, as a concrete political movement and ideology, to Williams's *Paterson*. Social Credit advocated the disbursement of state-sponsored credit money to workers, so that they could consume their way out of the Great Depression and permanently stabilize the capitalist economy. On a surface level, *Paterson* could be read as an endorsement of Social Credit. The poem's entire metaphorics of damming, draining, and overflow is derived from economic tropologies to be found in the pages of Social Credit journals such as *New Democracy*. As the poem progresses, however, it becomes clear that the redistribution of credit offers only a shallow imitation of the spontaneous social recalibrations Williams envisions, and Social Credit as a concrete "cure" becomes a foil against which Williams evolves much more nuanced and abstract models of spontaneous self-organization. These models of self-organization involve a social body capable of autonomous and counterbalanced acts of exchange— what Negri calls the "self-valorization" of the multitude, as opposed to forms of value exchange mediated by the state. I therefore reread *Paterson* as an attempt to figure these self-valorizing processes—the poem's images of androgynetic flowers and pregenital libidinal currents serving as an archive of modernist fantasies about a multitude capable of decentralized self-regulation.

In chapter 2, I show that Lewis's *Enemy of the Stars* similarly places fascism at the center of its symbolic economy. Lewis was attracted to European fascism for many of the same reasons that Williams was attracted to Social Credit. It promised to return to the social body the value and potency of which it was purported to have been robbed by international banking monopolies and their liberal-democratic political superstructure. But, as Reed Way Dasenbrock points out, Lewis was also deeply suspicious of vanguards of all kinds, including those of European fascism.[100] I turn to *Enemy of the Stars*, therefore, as a document of Lewis's ambivalences about fascist vanguards and the multitude they pretend to represent.

On a superficial level, the play seems to celebrate the protofascist Arghol in his attempts to educate the "son of the sensational masses," Hanp.[101] However, as the play progresses, this process of education becomes more and more sinister, until it becomes indistinguishable from the political puppeteering that Lewis condemns in the social sphere. At the end of the play, Hanp resists this process of emotional reengineering and murders Arghol, in a "political execution" about which Lewis evinces deep ambivalence.[102] But by examining some works that act as speculative extensions of the play—primarily "Physics of the Not-Self" and *The Lion and the Fox* —I show that Hanp represents processes of collective self-organization, resistance, and regicide that reappear throughout Lewis's creative and critical writings. These forms of self-organization all oppose the constituted power of parties, states, and their bureaucratic infrastructure, embodying what Negri refers to as "constituent power"— the multitude's immanent powers of association and counsel. Though Lewis is deeply skeptical of the multitude's ability to develop lasting, nonhierarchical institutions, I show that the "massed, organized, facultative personality" of *The Art of Being Ruled*,[103] the "public vituperator" of *The Lion and the Fox*,[104] and the "Not-Self" of *Enemy of the Stars*'s companion essay all emblematize a moment of constituent power to which Lewis continually returns us: a moment of spontaneous association that allows the multitude to resist the hypnotic sway of fascist vanguards and develop their own forms of political critique and organization.

In chapter 3, I show how Riding's political ontology revolves around her critique of vanguard social movements and their promises to unite the public and the private spheres by way of their representational apparatuses. For Riding, the image of the intellectual or the party emerging from some socially "unlocatable" stratosphere and then merging with the multitude is not one of social healing. Instead, this maneuver simply perpetuates the gendered split between the world of public values and the world of socially embedded existence. The former is reduced to a "male" world of experimental opinionizing and the latter is reduced to a "female" world of private sentiment.

In *Anarchism Is Not Enough*, "The Word 'Woman,'" and *The Telling*, Riding develops models of collective action intended to overcome this split between public and private, male and female, leader and led; these models center on "spontaneously generated" forms of order.[105] This kind of spontaneity, like that of the other modernists I examine, has little to do with private enclaves of feeling. In Riding's greatest work of utopian philosophy, *The World and Ourselves*, it corresponds to the "internal self-organization" (454) of councils of friends, communities, and workers. Riding's idea of internal self-organization thus anticipates the models of affect we see in contemporary multitude theory—forms of biopolitical creation that express collective powers to act and be acted upon. But Riding's modernist anxieties about the use of affect as an ideological weapon cause her to develop models of social affect that stress measure, proportion, and "mutual verifying"[106] more than the pure positivity of Negri's *cupiditas* and *amor*. Her poetry thus prompts us to imagine a form of social affect characterized as much by critique, mediation, and reciprocal limitation as by intersubjective creativity.

In chapter 4, I focus on Stevens's uncollected long poem "Owl's Clover," which he described as "a vaguely poetic justification of leftism."[107] In this work, the poetic imagination initially seeks to rival the organizational power of institutional communism, hoping to combine itself with the multitude, the better to direct and order it. But as "Owl's Clover" progresses, the poet comes into contact with an international assemblage of immigrant workers that is evolving its own organizational structures quite outside the jurisdiction of the poem's intellectuals and professional revolutionaries. This causes Stevens to reimagine the poet as just one force in a horizontal network of political agents, all of whom are moved by a collectively defined "logic of transforming certitudes."[108] And as in Riding's poetry, this vision of spontaneous self-organization stresses the negativity of disagreement, debate, and dialectical self-correction much more than the positivity of "being, loving, transforming, creating."[109] By recovering this image of a multitude that can accommodate negativity without degenerating into an aggregation of competing grouplets, I show how modernist forms of mediated spontaneity might serve as a corrective to the "phobia of the negative" sometimes evinced by multitude theory.

As a whole, then, this book recovers a lost debate within modernism about collective action in the early twentieth century and the extent to which it must rely upon institutional political apparatuses and their central, organizational wills. No doubt the seductions of such centralized wills are felt in all of the works I examine. These works often exhibit great attraction to what Sean McCann describes as the "pinnacle of feeling," the fantasy of a political executive "able through his gifts of imagination and rhetorical power to bond with people in way[s] that surpass[ ] not just political institutions and personal conflict, but representation itself."[110] And as Pericles Lewis points out, such images of redemptive individuality often align modernists with forms of national consciousness, to the extent that they represent themselves as "narrator-heroes who forge[ ] social realities in their own images."[111]

Ultimately, however, it is the political territory outside such leader- and nation-oriented identifications with which I concern myself most in this study. Jessica Berman's and Rebecca Walkowitz's analyses of modernist cosmopolitanism are thus close conceptual allies of this project. Berman's idea of a "being-in-common" that exists prior to "the adjudication of rights and responsibilities"[112] and Walkowitz's concentration on the politics that are encoded in everyday forms of "affect, manner, and self-consciousness"[113] both richly address what I might call the tropological resources of the multitude. These resources always exceed "the domain of public citizenship and the state,"[114] and thus constitute a reserve of perceptual modes, capacities, and powers on which modernism draws for the raw material of its speculative communities.

What I contribute to this conversation is an analysis of how modernists imagined such forms of attention, such aptitudes and desires, could come to organization without recapitulating hierarchically stratified regimes of power: how they might evolve themselves into institutions of self-government active across the social body as a whole. Imagining self-organization on this scale gives rise to very specific forms of optimism, anxiety, and theoretical self-correction. On one hand, it causes modernists to ask whether the multitude might evolve all the powers of critique, direction, and self-suspension embodied in the vanguard party, even without the centralized, bureaucratic agents who are supposed to personify these powers. On the other, it causes them to worry that this political ideal is nothing but a fantasy—one that all too easily conceals the process whereby popular leaders who *are* bent on accumulating power consolidate and centralize their rule.

Because of its concern with modernism's relationship to mass parties and mass movements, Michael Tratner's *Modernism and Mass Politics* is a particularly important forerunner to this book. Tratner's argument that modernism represents not so much a rejection of mass culture as an attempt to speak "the idiom of the mass mind" remains as relevant today as ever.[115] Particularly useful for my argument is his analysis of Joyce's changing attitude toward the masses. Tratner notes that whereas in his early work Joyce was attracted to the D'Annunzian ideal of a literature that would "ignit[e] a hidden explosive power within the masses" (119), in *Ulysses* "the artist does not have control over the fragments he collects" and is therefore unable "to incorporate others, to create a corporate or collective voice for a social order" (205–6). And though Tratner's study does not focus primarily on mass forms of self-organization, it provides extremely compelling glimpses of how modernism imagines the development of new social institutions from a mass base. Tratner reads Bloom and Molly's marriage, for example, as the emblem of newly developing institutional forms that "juxtapose socially structured pieces of various institutions and see what emerges" (215).

More recently, critics such as Nicholas Brown and Justus Nieland have added significantly to this reappraisal of modernism's relationship to collective life. Brown, for example, examines Wyndham Lewis alongside Ngugi wa Thiong'o, focusing on their shared interest in "the construction of a political subject, a concrete mediation between the individual subject and history."[116] Though Lewis's political subject is the fantasmatic "class of individuals," while Ngugi concerns himself with the far more concrete realities of peasant class consciousness, they both participate in the "eidaesthetic itinerary" that links modernism to the literature of decolonization. That is, they both strive to create representational ensembles capable of figuring, within the realm of sensual immediacy and cultural locality, the framing structures of global capitalism, whose total contextual scope is always in danger of appearing as an unrepresentable abstraction: the sublime of the modern world. Brown's analysis of the mystic substances and sublime objects of modernism as the inscriptions of a social rift that—in other contexts and places—becomes the site of overt collective agency thus anticipates the forms of political phenomenology that inform this study.

In *Feeling Modern: The Eccentricities of Public Life*, Nieland also develops a rich theoretical framework that allows us to see modernist experimentation as an attempt to join, rather than retreat from, modernity's forms of collective life. Especially useful for me is his attention to the prediscursive, unstructured modes of affect that intrigued modernist authors. While modernists were acutely sensitive to the role affect plays in the naturalization of public ideologies, Nieland also reminds us of modernism's obsession with the idea of "affect as a form of sensual responsiveness that eludes structure."[117] Building on this insight, Nieland develops a model of modernist collectivity that is closely related to the idea of the modernist multitude I develop here: a model of "publicness whose value lies precisely in its lack of positive, abiding content and thus in its capacity for the establishment of new social relations" (28).

This attention to modernism's utopian moments signals a vital development in New Modernist studies. In *Utopian Generations,* Nicholas Brown articulates it in his account of modernism's "negative utopias": utopias that are visible only as "a lack or contradiction in the actually existing social totality whose presence hints at an as yet unimaginable future" (22). Similarly, in *Feeling Modern,* Nieland locates modernism's utopian moment in the way it approaches affect's "openness to contingency and change" (25), and specifically in the way modernist works "seek[] to turn [their] own aesthetic innovations into rival technologies for shaping and structuring collective affects" (21). These insights allow both Brown and Nieland to read the structural elements of modernist works as maps of political energies—as speculative interventions into social divisions that still have not been bridged.

My analysis also tracks modernism's fascination with collective life as an unstructured, untotalizable ensemble, but its main focus is on precisely those moments when the prediscursive rhythms and nonstandardized experiential modes of the multitude seem capable of developing their own new orders, institutions, and organs of self-government. These moments are particularly destabilizing in modernist texts, precisely because of modernism's tendency to frame the artist as the bearer of the technologies of representation—as the figure who symbolically intervenes into the unstructured life of the multitude in order to map out its potential futures. All of the works I consider expose this model of literary agency as the aesthetic corollary of the party/class, leader/led antinomies from which they are trying to escape. So, without abandoning the terrain of the aesthetic, they evolve narratives of self-organization in which the technologies of representation are absorbed into self-mediating processes of the multitude itself, along with the "central minds" who once claimed them as their sole possession. In doing so, they vividly depict a condition that exists at the outer margin of most twentieth-century theory, but that was instrumental to the twentieth century's most ambitious revolutionary moments, from 1905 onward—a condition in which decentralized human networks develop their own directive organs, in which unstructured movements structure themselves.

My approach is thus in many ways a departure from the "politics as itself" trend that Douglas Mao and Rebecca L. Walkowitz identify as a principal feature of the New Modernist studies.[118] The focus on individuals as citizens and voters, on specific political leaders and government institutions, and on the specific effects of the mass media, is fairly remote from my analysis of modernism's often very abstract evocations of extra-legal self-organization. Nevertheless, the best examples of this growing body of criticism revolve around some of the same questions I address. Michael Szalay's *New Deal Modernism*, for example, brilliantly argues that for Stevens both insurance and poetry testify to the fact that planning, on both economic and literary levels, cannot evolve "intention-bearing wholes."[119] Many of Szalay's arguments are diametrically opposed to my own, for example, his contention that for Stevens "poetical and political acts of representation mistakenly endow abstract collectivities with the attributes of the human mind" (125). But the fact that we focus on the same question—whether "collectivities can rationalize and intend the economies they constitute" (126)—suggests that we are mapping out (in different registers, and with different conclusions) one of Stevens's central political anxieties, one that has precisely to do with the viability or nonviability of spontaneous organization as a political force.[120]

Questions I ask about the relationship of individuality to collectivity are also central to the interdisciplinary collection *Crowds*, in which Jeffrey T. Schnapp argues that photographers of early twentieth-century panoramas, like dictator-demiurges, are "at once immanent and transcendent with respect to the masses."[121] In a similar vein, Jobst Welge argues that in Rilke's *Notebooks of Malte Laurids Brigge*, "the interiority of the quasi-autobiographical protagonist is not a region shielded from the influx of the city"—that interiority here is instead an *effect* of "subject/crowd formations" that have been internalized.[122] In his contribution to this collection, Michael Hardt helps explain why the concept of the multitude might be preferable to the related ideas of the masses or the crowd in a study like mine. Referencing his work with Negri, which examines the ways the term "the masses" has been used to denote "an irrational and passive social force, seen as dangerous and violent because it [is] easily manipulable,"[123] Hardt explains that "the multitude," by contrast, is meant to evoke "a multiplicity of singularities that are able to act in common" and "autonomously."[124] For this reason, the term seems especially well suited to many modernists' fantasies about a spontaneous, decentralized social body capable of enacting the kinds of structural change that would render the external world worthy of modernist ecstasy.

Of course, in examining modernism's fantasies about the potential body of the multitude, one discovers something much more complex than sheer ecstasy. Works such as Ann L. Ardis's *Modernism and Cultural Conflict*, Tyrus Miller's *Late Modernism,* and Andreas Huyssen's lapidary

After the Great Divide all expose modernism's deep anxieties about mob sentiment and the mass media.[125] Mary Esteve's nuanced study *The Aesthetics and Politics of the Crowd in American Literature* shows how to American writers of the late nineteenth and twentieth centuries, the crowd represented not just "the incumbencies and potentialities of [the] polity's citizens" but a hypnotically suggestible mass, dangerously remote from the "abstract, disinterested, secular reason" imagined to underpin the liberal democratic public sphere.[126]

This book contributes to this expanding tradition of criticism by showing how multitudes—not just crowds or mobs—were a prime object of modernist fantasy. In doing so, it accomplishes several unique things. First, it retells the story of modernism as the struggle to represent powers of collective self-organization that lie outside established regimes of political representation. Second, it introduces spontaneity as an analytic category that allows us to read back and forth between theories of political spontaneity and some of modernism's most seemingly private, intimate meditations on creative spontaneity. Third, it develops a new conceptual vocabulary that allows us to see modernism's abstractions and difficulties as part of a speculative political language—one that is organized around questions of centralization and decentralization whose implications have begun to be felt in contemporary theories of democracy and post-Marxist political ontologies.[127]

All of this allows me to approach modernism's abstract creative processes as part of the mass political dynamics of the early twentieth century. Indeed, my overall claim is that modernist models of creative spontaneity dramatize the hopes and fears about *political* spontaneity that preoccupied so many thinkers in the early twentieth century. The very basic modernist idea that the artist's task is to lend organization to a set of volatile, spontaneous energies is, according to my analysis, part of an unconscious political narrative whose permutations are legible in most modernist works of art. In the works that I analyze, this unconscious political narrative is seized on consciously, thematized, and manipulated. This book is therefore less concerned with modernist works that aspire to *become* spontaneous, by integrating automatic procedures or art-alien materials into their formal ensembles, and more with works that approach spontaneity as something on the order of a myth, whose aesthetic and political implications must be explored.

This myth, summarily expressed, is that the organizational impulses of the artist could somehow *be*, or at least *imitate*, the virtual organizational processes of the multitude. Sometimes the modernist works I analyze try to convince us that the myth is a credible one, that the work of art could be *nothing but* the immanent associative logic of the multitude. At other times, they try to expose the forms of political deceit that this myth conceals. But in both cases, these works treat the problem of aesthetic spontaneity as a rescripting of social problems involving central, political apparatuses and the spontaneous collective forces for which they pretend to speak.

By foregrounding this complex synergy between modernism's models of aesthetic and political spontaneity, I hope to make visible an important literary undercurrent in Anglo-American modernism, one whose abstractions and difficulties point not to an entrenched subjectivity falling back on private emotional recompenses but rather to social worlds that exist beyond the party/class, leader/led, individual/collective antinomies of so much early twentieth-century political thought. These social worlds belong to political subjects and processes that exist at the very limit of modernism's figural resources; they are embodied in spontaneous organizational processes, leaderless multitudes, and horizontal systems of affiliation and valuation. Such subjects and processes literally *have no place* in the institutional political universes that form the backdrop of the works I examine. For this reason, we must locate them in the *virtual publics* to which these works bear witness—in the multitudes that exist on the political horizon of modernist literature.

1 RISING FROM NOWHERE

Self-Valorization in William Carlos Williams's Poetry

WHERE BETTER TO BEGIN a consideration of modernism and spontaneity than with William Carlos Williams's *Kora in Hell: Improvisations*? The very title of the book announces that its poems were conceived in an unpremeditated fashion. Improvisation, according to Williams, permitted him to "loosen the attention," allowing it to follow "a more flexible, jagged resort."[1] And *Kora in Hell*, which Williams often refers to simply as "my improvisations," embodies precisely such an "off-the-cuff" poetic method.[2] In creating the work, Williams resolved to "write nothing planned but take up a pencil, put the paper before me, and write anything that came into my head."[3] He did this "every day, without missing one day, for a year,"[4] and "at the end of the year there were 365 entries."[5] Extemporaneity, involuntariness—in short, spontaneity—was the touchstone of Williams's poetics in *Kora in Hell*.

And yet, it is not *Kora in Hell*, with its spontaneous intuitions and jagged resorts, that is the centerpiece of this chapter, but Williams's later, far more ponderous, epic poem *Paterson*. Why focus on *Paterson* rather than *Kora in Hell*? What does *Paterson* have to teach us about modernist ideas about spontaneity that *Kora in Hell* cannot?

My thesis is that *Kora in Hell*'s and *Paterson*'s very different models of creative spontaneity encode very different imaginations of the multitude, that the form spontaneity takes in each of these poems reflects Williams's changing sense of the multitude's own capacity for spontaneous organization and articulation. In *Kora in Hell*, the multitude appears primarily as an ineffable "beyond." It is represented as the earth out of which poetic composition rises, but it possesses few distinguishing characteristics of its own and no autonomous power of social organization. Poetic spontaneity in *Kora in Hell* is therefore defined in terms of the poet's mental journeys into the primordial loam of the multitude and his attempts to discover orders that they cannot articulate independently.

Paterson, by contrast, offers a far more complex portrait of the multitude. In Williams's epic, the multitude appears not just as an elemental murmuring that the poet draws on in his poetic improvisations but also as an interpersonal matrix with specific psychosocial blocks and capacities. One of *Paterson*'s primary goals is to situate these blocks and capacities within concrete structures of exchange and production whose history stretches back to the early colonial period in Paterson, New Jersey. The multitude therefore appears in *Paterson* as the product of a long history of divorces and alienations, beginning with New World slavery and the institution of wage labor in Paterson and continuing into more modern manifestations, such as the Haymarket Affair and the 1913 Paterson Silk Strike. In relation to a multitude such as this, possessed of its own actors, resentments, and oppositional tactics, the poet has greater difficulty imagining himself as a benevolent social visitant, improvising orders on its behalf. Instead, it is the credibility of this kind of benevolist poetic spontaneity itself that becomes the object of scrutiny in *Paterson*. Imagining the multitude as possessing its own history and organizational faculties causes Williams to define himself less as an organizer of the multitude's "raw material" and more as chronicler of the multitude's own capacities for spontaneous organization.

Of course, the image of the poet as a social healer does not altogether disappear from the symbolic economy of *Paterson*. Instead, it becomes one moment in a complex process of negotiation between the poet and the multitude, a process that Williams stages again and again in his epic. At one pole of this negotiation stands the image of the poet as an exponent, intuitively communing with the spontaneous pulsions of the multitude and evolving a concrete representational structure—the poem itself—in which the multitude might see its own dormant creative powers reflected. It is a poetic model that is central to *Kora in Hell*, but that resurfaces repeatedly in *Paterson*, where it is explicitly linked to the political project of *capitalist equilibration*, especially as articulated in the theories of monetary reform Williams was reading in the 1930s and 1940s. According to these theories, which Williams encountered in the Social Credit movement and in the work of the German economist Silvio Gesell, imbalances in the circuit of supply and demand could be spontaneously recalibrated if the productive effort of the multitude were continually returned to the multitude in the form of state-issued credit money. Williams's poetics of redistribution, in which the poet returns to the multitude its own latent productive capacities, in the form of a flexible, freely circulating ensemble of linguistic signifiers, therefore rescripts the redistributive logic of Gesell and the Social Credit movement, transforming its ideal of systemic equilibration into an ideal of poetic spontaneity.

However, there is another tradition of spontaneity at work in *Paterson* too, which came into existence through early twentieth-century theories of *political* spontaneity. This is the kind of spontaneity Peter Kropotkin has in mind when he describes "the spontaneous impulse of the masses" — that is, their ability to act and form complex associations outside of centralized governmental control.[6] According to this very different conception of spontaneity, order is not provided by centralized institutions of power but refers to "free agreements concluded between... various groups, territorial and professional, freely constituted for the sake of production and consumption."[7]

The question *Paterson* repeatedly asks is how this self-organizational capacity could emerge and sustain itself even in the absence of an individual nucleus, a central directive will. Though Williams was attracted to the Industrial Workers of the World as an example of spontaneous self-organization[8] and in 1923 even likened the "work" of his own poetry to Kropotkin's vision of spontaneous association,[9] he could point to no large-scale, living example of spontaneous self-organization when he began concerted work on *Paterson* in the late 1930s and early 1940s. Accordingly, Williams's political meditations during this period are a peculiar mixture of utopian longing and practical despair. At one moment, Williams will argue that "it should be... a great number of individuals in a free community" who bear responsibility for its "continual readaptation to circumstances," and at the next he will insist that "society, as an organism... takes no responsibility... and can take none."[10]

Paterson therefore stands at the crossroads of two models of spontaneity that are fundamentally distinct, but that often take on each other's characteristics and even blur into each other. The first model is a transcendent model of spontaneity, in that it depends on a strong, external will that restores to the multitude its spontaneity. In the guise of state-sponsored monetary reform, this model of spontaneity remains within the circuit of capitalist valorization, since it defines spontaneity as the multitude's ability to equalize its productive and consumptive processes, that is, to reconstitute itself continually as a productive body by making use of the buying power bequeathed to it. The second is an immanent model of spontaneity, one that resides within the associative processes of the multitude itself and that points beyond the displacements of capitalist valorization, toward something Michael Hardt and Antonio Negri describe as the *self-valorization* of the multitude. Unlike capital valorization, the self-valorization of the multitude inheres in "the virtual power of labor," which "exceeds itself, flows over onto the other, and, through this investment, constitutes an expansive commonality."[11] In other words, "self-valorization" refers to a process of value creation that eludes monetary measure and whose object is not the production of commodities but rather the reproduction of the multitude's own capacities: its communicative processes, affective networks, knowledges, and organizational know-how. Self-valorization therefore has a double existence, as the life-creating forms of association and exchange that exist alongside the capital relation *and* as an organizational and productive power that points beyond the entire regime of exchange value and its alienated modes of compensation.

In *Paterson*, this second model of spontaneity—the multitude's immanent forms of self-valorization—is often confused with the "spontaneous," systemic recalibration that state intervention is supposed to afford, as if the state could *return* the spontaneity of the multitude to it through monetary signifiers of its productive effort. At these times, Williams presents the multitude's self-valorization as no more than an aspect of capital valorization, just as, in Negri's terms, reformist ideology transforms self-valorization into "a liminal zone, meaningful only in terms of the reconstruction of a social totality."[12] At other times, however, Williams suggests that the capacities, talents, and organizational skill of the multitude cannot be dynamized and fulfilled through monetary compensation, since even a maximum of buying power will not restore the multitude to the decision-making processes, organizational initiatives, and technological infrastructures that shape their existence as producers of wealth. At these moments, in the fissures opened up by the inadequacies of monetary reformism, Williams asks whether it is possible to imagine a social order based on horizontal, extralegal associations of individuals, communities, and workplaces. In short, he asks whether the self-valorization of the multitude could be imagined as a large-scale force of social regulation.

Paterson provides no straightforward answers to this question. Indeed, for much of the poem, groups of individuals are represented as incapable of true, self-mediating spontaneity. Instead, they remain at the level of the "push-button behaviour-patterns" that Theodor Adorno describes in *Minima Moralia:* a plane of existence where "quick reactions, unballasted by a mediating constitution, do not restore spontaneity, but establish the person as a measuring instrument deployed and calibrated by a central authority."[13] Here spontaneity is possible only on an individual level; it exists only when the mediating powers of the subject combine themselves with the mute, inoperative collective and become its delegate. Thus emerges the image of artist as exponent, who merges with the multitude in order to elaborate its potentialities.

This Adornian model of spontaneity, which relies upon an individual, transcendent will for its coherence, prevails throughout much of *Paterson*, in its images of the poet as the receptacle, mediator, and redistributor of the multitude's latent powers of self-valorization. And yet, as the poem continues, Williams's emphasis is more and more on the failure of this model of poetic redistribution. For the image of the poet as a wandering, improvisatory figure, cross-fertilizing the multitude with his spontaneous intuitions, the image of an immanently self-fertilizing multitude comes to be substituted. In the process, the idea of poetry as a transcendent measure of the multitude's possibilities comes to be associated with the draining of the multitude's immanent productive vitality. The transcendent spontaneity of the poetic genius and centralized political leadership, with their promises to synthesize the pulsions of the multitude into an articulate representational system, comes up against its limit: the immanent spontaneity of a multitude capable of effecting its own social calibrations, outside any currently legible representational system or valuative measure.

In the readings that follow, I will show how these two very different models of spontaneity clash, combine, and condition each other, producing hybrid models of agency in which distinctions between leader and led, production and reception, actuality and potentiality erode almost beyond recognition. What these new models of collective agency make visible is a multitude defined not just by its concrete patterns of existence but also by virtual capacities that Williams can evoke only by way of the most strenuous imaginative effort.

The Raw Material of the Mind

Thinking about the status of spontaneity in *Kora in Hell* will help us construct a baseline against which to measure the models of creative agency—both individual and collective—that appear in Williams's poetry. In *Kora in Hell*, spontaneity is fundamentally an *individual* attribute—its primary value is that it allows the individual to break from habitual thought forms that stifle experience. The kind of unpremeditated attunement to experience that Williams describes in the preface to *Kora in Hell* takes on importance in the poem because it liberates the poet's senses from the conventional patterns in which they are trapped. Williams writes: "The senses witnessing what is immediately before them in detail see a finality which they cling to in despair, not knowing which way to turn. Thus the so-called natural or scientific array becomes fixed, the walking devil of modern life" (14). The fixed array Williams refers to here is the natural-seeming array of perceptual habits that come to condition the life of the senses. This array affords a scientifically correct perception of the world, since all of its data can be confirmed by way of empirical measurement. But this mathematized mode of perception, while it may admirably serve the interests of instrumental action, alienates the senses from an entire world of perceptual possibilities. All perceptual details that do not render instrumental action more efficient, that do not possess the finality of mathematical deductions, slip away from the senses and disappear into a dark netherworld of mental activity.[14]

In *Kora in Hell*, this perceptual netherworld and its dormant possibilities are represented by the Greek fertility goddess Kora, who has been transported to Hades and dwells there as queen of the underworld.[15] Kora, in other words, represents the poetic imagination, which exists in a shadowy, unconscious region beneath the bright, natural-seeming affirmations of everyday perception. Williams refers to this unconscious region as "the dark": "*That which is known has value only by virtue of the dark. This cannot be otherwise. A thing known passes out of the mind into the muscles, the will is quit of it, save only when set into vibration by the forces of darkness opposed to it*" (74). In this passage, Williams describes the way in which perception becomes habitualized; once a stimulus is known it becomes part of the fixed array of the senses. The reactions it habitually provokes become encoded at the level of the body, so that when this stimulus is encountered again, it gives rise to an immediate reflex without involving the creative energies of the individual will. Luckily, however, this world of fixed reactions can be "set into vibration" by the spontaneous forces of the unconscious mind. In *Kora in Hell*, Williams's method is to efface his habitual reactions as much as possible so as to allow these spontaneous interruptions to occur unceasingly.

This gives rise to a perplexing dilemma, however. Essentially, Williams's method is to suspend his familiar thought habits so that spontaneous intuitions might arise from his unconscious. But this means that Williams prepares the way for these spontaneous intuitions quite deliberately, attempts to magnetize them, so to speak, by clearing his consciousness of all familiar thought patterns. This means that these "spontaneous" intuitions are not exactly spontaneous, since Williams anticipates them, wills that they arrive, and seizes upon them continually in the act of artistic creation.[16] Williams's spontaneity, therefore, is not simply an overflow of emotion or sensation that comes upon him unawares. Instead, it involves a carefully maintained intellectual attitude that almost seems to involve two different mental agencies—two different poets, even— each going about his functions semiautonomously. On one hand, there is the poet who cleanses his mind and concentrates on keeping the field of consciousness open. On the other hand, there is the poet who immerses himself in the chaotic flux of unconscious sense data and communicates this unprocessed material to the first poet. The first poet, then, in his pristine and uncorrupted condition, begins to subject this raw material to his formal constructions.

As fanciful as this narrative might seem, it is precisely the figure Williams uses to illustrate the paradox of creative activity in the opening sections of *Kora in Hell*. In fact, he even has these two internal creative faculties banter with each other.[17] The "pure poet" says to the poet who mixes with the raw material of thought: "You think you can leap up from your gross caresses of these creatures and at a gesture fling it all off and step out in silver to my finger tips. Ah, it is not that I do not wait for you, always! But my sweet fellow—you have broken yourself without purpose" (34). The comments of the "pure poet" here indicate that some divide exists between the mind that constructs and the mind that gathers the raw material of life. If the pure poet could fathom any purpose in the explorations of the underground poet, it would mean that these explorations were not spontaneous after all. To qualify as truly spontaneous, these explorations must provide data that are not recognizable parts of the artist's conscious thought patterns. So the delicate mental balance that Williams's brand of spontaneity requires is one in which the pure poet must continually be surprised by the raw material that the underground poet manages to dredge up. The strangeness and clutter of this unconscious material is the only true hallmark of its authenticity, that is, of its status as a spontaneous mental product.[18]

But notice also how the pure poet is not just passively surprised by the undifferentiated data of sense experience that the underground poet explores. Instead, he actively recoils from the data in disgust. The alterity of the underground poet's discoveries awakens not merely bewilderment but also a peculiar kind of contempt in the pure poet. The pure poet even refers with disdain to the underground poet's "gross caresses of these creatures." But to whom is he referring? There has been no mention in this section of *Kora in Hell* of any creatures, human or otherwise, and the prevailing metaphor in the passage has involved aesthetic "cleanness" and "dirtiness," not distinctions between social status and forms of conduct.

But reading on, it becomes clear that the mud in which the underground poet moves has a social dimension as well, that it contains creatures with whom the underground poet associates and, consequently, that it is not just a site of mental flux and multiplicity but also a site of social flux and multiplicity. Moving indiscriminatingly amid the raw data of individual experience is, from the pure poet's point of view, akin to moving indiscriminately amid an uncultivated multitude of human beings. Indeed, the pure poet appears to make no distinction between perceptual multiplicity and social multiplicity. When the underground poet offers the music of this multiplicity to the pure poet and signifies that this music comes "out of the ground" (34), the pure poet replies contemptuously: "Is it this that you have been preparing for me? Ha, goodbye... *Encouragez vos musiciens!* Ask them to play faster. I will return—later" (34). The underground poet is thus figured as an earthy bandmaster, situated in a collective atmosphere of unconscious impulsions. The pure poet, by contrast, is figured as a pampered aristocrat who possesses an unrealistic faith in his egoistic self-sufficiency. Unable to discover a fit mental companion for his creative activity, he impiously asserts that he will "whistle a contrapuntal melody to [his] own fugue" (34).

What this vignette from *Kora in Hell* dramatizes, then, is the division between spontaneous impulse and formal construction. More than this, however, it suggests that this mental division somehow encodes a much larger social division. The spontaneous intuitions that artistic improvisation makes available are represented as a human multitude with whom the poet maintains a gross and undiscriminating sexual intercourse. And the formal consciousness that is capable of meticulously shaping these collective undercurrents is represented as a fastidious aristocrat who turns up his nose at the unrefined raw material with which he is presented.[19] So why does Williams present the divisions of the creative mind in terms of these class divisions?

Theodor Adorno helps provide some answers to this question in his meditation on the roles of expression and semblance in artistic spontaneity. In *Aesthetic Theory*, in a dialectic that closely parallels Williams's creative drama, Adorno describes expression as the collective dimension of art, as the heterogeneous, social raw material that art seeks to express, whereas semblance corresponds to "form in the broadest sense" and represents the autonomy and critical capacity of art.[20] "Expression," therefore, "approaches the transsubjective; it is the form of knowledge that—having preceded the polarity of subject and object—does not recognize this polarity as definitive" (111). As in Williams, however, there is a danger implicit in this fusion of the individual with primal, transsubjective impulses. Without the guiding hand of artistic semblance, this intercourse with the *membra disjecta* of society could "regress[ ] . . . to chaotic regularity" (109)—that is, remain an unorganized, sensuous flux.

The thought categories that Adorno deploys to describe the dynamics of artistic creation therefore inscribe the social divisions between collective impulse and individual construction that we find in Williams. Transsubjective expressive elements provide the raw material of art, but there is no guarantee that this "*membra disjecta* will somehow unify" (108). On the other hand, the autonomous artistic will that is supposed to liberate these social elements from their facticity is always in danger of separating itself from them and becoming a detached formalism. Indeed, describing the "system-driven music" of his contemporaries, whose desire for aesthetic autonomy often reduces them to mathematized lifelessness, Adorno clearly resurrects Williams's image of the prophylactically egoistic composer.[21] As an antidote to this, Adorno describes a form of "spontaneous listening" the composer should perform, in which "the ear's form of reaction . . . passively appropriates what might be termed the tendency inherent in the material."[22] He elaborates on this ideal in "Toward an Understanding of Schoenberg": "At every level in Schoenberg, forces of a polar nature are at work—the forces of unrestrained, emancipated, authentic expression; and the force of a through-construction that attracts to itself even the least detail, the fleeting tremor."[23] For Adorno, these seemingly contradictory forces "have a secret common root," namely, "musical spontaneity."[24]

For Adorno and the Williams of *Kora in Hell*, then, "spontaneity" refers to an artistic ideal in which collective impulse and formal construction are in perpetual dialogue. This dialogue, initiated by the artist and sustained by his or her intuitive "probing in the darkness," is aimed at liberating transsubjective impulses from their irrationality—at "organiz[ing] what is not organized."[25] But as Adorno repeatedly stresses, it is only a transcendent social agent, tactically removed from transsubjective currents, who can perform this liberation on behalf of the multitude. As a consequence, artistic spontaneity comes to replicate, in its internal structure, the social divisions it seeks, in principle, to overcome. Incapable of organizing itself "from below to above" (220), the multitude is recast as an ensemble of productive forces that must be harnessed and directed by a representative of "the most progressive consciousness, which today is exclusively that of the individual" (42). Responsibility for the mediation and integration of collective impulses can, according to this schematic, only reside in strong, tactful individuals capable of exerting "control over the material" (59).

No doubt, both Adorno and Williams try to avoid the authoritarian implications of this agential model by foregrounding what Adorno, in *Aesthetic Theory*, calls "the latent collectivity of . . . subjectivity" (86)—that is, the presence in the individual of "mimetic preindividual elements," by virtue of which "every idiosyncrasy lives from collective forces of which it is unconscious" (42). Indeed, in his *Autobiography,* Williams defines Kora as an expressive force that is simultaneously subjective and objective:

> Damn it, the freshness, the newness of a springtime which I had sensed among the others, a reawakening of letters, all that delight which in making a world to match the supremacies of the past could mean was being blotted out by the war. The stupidity, the calculated viciousness of a money-grubbing society such as I knew and violently wrote against; everything I wanted to see live and thrive was being deliberately murdered in the name of church and state. . . . It was Persephone gone into Hades, into hell. Kora was the springtime of the year; my year, my self was being slaughtered.[26]

Williams's response to this dire condition is to seek out the principle of historical rebirth where it is hiding, and it is hiding both in the suppressed creative energies of the world's populations and deep within Williams's own psyche. In other words, he recognizes a continuum of sorts between the creative energies buried in his own unconscious and those that are latent in the multitude, so much so that the spontaneous impulsions Williams discovers in his own mind seem instinct with the collective energies that he hopes to see bloom in the social arena. Williams's descent into the impulses of his own mind is therefore performed not merely in the service of some individualistic psychic research. Instead, he hopes that his improvisations might simultaneously liberate the spontaneous creative energies that are lying dormant in the social body and lend them a publicly recognizable shape.

As we have already seen, however, this liberation narrative contains a profound schism. When the multitude spontaneously creates its own collective music, the formal capacities of the poet detect only a rude cacophony from which they withdraw. And conversely, if the poet's improvisations do manage to rescue some spontaneous intuitions—carrying them from the underworld of the mind into the light of conscious thought—their nature is immediately distorted. They are interpreted according to habitual thought categories and become the possession of the conscious mind. Williams likens this process to the way that "*certain pestilential individuals, priests, school teachers, doctors* [and] *commercial agents,*" whose professions cause them to live among the poor, ignore the "*ancient harmonies*" of the multitude, which "*in their ignorance*" these professionals believe are merely a "*confused babble of aspiring voices*" (43–44). These professionals try to "possess" the poor with their own worldviews, believing that this will liberate them from their social marginality. Concerning this bankrupt rescue narrative, Williams comments: "All things brought under the hand of the possessor crumble to nothingness" (20).

Kora, then, as the representation of the multitude's spontaneous music and the artist's unconscious creative powers, is destined to remain in the underworld. Williams's ironic statement "perhaps we'll bring back Eurydice—this time" (20) testifies to this. Eurydice disappeared before the backward glance of Orpheus, just as the pulsions of the unconscious disappear before the shaping powers of the conscious mind. So the poet, by virtue of his underground persona, may maintain a perpetual dance with the spontaneous impulses that reside in the dark of the mind. But neither the poet's fugitive intuitions nor the collective creative impulses with which they are intertwined can survive conscious scrutiny.

We are therefore left with the Adornian paradox of a collective subject that is the source of artistic spontaneity, but that lacks any organizational force of its own and must therefore have its own potentialities restored to it through the benevolence of a transcendent social actor. According to this model, spontaneity is located not in the multitude itself, as a force of creativity, organization, and self-valorization, but rather in the formal tact of creative individuals, lending their constructive capacities to the multitude, to show it what it might become.

Spontaneity and Intransigency

Kora in Hell thus leaves us with a number of tantalizing questions that seem unanswerable within its own symbolic economy. For example, why does it seem so natural to associate the chaotic flux of perception with the chaotic flux of the multitude? Moreover, why do the poet's constructive faculties seem to play either the role of the detached aristocrat or the misguided benefactor of the multitude? What larger social intransigency does this creative scission encode? And finally, why is it that the life of the imagination comes to carry such loaded political connotations in the first place?

According to my analysis, *Paterson* is able to offer some surprising answers to these questions, because it explores the social dimension of spontaneity much more thoroughly than *Kora in Hell* does. In Williams's early improvisations, the categories of creative intuition certainly are politicized, but in *Kora in Hell* Williams does not ask why the multitude so often tends to be represented as an unconscious flux, nor why the spontaneity of the creative mind is so often represented as deriving its energy from this mobile, collective force. *Kora in Hell*, therefore, primarily *enacts* certain dilemmas of modernist spontaneity, whereas *Paterson* enacts them and speculates about many of their social, historical, and psychological underpinnings as well. It is true that at times, *Paterson* seems to endorse unironically the image of the poet as a benevolent liberator, merging with the spontaneity of the multitude in order to articulate the new social vocabulary that lies dormant within it. But at other times, Williams's epic explores the social, historical, and psychological foundations of this modernist myth so relentlessly that the poem becomes a speculative map of the real social contradictions and fantasmatic compensations that the idea of spontaneity encodes. In this capacity, *Paterson* moves far beyond the image of the modernist as a blind dancer amid the impulsions of the collective unconscious. What it evolves instead is a new kind of epic quest. Williams's epic is one that seeks to discover the systemic social forces that divide the multitude from itself. The object of its quest is to reveal the social intransigencies that precede and frame the "free play" of creative spontaneity.

Some excellent criticism has begun to highlight these sociopolitical dimensions of Williams's epic. Notably, Fredric Jameson devotes the first chapter of his *Modernist Papers* to *Paterson*'s "poetics of totality." In his account, *Paterson*'s ambition to project "America as a telluric or chthonic reality" is undermined by the epic's swift and unsteady modulation between a multiplicity of "documents and voices" drawn from daily newspapers, oral histories, works of anthropology, epistolary correspondence, economic data, and so on.[27] The formal imbalances and infelicities of Williams's poem thus frame Paterson's population less as a self-determining epic community than as a flux of "American lives and experiences [that] are also the absence of voice... the lack of even those multiple subjectivities that could alone sustain and subtend the Bakhtinian vision of a kind of spiritual democracy."[28]

Michael Tratner too stresses the social blocks and failures that *Paterson* incorporates into its epic vision. In *Deficits and Desires: Economics and Sexuality in Twentieth-Century Literature,* Tratner focuses on "the blockage of free fluid flow" in Williams's sexual and economic imagery, arguing that Social Credit, for Williams, promised a comprehensive release of generative energy.[29] But since this generative energy, this "abundance waiting to be released," is far greater than the poet's own meager energies, Williams leaves us with an image of poets "unleashing forces far beyond their comprehension" and "danc[ing] contrapuntally to everything around them."[30] According to the ideology of Social Credit, this abundance, this generative energy, is nothing less than the total productive power, aesthetic sense, and capacity for innovation of the social body. It makes sense, then, that Williams often stages the failure of his individual creative powers in the face of this massive generative network. It is hard to imagine a spontaneous individual dance, however complexly contrapuntal, that could reorganize and direct such a massive creative ensemble. Indeed, Tratner correctly notes that unlike Pound, Williams is unattracted to images of strong, individual leadership and often "seems against centralized government altogether."[31] Fashioning a poetic persona in whom all social contradictions could be spontaneously resolved is therefore anathema to Williams's poetics in *Paterson.*

Nevertheless, there is another form of spontaneity operating at the margins of Williams's epic, in spaces opened up by the failures of agency Jameson and Tratner so aptly document. This kind of spontaneity belongs to the generative energy of the social body itself—to what Paulo Virno, following Marx, describes as the "general intellect" of society: "the communication, abstraction, self-reflection of living subjects."[32] What C. H. Douglas and other Social Credit theorists imagined as a cultural inheritance—that is, an accretion of cooperative forms and productive know-how—becomes, in this very different political vision, an agent in its own right: a network of social producers capable of directing and recombining its own productive energy in highly differential ways.

But as we shall see, Williams strains his imagination to its limit attempting to visualize such a form of collective spontaneous agency, often resurrecting the figure of the poetic genius or the Social Credit technocrat to fill in the gaps of his political vision. In my readings of *Paterson*, it is this struggle on which I focus, the struggle of a political imagination that seeks to delineate forms of leaderless, collective *autogestion*, but that often uses the spontaneities of the individual poet to evoke them—the struggle to depict the social body as a self-restoring complex, but one that is difficult to imagine in the absence of some form of centralized direction, however shadowy and indirect.

A good place to begin an examination of this struggle and the differing ideas of spontaneity that attend it is *Paterson* II, where the agon between individual and collective forms of agency, like so many modernist agons, is represented as a technically complicated dance.

Libidinal Distributions

This dance begins in *Paterson* II, section I, when Williams's poetic persona starts moving impulsively through a park that is filled with workers recreating on a Sunday afternoon. Here, Williams employs a trope that is already familiar from *Kora in Hell*, that of the multitude as a group of earthy musicians. But in *Paterson* II, the movement of the poetic imagination through the shifting timbres of collective life is tracked much more closely, and the glancing movements of the multitude are figured much more explicitly as the source of his spontaneous poetic intuitions.

At first, Williams represents the multitude's movements as the unpredictable flight of grasshoppers in the park: "before his feet, half tripping, / picking a way, there starts   . / a flight empurpled wings!"[33] These movements continually elude Williams's poetic "feet," but even as they expend their energy and disappear into the "coarse cover," they "leave, livening the mind, a flashing / of wings and a churring song" (47). In other words, Williams's poetic process is guided by the complex, improvised music of the park's earthy inhabitants.

Where this narrative departs significantly from *Kora in Hell* is in Williams's attempts to discern the reason for the split between his own improvisations and the ungraspable "living presence" (47) that animates them. In a telling departure from the epistemology of *Kora in Hell*, Williams is not content to regard this split simply as a phenomenological given, a scission between the mind that intuits and the mind that constructs. Instead, he suspects that this creative schism may mirror some interpersonal schism that exists within the social body itself. He writes:

> among
>
> the working classes SOME sort
> of breakdown
> has occurred. Semi-roused
>
> they lie upon their blanket
> face to face,
> mottled by the shadows of the leaves
>
> upon them (51)

Here Williams isolates a single proletarian couple that is meant to represent the collective self-estrangement of the workers in the park. In this section of the poem, such self-estrangement is represented in primarily psychosexual terms. Accordingly, the male member of the couple is described as a "flagrantly bored and sleeping" "lump," and the female member is described as "stir[ring], distraught, / against him—wounded (drunk), mov[ing] / against him ... desiring" (58). In other words, there is a libidinal disconnect between the couple. Even though the collective life of the workers in the park is represented as a promiscuous flux, shot through with renovating possibilities, the couple Williams isolates is incapable of actuating this vitality. Their "semi-roused" posture is meant to evoke this condition of psychosexual ambivalence. Some gap separates the two lovers that prevents them from being a functional, fully roused couple.

In this context, the task of the poet is to discern the sources of this interpersonal alienation and to provide a language capable of translating the potential vitality of the multitude into a concrete, vivifying force. This task is personified by an evangelist who seeks to gather the atomized figures in the park together, to "marry" them to each other and, in so doing, to overcome their condition of alienation. Once again, the sexually ambivalent couple in the park comes to represent the workers around them, as well as their atomized state. Now, however, the male of the couple is fast asleep, and his sexually unresponsive, dormant form comes to represent the multitude's inability to wake to a sense of its own potency. The evangelist is therefore in league with the female of the couple, since both figures are attempting to rouse the dormant vitality of the sleeping man. As part of this bizarre seduction, the voice of the evangelist enters the sleep of the male lover

> until there moves in his sleep
> a music that is whole, unequivocal (in
> his sleep, sweating in his sleep—laboring
> against sleep, agasp!) (59)

Nevertheless, the male lover "does not waken" (59), and the dream of plenitude he glimpses is not translated into actuality.

So what does this much more detailed representation of the poet's contact with the multitude tell us about Williams's ideas about spontaneity in *Paterson*? For one, it suggests that Williams now approaches the music of the multitude less as a free play of improvisatory forms than as an internally divided complex. At first, the spontaneity of the multitude is represented as a wild, unstructured flight of insects, an improvised pattern of transecting movements whose energizing force is closely aligned with the vital forces of nature. But what at first appeared as an unstructured play of vital forces later reveals itself to be a fairly limited set of libidinal patterns that are rigidly structured around a schism that runs through the interpersonal existence of the workers in the park. In other words, the spontaneous, promiscuous libidinal patterns of the park are *organized* around a constitutive lack that the circulation of libido cannot heal over. Spontaneity, then, exists within certain socially defined limits. In fact, everything spontaneous about the workers' interactions begins to seem like an agonized attempt to overcome some psychosexual intransigency that prevails within their theater of social activity.

Moreover, the mediations of the poet, which are aimed at overcoming this psychosexual intransigency, are represented as inadequate, not because the poet distracts himself with egoistic journeys such as those undertaken by the pure poet of *Kora in Hell* but because of some blockage at the level of the multitude itself. The spontaneity of the multitude is somehow damaged or wounded, and by the end of *Paterson* II, it is clear that the poet is unable to cure this condition through improvised formal arrangements. Instead, he must embark on a different kind of poetic project, one that involves tactically removing himself from the immanence of the multitude in order to track down the origin of the blockage that is at the center of its interpersonal exchanges.

In other words, the very category of spontaneity is coming into crisis in *Paterson*, and the idea of modernist intuition as an improvisatory surrender to the spontaneity of the multitude is coming into crisis along with it. Instead of asking how the sensibility of the poet can become earthy enough to provide an immediate transcription of the multitude's spontaneity, *Paterson* begins to ask, What is missing from the spontaneity of the multitude such that the poet, in his or her intuitive excursions, is supposed to act as its restorer, its redistributor? Moreover, why does this restorative, vital principle seem *dormant* in the social body, that is, purely potential: a part of its collective dream thoughts, but not part of its living patterns of exchange? What is the history of this separation, this wound around which the spontaneities of everyday existence are organized?

Credit and Reinvestment

In a 1936 essay titled "A Social Diagnosis for Surgery," Williams provides some clues to his ideas about the scission that drains Paterson's collective body of life. He describes "a cancer of the body politic" that is "draining out [its] life faster than [it] can replace it by what [it] eats."[34] This structural imbalance has been created by what he calls "credit monopoly and kindred monopolistic trends."[35] In other words, there is something about the monopolization of finance capital that compromises the "health of exchange."[36] For Williams, this is because such private caches of credit money represent quantities of value that have been withheld from the population at large, diminishing its buying power and preventing it from absorbing, through consumption, the full value of the commodities it produces. According to this account, the disparity between wages earned and commodities produced leads to crises of overproduction. If consumers are unable to realize the value of the sum total of commodities produced, factories will become unprofitable; this will lead to layoffs, and these layoffs will even further diminish effective demand, setting in motion a rapid downward spiral that Williams understood to be the underlying dynamic behind the Great Depression.

According to Williams, the solution to this progressive diminution of the population's buying power lies in "the socialization of credit money."[37] According to this scheme, all workers would be immediately paid the full value of the commodities they produced, in the form of credit slips issued by the government. This would restore health to the social body by allowing it to fold back into itself all of the value it creates in the process of commodity production. And it would restore health to the capitalist system as a whole, since industrialists would have immediate access to all the value realized in the consumption process, rather than having to fuel the next production cycle with private, interest-bearing loans. Theoretically, this would allow for a new kind of social vitality and would restore the lost spontaneity of the social body. No longer would the energy of the body politic remain dormant within it, unable to be realized within a theater of reciprocal exchange relations. Instead, libidinal-economic fluidity would be restored to the socius; it would possess the capacity to reinvest spontaneously the sum of its productive efforts.[38]

In *Paterson* IV, Williams provides an image of the ways in which this credit scheme could restore the spontaneous vitality of the multitude. The image is of the local, distinctive labors of individuals being returned to them as an abstract, universal potency—a collective energetics in which spontaneous creations and exchanges could be continually consummated.[39] Williams writes:

> Credit makes solid
> is related directly to the effort,
> work: value created and received,
> "the radiant gist" against all that
> scants our lives. (185)

In this passage, Williams offers credit as the cure for the wound that exists in the social body. Credit would provide the medium in which the productive effort of Paterson's individuals could be mirrored and fecundated by other members of the social body, effectively allowing them to recover and articulate themselves *as* a social body. Accordingly, this cure extends beyond the realm of merely economic exchange. If the effort behind individual work cannot be reflected by the productive efforts of society as a whole, then no mutually generative exchange can occur at the levels of language or sexuality either. The terms, the signifiers, that would enable such exchange are no longer distributed amid the social body as a living, expressive element. Instead, such terms and signifiers are drained of their life and returned to the social body as a dead medium in which its own capacity for spontaneous, reciprocal articulation is no longer present. Credit, then, promises to restore the sexual, linguistic, and economic motility that would allow the social body to become a spontaneously self-creating complex.[40]

What is most interesting about this model of social restitution, however, is that its structure is almost identical to the forms of *poetic* mediation and redistribution whose *failure* Williams uses the evangelist to represent. Like Social Credit, the evangelist's agency is an external force that inserts itself amid the social body, promising to restore its energies. But, as we have already seen, this form of social mediation fails. It fails to wake the dormant social body to its own vitality, because it confronts some structural intransigency within the social body itself. At the level of *Paterson*'s overt polemics, this intransigency is simply the population's lack of access to credit money. But if this were all that is at issue, Social Credit and the evangelist's forms of external mediation would be perfectly adequate, and *Paterson*, presumably, would be a much shorter poem. In fact, Williams intuits that these forms of external mediation are thoroughly inadequate, and it is at the level of *Paterson*'s symbolic economy, rather than at the level of its political arguments, that this becomes obvious. In other words, *Paterson*'s symbolic economy, with its deities, presences, and symbolic landscapes, constitutes a speculative social topography against which various forms of mediation and redistribution are measured.[41] And Social Credit and poetic "redistribution" both fail this speculative test.

The "Blocked" Multitude

To understand these failures of agency, it is necessary to understand what the redistributive mechanisms of Social Credit and the poetic "redistribution" of the evangelist *fail to account for*—what lies beyond them on both the conceptual and material levels. In *Paterson* II, this beyond is represented as a sleeping male deity who resides at the bottom of the Passaic Falls, well beneath the park where Paterson's workers are recreating. The fact that he is sleeping suggests that he is a colossal double of the dormant worker in the park. And the efforts of the evangelist, as well as the worker's female companion, to rouse the male worker are therefore, in a sense, attempts to rouse his monumental divine counterpart. Who, then, is this profounder sleeping figure, of whom the male worker is just the local representative? He is clearly meant to represent some fundamental aspect of Paterson's social geography, for Williams names him "Paterson" and opens his poem with a description of him:

> Paterson lies in the valley under the Passaic Falls
> its spent waters forming the outline of his back. He
> lies on his right side, head near the thunder
> of the waters filling his dreams! Eternally asleep,

> his dreams walk about the city where he persists
> incognito. Butterflies settle on his stone ear.
> Immortal he neither moves nor rouses and is seldom
> seen, though he breathes and the subtleties of his
>   machinations
> drawing their substance from the noise of the pouring
>   river
> animate a thousand automatons. Who because they
> neither know their sources nor the sills of their
> disappointments walk outside their bodies aimlessly
>   for the most part,
> locked and forgot in their desires—unroused. (6)

Notice how in this passage the male giant is "eternally asleep" and yet at the same time conceives "machinations" that "animate a thousand automatons." This suggests that the giant's unconscious mind somehow generates the everyday reality of the workers in the park—that the workers themselves, in fact, are dreamed into existence by him. The position, then, from which the workers' collective life is structured is removed from them. It is not a function of their own vital capacities and, in fact, seems to be a location where their vital capacities are trapped, dormant. Within the realm of their everyday existence, only the amount of energy that will allow them to resume their lives of automated labor and alienated sexuality is returned to them.

In this passage, then, it is easy to detect some of the economic motifs that obsessed Williams in the 1940s. The waterfall, whose kinetic energy continually drains into the valley below, represents all of the energy that is drained from workers in the production process, energy that is not fully returned to them in the form of spending power, but that is instead contained, dammed up, in the recumbent figure of the sleeping giant. This metaphorics of draining and damming is omnipresent in the economic theory Williams was reading, as is Williams's figure of dormancy. In the economic works of Silvio Gesell, C.H. Douglas, and Ezra Pound, credit is represented as a great dormant force that need only be discovered by legislators and put to work.[42]

But there are also many aspects of the above passage that cut against the metaphorics of Social Credit and even thoroughly undermine it. For example, the dormant giant is positioned in the exact location occupied by the famous silk-spinning and dying factories of Paterson, New Jersey. The factories, like the giant, were sprawled by the side of the Passaic River beneath the falls. The giant's "machinations" and "automatons," therefore, are clearly meant to evoke the industrial processes animated by the energy of the waterfall. George Zabriskie makes this connection clear: "As the waters of the Falls drive the electric motors of the factories, as they once drove the undershot water wheels, so do they drive the thoughts of the sleeping giant, Paterson."[43] The vital energy of the workers, then, is penned up in the industrial apparatus itself, not just in the coffers of private financiers. Williams's imagery, therefore, destabilizes the ideology of Social Credit in a fascinating way. For if economic crisis is not simply the consequence of correctable blockages at the level of finance, but rather involves structural contradictions at the level of production as well, then solutions that operate strictly within the realm of redistribution and consumption are doomed to failure.[44]

The consequences of such a failure for modernism, and specifically for modernist figurations of spontaneity and social mediation, are difficult to overestimate. For if restoring the vital, self-creative energies of the social body required only an act of fiscal legislation, then this restorative function could be carried out by enlightened leaders acting benevolently on behalf of the multitude. Poundian forms of social mediation, for example, in which individuals of great insight and *virtu* can singlehandedly break the credit monopolies that block social exchange, would constitute a credible social cure.[45] If, however, as Williams suggests, the multitude's energies are trapped within an industrial apparatus whose functioning is structurally removed from their collective will, then no legislative actions concerning redistribution or credit could offer the kind of restitution Williams desires. Instead, it would be necessary to imagine a structural transformation in which the multitude would reclaim creative energies that had become sedimented in a rigid, unresponsive industrial apparatus. Anything short of such a structural change would mean that the multitude would continue to "walk outside their bodies" as substanceless cyphers, signifiers of an alien productive force that animates their every step.

It is at this point that *Paterson*'s symbolic economy points away from models of capitalist equilibrium and toward what Negri describes as the self-valorization of the multitude. According to Negri, this process of self-valorization is "the time of living labour that traverses the whole of society, and that carries and explicates the productive overdetermination that cooperation has determined and determines."[46] In other words, self-valorization is the process whereby the multitude uses its talents, capacities, and activities to enrich its own collective being, rather than simply to provide fuel for the process of capital valorization. Self-valorization is thus simultaneously "inside and outside of capital."[47] Inside, in that its creative potentialities come into being only after large-scale industry has become the productive foundation of society, transforming labor into an abstract, mobile force and determining in advance its patterns of productive cooperation. Outside, in that through this process of socialization, the multitude discovers in itself needs, capacities, and organizational powers of a quality and scale that are completely incommensurable with the capital relation. So, as Negri explains it, self-valorization is simultaneously an actual process of organizational networking and communicative interrelation as well as a virtual capacity for self-rule that points toward as yet unrealized modes of productive coordination.

Locating these powers of self-valorization, however—showing how they explicate the powers of human cooperation embodied in capital, while at the same time exceeding and subverting these—presents formidable conceptual difficulties. One danger would be to identify such forms of self-valorization with idiosyncratic lifestyle practices, what Negri calls "the privilege of experiments in living which always come to nothing."[48] Throughout their work, Hardt and Negri make it clear that fantasies about "the simple life"—the desire to return to the production of use values on a small scale—has nothing to do with self-valorization, properly conceived. The latter, in fact, can be grasped only at a level of generality that encompasses the multivalent, expansive flows of capital itself. And yet, at this level of generality, it would be easy to mistake any struggle for a better life for self-valorization, *tout court*, even struggles for monetary reform such as Williams endorsed, which rely on fantasies of a perfectly harmonized, unantagonistic capitalism.

In the political pamphlets compiled in *Books for Burning*, Negri addresses this difficulty directly. He admits that "in a given relation of antagonism, workers' processes of self-valorization operate alongside capitalist coercion" (201) and even claims that "the struggle over public spending" provides the multitude "the possibility of materially grounding its own productive unity—of opposing exploitation by means of self-valorization" (250). But he insists, against Keynesian and socialist models of state intervention, that the multitude's self-valorization cannot be contained and stabilized simply by public spending. "Infrastructures, services, education, housing policies, welfare policies, etc. multiply and determine an ever-wider context for the process of self-valorization" (256). But these goods and services remain merely a *context* for the process of self-valorization, a backdrop for the multitude's autonomous creation of "needs, free time, and civilization" (201). This autonomous creation thus exists as a countersphere within capitalist civilization, possessing its own logic and modes of agency.

To bring this countersphere to view more clearly, Negri traces a path that, in his own way, Williams also traces in *Paterson*. Negri begins, in *Marx beyond Marx*, by focusing on monetary circulation and the theories of monetary reform that would, with the help of Silvio Gesell and C. H. Douglas, influence Williams so profoundly in the 1930s and 1940s. Negri then interrupts this narrative of reimbursement and equilibration, confronting it with everything it cannot equalize, resorb, and include, namely, all the processes of collective self-valorization that become more and more vivid in the course of Williams's epic. Negri (following Marx) thus deploys a strategy of interruption that we will encounter repeatedly in *Paterson*, a strategy that defines self-valorization as a limit or excess of capital itself: as all the powers of collective association, recombination, and self-organization that could never express themselves in the capital relation, even if they were fully recuperated at the level of "buying power." It is as if these virtual capacities can be made tangible only after an exploration of the fantasy that monetary circulation *could* provide an adequate measure of the multitude's recombinative power.

This fantasy is that of "a revalorization of a pure, deployed, and abundant circulation" (26), or, as it appears in the Marx text Negri is explicating, the fantasy of "*proportionate production.*"[49] In the *Grundrisse*, proportionate production is an imagined state of economic equilibrium in which production and consumption would be perfectly equalized, an ideal rooted in the economic theories of Pierre-Joseph Proudhon, which Williams would encounter via the works of Silvio Gesell and the Social Credit theorists. The idea is that a reorganized banking system would compensate workers with time chits representing the numbers of hours they worked. Theoretically, this would allow workers to buy back the full value of the commodities they produce, providing industry, in turn, with a steady supply of immediately reinvestable capital. As Gesell argues in *The Natural Economic Order*, this would free industrialists from the necessity of undertaking interest-bearing loans, which then require them to exact from their workers a surplus value proportionate to the rate of interest they must repay. Gesell explains: "Money... lays down this obvious condition for the construction of a house, or a factory, or ship, that the house must be able to exact from its tenants, or the factory from its workmen, or the ship from its freight, the same interest that money itself can at any time exact from the wares" (390). Eliminating money interest would therefore eliminate the need for industrialists to extract surplus value, and in this way "the means of production will lose their capitalistic character" (35), allowing any skillful "technician" to become a manufacturer and allowing humanity to "develop[ ]... its full powers" (34).

This is the vision of unfettered and self-renewing human exchange that animates much of *Paterson*, and that prompted Williams to extol Gesell's "plan to secure an uninterrupted exchange of the products of labor, free from bureaucratic interference, usury and exploitation."[50] But it is also a vision that *Paterson* continually interrupts, confronting it with images of pent-up creative energies, inflexible command structures and class divisions that remain troublingly external to Gesell's monetary utopia. Marx employs a similar strategy of interruption when he asks how the bank that issues money against *all* commodities produced, so that consumers will have sufficient buying power to absorb all of them, could possibly be imagined to be indifferent to matters of industrial policy. As Marx points out in the *Grundrisse*, such a bank would be "the general buyer and seller" of all commodities, since under this regime, all producers would "not await the chance arrival or non-arrival of a buyer, but go immediately to the bank, unload their commodities on to it, and obtain their exchange value symbol, money, for them" (155, 154). This would present the bank with the prospect of an inevitable and catastrophic currency crisis, since it would be compelled to issue currency against all enterprises, regardless of their competitiveness. In reality, the bank would "have to determine the amounts of labour time to be employed in the different branches of production... because, in order to realize exchange value and make the bank's currency really convertible, social production in general would have to be stabilized and arranged so that the needs of the partners in exchange were always satisfied" (155). In this way, the utopia of free circulation is transformed into one of the two political forms from which it had been striving to differentiate itself: either "a despotic ruler of production and trustee of distribution" (i.e., a totalitarian state, which Marx here submits to a proleptic critique) or "nothing more than a board which keeps the books and accounts for a society producing in common" (i.e., a collectivist government that would presuppose "the common ownership of the means of production") (155–56).

What reappears in Marx's critique—the problems of organization, decision making, and the methods of measuring value—are precisely the problems grouped under the category of self-valorization in Negri's thought. The attempt to solve these problems by "disappearing" them within the realm of monetary circulation only causes them to return with greater force and clarity. The question of self-valorization is posed again as the question of how the multitude could set its own priorities, distribute its productive energies, and create models of communication and exchange in the absence of the state and the falsely neutral measures of value that appear in Proudhon and Gesell. What at first appears as an intransigency in the capitalist system—its inability to equalize exchange or eliminate command from the production process—thus becomes a prompt for speculative inquiry, an attempt to grasp what the preconditions *would* be for a social recombination on this scale.

This is precisely the shift that *Paterson* performs as it poses ever greater challenges to Social Credit's models of equilibration. It is as if Williams must enter into the byways of the circulation process, beginning, like Marx, with an exploration of money and the grandiose fantasies of equilibration it inspires, in order to see more clearly the blunt realities of fixed capital, the division of labor, and the state monopoly on legitimate violence—in short, everything that monetary reform cannot dissolve. The most striking emblem of this shift is *Paterson*'s evangelist, who represents both the dream of money as an almost magical force of social potentiation and the bloody realities of primitive accumulation, state violence, and capitalist command that money so effectively conceals.

In *Paterson* II, the evangelist is first introduced as a benevolent figure attempting to restore the libidinal-economic fluidity of the multitude. He recounts a self-congratulatory narrative about his accumulation of capital and the command he later receives from God to "give away [his] money" (70). He then moves among the multitude, making "a wide motion with both / hands as of scattering money to the winds" (73). This image of scattering clearly links the evangelist's redistribution to some form of collective sexual fertilization. It is as if the evangelist is returning to the multitude the vital energy that they require in order to reconstitute themselves as a dynamically connected, potentiated social body.

In the economic realm, this redistribution is supposed to make possible the marriage of each worker's productive efforts to the productive efforts of the city as a whole. What the evangelist offers is the medium, the element, the terms that would allow the multitude to find its productive efforts reflected and potentiated within its collective body. His success would thus represent the success of redistribution as a social cure, the success of Social Credit.

But as the minister symbolically scatters money amid the population, it becomes clear that returning the multitude's vital energy to them in the dead medium of money will do nothing to wake them to their creative potential. In fact, this quantification of their productive energy is hardly distinguishable from the originary act of violence that transformed Paterson's smallholding farmers into a drift of quantifiable labor values. Accordingly, as the minister scatters the money that is supposed to heal the wound in the social body, the multitude is not healed and does not wake from its living death. Instead it is merely reinstituted as an "amnesic crowd (the scattered), / called about" (60). In other words, the minister and the Social Credit cure that he represents suddenly seem complicit with the historical processes that defined Paterson's inhabitants as so many atomized nodes of exchange: vital forces to be tapped and "compensated."

Through a kind of anamorphic turn, the minister's failure helps make visible everything that cannot be returned to the social body through the mechanisms of money and credit. As he continues his self-congratulatory reverie, symbolically disburdening himself of all the values pent up in Paterson's industry and anticipating the rebirth and fulfillment that will be visited upon Paterson's inhabitants as a consequence, Williams interrupts him with narratives and images evoking the violent economic divisions that are the backdrop of the minister's displays of benevolence. When the minister claims to "bring / the riches of all the ages to you here today" (66), echoing C. H. Douglas's idea that credit will make the entire population heirs to the accumulations of cultural knowledge and wealth embodied in industry, Williams interrupts with a historical narrative of Alexander Hamilton's struggle to prevent popular control of this "cultural heritage." Williams stresses that Hamilton "never trusted the people, 'a great beast,' as he saw them" (67) and then tells of Hamilton's ambition to transform Paterson, New Jersey, into "a great manufacturing center" financed and controlled by federal rather than local entities (70).

The story Williams tells, then, is about Hamilton's desire to centralize not just finance capital but industrial capital as well, that is, his attempts to "harness the whole, young, aspiring genius" of the nation "to a treadmill."[51] The narratives and images Williams interposes as commentaries on the minister's sermon, therefore, emphasize the wedges that have been driven between the multitude and the forces of production that shape their conditions of existence, not just between the value of their products and the wages they receive for them. The image of John Johnson being hanged for the murder of the Van Winkle family exemplifies the primordial trauma of this form of primitive accumulation; as a "laboring farmer... employed by some of his neighbors in the same capacity" (197), Johnson represents an impoverished, landless population separated from the "sleeping capital" shut up in the private property of a family whose name, in the American folk tradition, is synonymous with dormancy. Worse yet, the crowd that gathers "on Garrett Mountain and adjacent house tops to witness the spectacle" (202) exhibits a morbid fascination with the consequences of their own dispossession. Rather than gathering their creative energies to resist the dynamics of primitive accumulation in which John Johnson is ensnared, they prefer to watch "April! in the distance / being hanged" (72).

Later in Williams's epic, this image of the multitude's ritual sacrifice of its own creative vitality is juxtaposed with the image of a Dutch farmer who maintains a rich qualitative relationship to his own productive energies. Williams's versified rendition of a narrative history of Paterson tells of a man who, during a cholera epidemic, "refused to bring his / team into town for fear of infecting them / but stopped beyond the river and carted his / produce in himself by wheelbarrow" (194). The Dutch farmer represented here possesses a relationship to his labor and the exchange process as a whole that is far richer than anything that is possible in the deskilled and spiritually numbing world of automated labor. He is included in *Paterson* as an example of all the human powers of understanding, care, and reckoning that are destroyed by primitive accumulation and that cannot be restored through the redistribution of quantities of credit money.

This is why Williams eventually exhibits the minister as a false savior, indicating that his "harangue hung featureless / upon the ear" (70). Essentially, the minister is unable to attend to the qualitative "features" of the members of the multitude he addresses, transforming them instead into a mass of faces that are as blank and impersonal as the dollar bills he pretends to disseminate among them. This attempt to transform Paterson's workers into so many qualityless nodes of exchange, therefore, backfires on the minister. Williams suddenly describes him as "outnumbered" (72) as he "addresses / the leaves in the patient trees" (72). The purely quantitative definition of the workers as exchange values—as endlessly proliferating, undifferentiated "leaves" of currency paper—suddenly evokes the inevitable failure of money to restore the morcelized social body to the qualitative disposition of its forces. The trees as "patients" awaiting a cure for the primal wound that exchange value has exacted have suddenly become murderously "patient" spectators to the phony monetary sacrifices made by the evangelist.

Ultimately, the evangelist is associated with a "cold blooded / murderer" (72) who was hanged when Paterson was still being transformed from an agrarian economy into an industrial one. Like this primordial murderer, the evangelist is subjected to a symbolic hanging by the crowd that has gathered about him. To add insult to injury, his body is sent downstream, where the evangelist undergoes a "second death" by water. Williams writes: "*Le / pauvre petit ministre,* swinging his arms, drowns / under the indifferent fragrance of the bass-wood / trees" (82). In an uncanny way, the manner of the evangelist's death casts a final judgment on the form of social mediation he represents. The arm motions he makes while drowning obviously mirror his arm-swinging disbursements of money to Paterson's workers. But the evangelist cannot accelerate this gesture enough to keep pace with the current of the river and the much more massive arm swinging of the industrial waterwheels that churn in the river where he meets his end.

The image of the strong, individual leader equalizing social exchange by accelerating monetary compensation therefore fails in *Paterson*. Instead, what Williams's epic tends to focus on are all of the repressed historical traumas and unseen structural estrangements that make such easy solutions impossible. For Williams, it is only by waking to these traumas and estrangements that Paterson's multitude will be able to restore its lost vitality. But how to represent the psychic life of all that is historically forgotten? How to recount the history of an absence?

The History of the Ineffable

In a passage that he expunged from the final typescript of *Paterson,* Williams provides a clear description of the kind of originary violence that persists, largely undetected, in America's structures of trade and governance, rendering the evangelist's efforts at social equalization futile. The scene he sets is of George Washington's Ringwood estate and "the ironworkers' cabins, the charcoal burners, the lime kiln workers" that are clustered in the forest nearby, "hidden from lovely Ringwood" (12). These two locations represent an unstable duality that lies at the origin of America's national history: "a bold association of wild and cultured life" that "grew up together" (12) in the early years of the country's existence. Washington's idyllic Ringwood Manor obviously represents the cultured side of this equation. But its "ease" is threatened by a "wild" assemblage of wage laborers and slaves who are transforming elemental iron ore into "links . . . for the great chain across the Hudson" (12).

This chain, which prevented the British navy from advancing up the Hudson river, and which was a decisive element in America's victory over the British, stands as a symbol of America's primal emergence as an independent national entity. But Williams emphasizes that this chain was forged by workers who were themselves still in chains. Slave labor provided for the accumulations of wealth America required if its bid for national autonomy was to be successful. Therefore, even America's most originary act of self-constitution is completely inseparable from a primal violence that cannot be contained or expressed within the logic of Washington's heroic republican ethos. Consequently, Williams retells America's history as one of trauma and abandonment.

He writes of the area surrounding Ringwood:

> Certainly you would say under these calm trees—
> There's no violence here: rapine, harlotry,
> disease and abandonment—
> engrafted on the wild. Hamilton, violence at
> his birth, drawn toward violence, to die also
> by violence. Violence in the earth. Iron
> lightnings from the earth. Thunderbolts of steel—
> dug by primitives, by slaves—enkindled
> by strange fires, illicit, unrecognized—[52]

The strange, illicit, unrecognized fires of this passage refer to the heavy labor required to extract and process iron ore, but they also clearly refer to the illicit sexual violence that was the traumatic support of the American slave economy. For Williams, the forcible induction of black slaves into sexual relations with their white masters represents a primal and traumatic "energizing" of the capitalist system—one that allows for an expanding mass of slave laborers to be reproduced without cost to the master. What is horrifically "strange" about this method of wealth production is that in it sexual terror is translated immediately into the disposable energy of the system as a whole. Capital amassed in this fashion bears within itself, with none of the mediations of the wage system, the unspeakable violence that lies at its origins. And this procreative terror then transfers its traumatic charge, through the laboring bodies of the slaves it produces, to the "thunderbolts of steel" that will come to form the material infrastructure of industrial capital.

So, for Williams, just as iron ore originally extracted by slaves is melted down and transformed into the factory infrastructure one sees all around one, so too did capital produced in America's slave economy, through concentration and reinvestment, come to constitute a traumatic and ever-expanding economic "charge" that renews and revitalizes the capitalist system. In other words, Williams insists on reestablishing the continuity between contemporary systems of exchange and the primordial social violence that every cycle of exchange has carried within it up to the present day. This primordial social violence, for Williams, haunts our everyday circuits of exchange, rendering systemic stability impossible on both an economic and a psychic level.[53] The image to which *Paterson* continually returns is that of an original violence meant to introduce an energic support to the system of exchange, which institutes itself as the perpetual present of a system that is for that reason unable to contain and harmonize the energic surpluses it carries. A healed social body, capable of spontaneously equalizing supply and demand, wealth and consumption, is unthinkable in this economy, since this economy supports itself on the disparity between what workers produce and what they receive as "compensation" for their efforts.

In *Paterson*, the Passaic Falls embodies this paradoxical idea of a systemic support that is at the same time a systemic failure or crisis. In an early representation of the falls, Williams repeats the image of the lightning stroke that he uses to represent the illicit extraction of capitalism's primal charge from slaves. But now this lightning stroke has become a permanent and quotidian feature of Paterson's social landscape. "Succeeding hordes" (8) of water represent Paterson's workers, reimagined as masses of energy that will fuel the factories below. The lip of the falls represents the moment when, on their way to fuel this industrial apparatus, the multitude are suddenly deprived of the power they imagined themselves to possess in the park above, when their spontaneous perambulations and libidinal exchanges are suddenly revealed to be "unsupported" on a systemic level. Lacking a common social language, a common medium of exchange, a reciprocal libidinal economy, they become like helpless droplets of water. They

> fall, fall in air! as if
> floating, relieved of their weight,
> split apart, ribbons; dazed, drunk
> with the catastrophe of the descent
> floating unsupported
> to hit the rocks: to a thunder,
> as if lightning had struck (8)

In this passage, the falls stands as a symbolic nexus of loss, uniting the processes that continue to drain value and labor from Paterson's workers with the earlier historical processes that first constituted Paterson as an industrial center of colonial America. What Williams hopes to make visible in this way is that the separation of Paterson's workers from the disposition of their vital energy is a phenomenon that has a history. The image Williams presents is of individual productive efforts failing to meet with any counterbalancing support, and therefore fanning out endlessly, like the skeins of silk produced by the factories below. But what might seem like a purely contingent loss of agency, occurring as a consequence of chance imbalances of exchange, or because of subjective deficiencies of spontaneous energy, is in fact part of a complex system of value extraction that was forcibly imposed on Paterson's population long ago. And because this inaugural act of violence came to be coded in the laws and norms governing social life in modern America, the history of this original, constitutive separation came to be repressed.

What is at issue here is what Werner Bonefeld calls "the permanence of primitive accumulation": the fact that "the slavery, theft, etc. that first constituted capitalism" is not just a moment in the "antediluvian existence" of capital, but is "shifted from the prehistory of capital into the present, into a moment of its reality and of its present activity, of its self-formation."[54] Bonefeld focuses on this *institutionalization* of primitive accumulation—the way it "persists, within the capital relation, as its constitutive pre-positing action."[55] And in *The Micro-Politics of Capital*, Jason Read helps explain how the overt violence that attended the expropriation of smallholding farmers must constantly reproduce its effects through "a new type of violence... monopolized and standardized by law and the bourgeois state."[56] From this *institution* of primitive accumulation as a normalized "moment" of capital accumulation is "derived the eternal right of capital to the fruits of alien labour, or rather its mode of appropriation is developed out of the simple and 'just' laws of equivalent exchange."[57] In this way, primitive accumulation becomes part of a complex of contemporary social relations that forcibly ensures the principle of capital's self-reproduction while permitting its violence to "disappear... into the quotidian relations that the law makes possible."[58]

In *Commonwealth*, Hardt and Negri similarly argue that primitive accumulation does not simply give way to capitalist production according to a progressive historical narrative. Instead there is "a constant back-and-forth movement in which primitive accumulation continually reappears and coexists with capitalist production";[59] they cite Jason Read's work in this connection. But for Hardt and Negri, primitive accumulation should also be viewed as the motor of labor's increasing socialization and potentiation. The traumatic destruction of traditional cultures and production techniques, the definition of labor as a nonspecific, abstract quantity, rather than a specific, qualitative exercise, allows for a conception of "the abstract collectivity of labor," that is, of "creative worker subjectivity, in the potentiality it possesses of being a source of all possible wealth."[60] Through the generalization and multidimensionality it acquires in this process, *abstract labor* comes to signify the possibility of a general, creative self-organization of the multitude, that is, the possibility of self-valorization.

And yet, *as* abstract labor, the creative potentiality of the multitude confronts an indissoluble obstacle. It is the same obstacle we see in the "blocked" multitude of *Paterson*, namely, the fact that as exchange value, the multitude is unable to exercise its own self-organizational potency as generally and variably as it is capable of doing. *Paterson*'s workers circulate like currency, with all of the freedom and flexibility that money allows, but also with its inability to fulfill and equalize the value it carries. In *Labor of Dionysus*, Hardt and Negri describe the desire, which Williams inherits from Proudhon, Gesell, and the Social Credit movement, to make money equal to the value of all circulating commodities, and thus to make abstract labor equal itself. This would be "a situation in which profit and interest are reduced to zero, and in which the monetary relation... would disappear, since money would be reduced to a mere accounting unit, simply a general symbol of equivalence between commodities produced."[61] What this account leaves out, however, are the relations of ownership and command that persist within this fantasy of a steady-state, self-equilibrating economy. While social labor is animated by a massive complex of alien fixed capital and alien directive power, its creative, organizational potentiality can never be fully recuperated. Instead, "the elementary and spontaneous movements of labor-power" begin to constitute an oppositional countersphere, and "a neurosis of the mobility and the rupture of the law of development that abstract labor accumulated at a social level determines and takes hold of the entire society" (114).

For Negri, the only cure for this neurosis is for abstract labor to exist not merely as a function of monetary circulation and unequal exchange but also as an agent in its own right, capable of spontaneous association not just at the level of circulation but also at the level of production. This "deepening of productive cooperation" such that it becomes "a constituting praxis" is the way Negri imagines a comprehensive recuperation of the creative energies of abstract labor, "creative energies that the universality of cooperation in production, that the successive displacements of production have produced, have enormously enlarged."[62] According to this trajectory, abstract labor first suffers the "reduc[tion] of the subject to a mere quantitative entity and a purely numerical existence in the market," but in the process develops "abstract qualities" that "are linked within the universality of communicative potential" and that allow it to "act[ ] ... upon the totality of the conditions of production and reproduction of the social."[63] The damaged or incomplete spontaneity of the multitude, expressed within the neurotic circuits of unequal exchange, accordingly becomes spontaneity in the strong sense, that is, *self-valorization:* "the capacity of the social body to present itself as the activity that regulates universality."[64]

Within *Paterson*'s symbolic topography, the process whereby the wound of abstract labor becomes a potential for self-valorization is imagined as a leap from the upper realm of circulation to the lower realm of production, a retrieval and resorption of everything that is currently drained from the interpersonal body of the multitude. And indeed, *Paterson* presents us with many such images. There is the image of the poet as a bee, attempting to "tongue" the beauties of the multitude—to capture and articulate them before they fall away, like the falls' droplets of water. And there is the image of Sam Patch, whose cliff dives bizarrely enact the leap from the upper realm of circulation to the lower realm of production; indeed, it is the impulse to *retrieve* lost items—a rolling pin, a pet bear—that often motivates his leaps. But as in the Adornian model of spontaneity we examined in relation to *Kora in Hell*, such leaps posit the individual as a deputy of the multitude. They are performed on the multitude's behalf and elicit only passive spectatorship from them. The fact that both attempts to recuperate and revalorize the multitude fail (Williams's flowers "wilt and disappear" [11]; Sam Patch perishes when he strikes the water of the Passaic) suggests that Williams places little faith in such individual displays of spontaneity.

And yet, for much of *Paterson*, collective forms of spontaneity are equally difficult to imagine. The image of the multitude falling through air is not that of a self-mediating leap and holds little promise of recuperating all the values that are displaced in this process. Instead, it is an image of a vast social incontinence—the site of a collective loss, where the multitude not only surrenders its own powers of spontaneous organization but also actually derives a perverse pleasure from doing so. Williams represents these collective powers as a massive liquid force, which the multitude orgasmically surrenders, or pisses away, in the "conveniences" (60) of the park above the falls. And the sound of this willed, collective disburdenment is indistinguishable from that of the falls itself.

In this deeply unspontaneous ritual of collective self-dispossession, workers queue up—at the direction of a traffic cop, no less—in order to "relieve[ ]" (60) themselves of a collective tension: the troubling sense that partially dawned on them that afternoon that beneath all of the "complex voices" (60) of the park, there existed a single voice—their own—that could be collectively articulated. Instinctively avoiding the collective effort such an act of self-discovery would demand, the multitude accepts the compensatory pleasures offered by the traffic cop: that of being "good dogs" (61). In a masochistic display, the multitude assents to the draining of their spontaneous powers of association.[65]

As the symbolic economy of *Paterson* develops, then, the image of a genuinely spontaneous social body becomes that of a multitude that *does not release* its internal tension, however gratifying such a release may seem at the moment. Or rather, it is the image of a multitude for which the release or "floating" of productive effort is immediately a collective resynthesis of this effort, a distribution of its energy across the social body, rather than an abandonment of this energy to an alien productive apparatus and the monetary compensations it provides. This vision is far more radical than that of Gesell and Social Credit, for it could be realized only if the multitude and the productive apparatus animating it were not socially divided, but part of a self-mediating continuum. Williams provides no concrete images of what such a continuum would look like in *Paterson*. Indeed, the image of such a spontaneously self-mediating multitude emerges only behind the back of Williams's strained engagement with monetary reformism, in its gaps, inconsistencies, and false premises. But what Williams does provide are a number of abstract emblems of such an imagined state of spontaneous self-mediation. What these emblems invite us to imagine is a release that is at the same time a taking-up, an expenditure that is at the same time a reception, in other words, a simultaneous circuit of values produced and values received. In these moments, Williams ushers us away from a transcendent model of spontaneity, based on the external directive will of the state, the artist, or the Social Credit functionary, and begins to imagine an immanent process of self-valorization.

To imagine such a process of spontaneous self-calibration, Williams draws on the sphere of libidinal economy, where the distribution of erogenous zones and innervations across the individual body prefigures what he would like to discover on the part of the multitude.

Androgynetic Generation

In order to picture an economy in which discharges are at the same time renewals or excitations, Williams repeatedly conjures the images of polymorphous bodies whose erotogenic surrenders are at the same time reinvestments of energy. These images serve as psychosexual emblems of what Williams has difficulty imagining concretely within the sphere of material production and distribution. This figuration of the multitude as a collective libidinal organism is one Williams borrows in part from Wilhelm Reich, whose *The Function of the Orgasm* Williams was reading in 1946 while he wrote *Paterson*. In particular, Williams borrows from Reich the idea that barriers to spontaneous libidinal-economic circulation in the multitude are simultaneously barriers to their capacity for spontaneous political association. Referencing Reich in a note to Kenneth Burke, Williams explains the difference between authority-blinded workers, like those depicted in *Paterson* II, and the psychosexually "complete" man. According to Williams, such a man does not have to *ask* someone else (the politician) to lend him something, to "grant" him equality with others. He does not need a Fuhrer, a Duce. Those bastards can only practice their arts on an incomplete man (robbed by the cute bankers, by the nifty systems by which men are always robbed).[66]

Notice here how Williams aligns psychosexual and economic forms of completion. The bankers' privatization of what should be a public possession—credit—interrupts what should be a spontaneous biosocial circuit, leaving the multitude searching for fantasmatic compensations for its lack: a Führer, a Duce. Imagining what restored "bio-psychic motility"[67] would look like, however, is a more difficult task, which leads Williams into some bizarre territory. Writing to Burke, he compares such social potency to the experience of orgasm:

> The function of the orgasm is not nookie, not pleasure but the (the words fail me) summatization, the recurring assertion of the psycho-somatic individual as one, as a whole. It resynthesizes (at its best) the at-loose-ends man into the individual. . . . It also "recreates" the man, theoretically makes him want to assume responsibility (since his world is completed in that cycle—that's what he knows).[68]

This idea of orgasmic "resynthesis" is quite counterintuitive. It seems a direct contradiction of the image of the self-relieving multitude of *Paterson* II, whose collective, ecstatic surrender of responsibility is depicted—like the falls itself—as a noisy collective orgasm. Here, however, the orgasm represents the opposite of "relief" and complacency. Williams's use of words such as "summatization" and "resynthesize" suggests that he is describing not so much the singular moment of orgasmic release as a state of simultaneity in which energic discharges are immediately taken up by the social body as a moment of its "responsible" self-mediation. It seems that what Williams has in mind is a biopsychic circuit that immediately converts the "summit" of energic release into the resorptive "summation" of these energies by the reciprocal activity of society as a whole.

Of course, Williams stresses that this image of spontaneous self-summation is a futural vision, incommensurable with the economic relations of his day and the libidinal blockages with which they are coextensive:

> We're not talking about the present day world, the present day world is almost entirely neurotic in its make-up; we're talking of a biologically functioning world in which relationships between the sexes are uninhibited by "property" let us say.[69]

In other words, what Williams is trying to imagine is a condition in which women and men could continually reintegrate sums of productive energy into the social body, rather than allowing them to pool up in private coffers or alienated work processes. Such self-regulation would thus be spontaneous not in the sense of being a drunken or ecstatic surrender, but rather in the sense of being a collectively sustained form of attention and recalibration.

In *Paterson* IV, Williams explores this new, collective idea of spontaneity in some fascinating ways. Rather than representing the damaged spontaneity of the multitude as a wounded female body that needs to be phallically fulfilled by the redistributive force of the poet, Williams introduces an imagined plurality of brides whose metonymies of erogenous excitation elude relief in exactly the way Williams hopes the multitude might. Drawing on his knowledge of Freudian psychoanalysis, Williams reimagines the social body as a spontaneously self-organizing complex of pregenital excitations, which refuse to be unified under the heading of an external, phallic agent, however benevolent the intentions of that agent may seem.[70]

Williams names some of these brides. There is Alma, for example, "who wrote a steady / hand, whose mouth never wished for / relief" (191). And there is Nancy,

> who never smiled more
> than was sufficient but whose broad
> mouth was icy with pleasure startling
> the back and knees! whose words were
> few and never wasted (191)

The libidinal economies of these brides belong to the realm of "forepleasure" in Freudian terminology—that is, a type of excitation that is not discharged but renews itself promiscuously in erogenous zones not governed by the phallic logic of "end pleasure." This is essential, since the collective discharge or "relief" of the falls represents the removal of creative energy from the body of the multitude and its transformation into qualityless kinetic energy by the factories of the lower Passaic. Alma's libidinal economy, by contrast, is not punctuated by a discharge or relief of energy, a spilling over of energic quantities that she is unable to resorb and mediate. Indeed, Williams suggests that her libidinal innervations are matched only by her steadiness of hand, as if having a steady hand— the ability to maintain continuity even amid variation—is somehow similar to the play of excess and containment expressed in Alma's desiring economy. With Nancy as well, abounding excitations never exceed her capacity for "measured" articulation in speech and comportment. These brides thus do not operate according to a phallic libidinal economy, where continual energic losses are returned fantasmatically in the form of fetishized objects. Instead, self-loss, self-abandonment is imagined here to be functionally equivalent to self-possession, to a measuring out of libidinal currents across the organism as a whole. As models of social exchange, then, these brides represent a multitude capable of immediately relaying value from one component element to another, of spontaneously coordinating the production and reception of social effort.

Williams's emphasis here on pregenital erogenous zones—the mouth, the back, the knees—thus signals a shift away from a wounded, lacking social body in need of phallic restitution and toward an imagined social body that is innocent of or remote from such traumatic excavations. The "Nancy" above, for example, is an incarnation of Nancy Cunard, who in Williams's *Autobiography* represents "an experience remote, childish, like the very first feelings of love, unassociated with sex."[71] In other words, she is associated with forms of desire that are beyond the tortured negotiations of "mature" phallic sexuality—forms of desire that are more primordial and perverse, but also more physically integral. Williams associates this form of desire with women more than men, since for him women are far superior to men in their ability to combine physical desire and self-mediating poise. As Williams writes, "Men are the technical morons of the tribe, women keep some proportion, remain sound even in debauchery, relate the parts to a whole, act, that is with the body, the related parts, together, not a part of it, as to be sure, they must survive."[72] Parsing the strange syntax of this sentence leaves us with the proposition that women such as Cunard act, bodily, the related parts (of the tribe?) together to form a whole. That is, they achieve precisely that social resynthesis and summatization that is denied to phallic discharge. While the latter releases social surplus and social responsibility from the ordinary circuits of exchange while producing an arousing *illusion* of containment and proprietation, Williams's brides sustain a permanent, bodily acting-together of particulars that resorbs social surplus in a way that has nothing to do with containment or property. Instead, loss and externalization seem to be folded back into the matrix of the social whole, not through the detour of redistribution, but rather through some process of propertyless appropriation, a loss that is immediately an innervation, a "soundness even in debauchery."

With this image, Williams moves beyond the figural limitation that Gilles Deleuze and Félix Guattari attribute to Reich: his difficulty in "determining the insertion of desire into the economic infrastructure itself, the insertion of the drives into social production."[73] In *Anti-Oedipus*, Deleuze and Guattari observe that Reich sees "reactionary mass investments" (119) as the product of inhibited desire, but revolutionary investment as the workings of economic rationality; therefore, he is unable to see the impulse to revolt as anything but the restoration of rational economic interest on the part of the multitude. Williams, by contrast, offers a positive image of what Deleuze and Guattari call "desiring-production": an investment of flows, energies and intensities that predates and subtends the functional organization of desire. As Elizabeth Grosz points out, this idea of desire as that which "makes things, forges connections, creates relations, produces machinic alignments" moves us away from the model of desire-as-lack, which privileges the image of the phallus as the imaginary compensation for a primordial lack that is chronically gendered "female."[74] And yet Williams does not reject the category of lack in its entirety. Instead, he historicizes its genesis, determining its psychic phylogeny in the separation of humanity's creative powers from its ability to mediate and direct productive activity. This means that for Williams, the insistence of lack is not dissipated through reference to pregiven, primordial flows and intensities alone. Instead, his emphasis is on a distinctively modernist process of mediation, whereby reserves of ungoverned creative energy achieve organization within a reciprocal and evolving social system. So what Williams adds to Reich's thought is less an image of deterritorialized seepages undermining molar orders from within than the image of a comprehensive process of self-organization, in which the productive energies of the multitude develop themselves institutionally, but without the losses, traumas, and rigidities that characterize institutional life under the rubric of capitalist valorization.

Williams's brides emblematize this ideal of internally reflected mediation, the ideal that "effort, / work" should express the synchrony of "value created and received." The mutual excitation of pregenital erogenous zones, such as the women's mouths, has exactly this character of sustained and chiasmatic creation/reception of value. And Williams distinguishes his mediatrix figures from women "too drunk / with it—or anything—to be awake to / receive it" (191). In other words, it is not an infantile polymorphism Williams seeks, in which each drive chaotically follows its own separate path toward satisfaction. Instead, what Williams seems to be aiming at is what Teresa de Lauretis describes as "a sexuality of component instincts, which, unlike infantile polymorphous perversion, is inclusive of phallic and genital drives but, unlike 'normal' sexuality, is not bound to a necessarily phallic, genital, and heterosexual primacy."[75] Williams's nonproprietary model of exchange thus seems to involve a continuity of physical intentionality sustained *amid* the multiple surrenders and innervations of pleasure production—pure effort, in other words, that is synonymous with pure surrender. This is less a nonorgasmic than a permanently and consciously orgasmic economy.

But the gendered character of this new desiring economy suggests that there is something incomplete, one-sided, or transitional about it. As Williams suggests, it is precisely *because* women are marginalized in his society, precisely because "no locus is *permitted* them in the society in which they should be active members," that what is "valueless (priceless)" in them[76]—that is, their sexuality—achieves its status as the harbinger of a socially integral beyond. It is precisely because Williams's brides are "not part of" the tragicomic inflations and depressions of phallic libidinal economies that their surrender to their rhythms can be viewed as *partial*, part of a double attitude in which ridiculous displays of phallic virility are only half invested. This distance allows them, symbolically, to accomplish what the "virile" spectacles of *Paterson*'s celebrated cliff diver—Noah Faitoute Paterson—can only mimic: a ritualized resorption of the lost energy, desire, and language of the multitude. But it also makes them extremely alienated emblems of the multitude's imagined capacity for spontaneous coordination. It is precisely these women's dystopic struggles to survive in a world defined by phallic libidinal economies that invests them with whatever utopian function they possess. They prefigure that technique of standing apart amid self-surrender that the multitude is supposed to adopt on a collective level. But for Williams's brides, standing apart is a survival technique, not the free, collective process of self-calibration that it is meant to foreshadow.

Much feminist criticism of Williams helpfully zeroes in on his disturbing erotic investment in such alienated images of female mediation. For example, Williams's eroticization of the brides' survival mechanisms mirrors what Sandra Gilbert and Susan Gubar call his "voyeuristic absorption" in the other forms of gendered violence *Paterson* represents.[77] And Cristina Giorcelli argues convincingly that behind Williams's seemingly generous depictions of women as mediator figures is the imperative that women "donate themselves wholly and 'forthwith'... like abiding, self-effacing, ever generous lovers."[78] According to this logic, the female deity of *Paterson* I is analogous to the Virgin of *Paterson* V; as "the creator of The Word by Whom she was created," Mary is "only an intermediary," a "vessel" in a closed circuit of male exchanges.[79]

It is difficult to sort out the utopian from the dystopian in this mélange of gendered bodies and fantasies. The images of collective spontaneity above are supposed to evoke a social body capable of exchanging quantities of productive effort in highly fluid ways. But as Luce Irigaray notes, it is no accident that "woman" so often comes to represent such depersonalized mediating functions: "Off-stage, off-side, beyond representation, beyond selfhood," "woman" too often represents a "reserve supply of *negativity*" which supports the rearticulation of desire.[80] This is because, for Irigaray, "*women-as-commodities are... subject to a schism* that divides them into the categories of usefulness and exchange value; into matter-body and an envelope that is precious but impenetrable, ungraspable, and not susceptible to appropriation by women themselves; into private use and social use."[81]

"Woman," in Irigaray's analysis, is thus divided along the same lines as *Paterson*'s social topography. The falls of the Passaic stand as the scission that divides the upper valley, where workers circulate mechanically, from the industrial apparatus below, which is inaccessible to them. The falls is thus the perfect emblem of a society in which the qualities of activity and passivity, production and reception, are divided temporally, sexually, and socially. And Williams's imaginary solution to this problem is actually quite similar to Irigaray's. He elevates "woman," as the sex that suffers this division most acutely, into the social "operator" whose internal doubleness signals a radical potentiality:[82] that the social body could fold all extraneated energies back into itself, embracing them in an internally reflected play of values. As Irigaray puts it in *This Sex Which Is Not One*, this would mean that the commodity-body, whose valuative standard is an external "surplus-value" (178) that constitutes it as the "mirror" and "supporting material" of phallic "speculation" (177), could collapse this externality into its own activity and create something like a "*mirror that copies it so that it may be at once itself and its 'own' reflection*" (176)—a condition in which "use and exchange would be indistinguishable" (197).

Williams's brides thus stand in for a process of social resorption and *rabattement* that, even in highly speculative contemporary philosophy such as Irigaray's, is difficult to imagine except as a function of gendered divisions that separate society into an artificial hierarchy of functions. There are moments in *Paterson*, however, in which Williams attempts to imagine the multitude's self-reflective powers as something even more primordial than these gendered mediations, indeed, as something even more primordial than sexual difference itself. For Williams, the prototype of this primordial social ontology is to be found only amid "childhood's / lecherous cousins" (188), that is, amid the component drives as the ambivalent protagonists of childhood sexuality. According to Williams, we should not dwell on the privileged trio of component drives, but remain alive to the "connivance," the "convoluted forms" (188) of pregenital sexuality, the complex claim of the entire body's erotogenic potentiality. In this vein, Williams writes, "Man and woman are not / much emphasized as / such at that age: both / want the same / thing. to be amused" (189). Women's bodies here no longer (or do not yet) mirror the traumatic social extraction of value in which men "discover" their desire as a loss continually eliciting compensation, cure, and redemption. In the face of these agonized "adult" rituals, the amused indifference of children appears as the profoundest "virtue" (188). Before this amused indifference, phallic sexuality and its overserious mystique of penetration and fulfillment is completely impotent.

In this image, then, Williams clearly abandons the idea of the poet as an individual, spontaneous force, single-handedly "holding together" and "scattering" the libidinal-economic energies of the multitude.[83] By *Paterson* IV, this model of individual spontaneity has clearly been aligned with the phallic pretensions of poetic "genius," according to which a virtuosic individual, a "Faitoute," "does it all" on behalf of the multitude (or, alternately, "makes everyone": *fait toute*). Abjuring this model of spontaneous individual synthesis, Williams leaves us with a legend that reappears throughout book IV, section III: "*La Vertue / est toute dans l'effort*" (188). In other words, "responsibility" for the reciprocal ordering of the social body can now be conceived as "in" the labor, the effort—simultaneously productive and receptive—of the multitude itself.

This new kind of collective spontaneity is represented as a state that is neither male nor female, neither productive nor receptive alone, but both, simultaneously. Williams imagines it as a collective "hermaphroditic state" or "androgynetic generation,"[84] in which the social body appears as a "composite / dandelion that / changes its face overnight. Virtue, / a mask: the mask, / virtuous" (188). Not definable in terms of female and male, the dandelion is a "composite" that alternates between a receptive, absorptive role and a productive, dispersive role. As a species, it enacts these roles simultaneously, just as in Williams's ideal libidinal economy production and resorption of value would constitute a differential simultaneity. The flower is simultaneously the proprietor and the relayer of the conditions of exchange, and each of its roles is transient, a mask, by which Williams means that there is nothing behind or external to it other than the spontaneous counterbalancing of exchange acts—no surplus value surreptitiously removing itself from the theater of exchange to become the external support of the system, a "private" staked out against the public alternation of masks.

Spontaneity in this context has far less to do with the poet's intuitive journeys into the multitude than with the multitude's own capacity to regulate the exchange of goods, services, talents, and forms of knowledge. Picturing how any social body could accomplish such large-scale exchanges in the absence of centralized leadership is a task almost beyond the imaginative powers of *Paterson* and of modernist literature in general. Nevertheless, the possibility of collective spontaneity on such a scale is the engine that drives Williams's speculative efforts in *Paterson*. The poem provides no concrete political images of the kind that we find in philosophers of spontaneity such as Kropotkin—images of workers' associations, mutual aid syndicates, and popular centers of direct exchange. Instead, we encounter pregenital erogenous zones, brides capable of discovering measure even in abandon, preadolescent bodies unfamiliar with the divestments and compensations of phallic sexuality, and androgynetic flowers. These are the wildly idiosyncratic emblems of a condition Williams can barely bring into view: a multitude that is also a directive will, a discharge that is also a renewal.

Self-Valorization

The path that led us from *Kora in Hell* to *Paterson* has thus opened upon a model of spontaneity that involves more than the individual poet and the crude, murmuring multitude that is his raw material. Whereas *Kora in Hell* presents a multitude that seems ontologically incapable of self-direction, *Paterson*'s multitude is possessed of such a self-directive capacity but is prevented from expressing it by specific socioeconomic forces that Williams's epic sets out to name and describe. The shift is therefore from the modernist poet as a spontaneous genius, purveying the collective language that will restore the multitude to itself, to the multitude as a potentially self-organizing network of faculties, visible just beneath the surface of modernity's alienated systems of exchange.

That *Paterson* loudly proclaims the socially restorative value of Social Credit while undermining Social Credit's core principles at the level of its own symbolic economy is a testament to the intellectual strain Williams underwent in his attempts to think through the self-valorization of the multitude. Evidence of this strain is visible in each of the modernists I consider in this book, as well as in contemporary philosophers of the multitude, who tend to approach the concept only by way of highly abstract ontological meditations. *Paterson*'s modernist abstractions—its strange litany of part objects, errant drives, and metaphysical orgasms—could thus be approached as some of the twentieth century's early attempts to figure a political power that had no place within the era's regimes of representative government.

As we will discover in the chapters that follow, Lewis, Riding, and Stevens all find themselves at some point at the edge of a similar representational void. When this occurs, political positions they have noisily staked out for themselves—Lewis's schizophrenic proclamations about fascism and communism, Riding's defense of conservatism as the "intellectually official defender of idealism,"[85] Stevens's watery statement that he "is against the CIO and with the AF of L"[86]—tend to be replaced by a profusion of abstractions that simultaneously encode and exceed these authors' conscious political beliefs. The utopias that become visible in this process are thus rarely those of clear political argument. Instead, they are what Nicholas Brown describes as "negative utopias"—ideas of social order that become visible only through the gaps, inconsistencies, and voids of the current social order.[87]

Williams's utopia of component drives and spontaneous mediations emerged in precisely this way, out of his feverish and internally inconsistent wrangling with the ideology of Social Credit. Lewis's utopian impulses concerning the multitude—insofar as they can be detected at all—emerge in an even more intense struggle with the populist pretensions and betrayals of European fascism.

2 WYNDHAM LEWIS, CONSTITUENT POWER, AND COLLECTIVE LIFE

WE HAVE COME TO KNOW Wyndham Lewis as one of modernism's most vocal advocates of the stable, self-contained ego. In works such as *Time and Western Man* and *The Art of Being Ruled,* Lewis describes the ego as a static entity that "must cohere for us to be capable at all of behaving in any way but as mirror-images of alien realities, or as the most helpless and lowest organisms, as worms or sponges."[1] In other words, the ego is what prevents us from reacting in a purely mechanical, involuntary fashion to external stimuli. It should be regarded as a "static 'substance,'"[2] a stable position from which to analyze the flux of our environment. And as Vincent Sherry points out, this does not constitute a merely personal credo for Lewis. Shunning the ontological blurring of "acoustic empathy" and "demotic fellow feeling" allows one to resist the hypnotic effects of mass political movements.[3] Individuality and stability, it seems, are the last lines of fortification against the sensationalism of crowd-life.[4]

But what of the Lewis who writes in 1932 that "such artists as Shakespeare or Dickens are very little *individuals* at all—they are, as a matter of fact, a very great and numerous crowd"?[5] And what of the Lewis who writes in 1925 that "the expansiveness that manifests itself in inventive or expressive work... is not so very far removed from the consciousness of the crowd, for in multiplying itself a crowd is formed"?[6] In statements such as these, Lewis suggests that the artist's sensibility is not so distant from collective realities. In fact, it seems to serve as an embodiment or analogue of these realities. Indeed, in a 1932 essay titled "Physics of the Not-Self," Lewis describes a speculative organ that allows one to "participate... in the life of others outside [oneself]" and states, unironically, that "every altruism can be traced" to our ability to "go outside our self."[7]

These statements present us with a less familiar Lewis, whose ideas seem completely at odds with his well-known celebrations of the individual ego.

To understand this seeming contradiction at the heart of Lewis's thought, it helps to understand the difference between two distinct models of spontaneity that Lewis evolves in his work, since it is in his different conceptions of spontaneity that Lewis encodes many of his anxieties about the ego, the multitude, and the relationship between them. The first model of spontaneity is the commonsense one, according to which one acts on impulse, unpremeditatedly, giving oneself over to the impressions of the moment.

In works such as *Time and Western Man* and *The Art of Being Ruled*, Lewis critiques this idea of spontaneity and the notion that it affords access to creative impulses that are remote from the regulations of the individual ego. Modern philosophers, according to Lewis's critique, even suggest that such spontaneity allows one to be projected outside of one's own individuality, merging with a cosmic, vital power, an "indescribable creative gushing of the life-force" that becomes available only if individuals dissolve their selves and become receptive to it.[8]

But for Lewis, the occult life force that supposedly shapes human existence is merely a philosophical screen for the very real machinery of ideological repatterning that conditions the thoughts of the multitude. Spontaneity in this context simply means "renunciation of the *self*"[9] in the service of vast, irresponsible power systems. For Lewis, this means abdicating the critical power of the ego and surrendering one's ability to explain why any given phenomenon appears rather than another. In this situation, one will only be able to affirm, helplessly, that "anywhere in the world, or perhaps anywhere in the universe . . . men or oaks, for instance, might spontaneously appear."[10] Spontaneity-worship of this kind is for Lewis simply a mental training for the surrender of volition demanded by pseudodemocratic societies.[11]

However, there is another form of spontaneity we encounter in Lewis's work that he believes allows one to *resist* absorption by the mechanical rhythms of mass indoctrination and the philosophical pantheisms he believes to be their corollary. And this other spontaneity is not, as one might expect, a spontaneity of pure egoism—an expression of the "immediate" experience of the self. On the contrary, for Lewis, undiluted egoism cuts one off from the "concrete and 'material' world—which is all that is *common* to us."[12] Accordingly, Lewis associates genuine spontaneity with a "play of [the] instincts"[13] that occurs in the public realm. Spontaneity of this order *does* require one to surrender one's narrow egoism and participate in transsubjective patterns of existence, but this surrender of the self is not accomplished in order to merge one's consciousness irrevocably with the pulsations of cosmic sentiment. Instead it signals, first, a suspension of one's "fanatical hegemony with [one's] unique self-feeling"[14] and, second, an involvement of oneself in a public world in which many individuals coexist in an unpredictable play of qualities and forces.

In his philosophical work, Lewis makes a careful distinction between these two types of intersubjective involvement. The first involves an "immersion in the waves of the vital flux" and a desire to "merge us into a mutually devouring mass."[15] The second involves a "superficial contact of the exterior form" only—an action that affirms the proposition that human beings "are surface-creatures... committed to a plurality of being."[16]

In comparing the two very different models of spontaneity that we find in Lewis's philosophical work—the one involving "ecstatic cosmic raptures"[17] and the other involving more local social journeys into a "nonassimilable universe"[18]—we find that they correspond to very different ideas of collective existence. In *Time and Western Man*, Lewis notes that merging one's consciousness into a "pantheistic immanent oneness of 'creative,' 'evolutionary' substance" means becoming an unthinking political reaction-complex (166). The collective existence imagined here is that of self-styled "men-of-action," who are "plunged from one discontinuous, self-sufficing unit of experience to another... in moods of undiluted sensationalism; the ideal slave[s] and instrument[s] of any clever and farseeing person—who, of course, is the *real* man-of-action" (20).

The second form of spontaneity, however, which involves walking abroad in a "common world in which we all meet and communicate" (181), involves a nonstandardized play of social instincts. In *The Art of Being Ruled*, Lewis describes it as "an impulse to new life," which is creative in that "new and organizable elements come into existence every year, present themselves for valuation, and invite to new combinations" (351). In this context, what is common is precisely the matter for public contestation, hence the spontaneity of this contestation is not borrowed from some occult, nonhuman force, but in fact corresponds to an intersubjective logic that is in the process of being defined.

This dimension of Lewis's work, which involves realms of experience quite remote from the strong, central ego, has received some exacting and sensitive critical attention. For example, in *Modernism and the Fate of Individuality,* Michael Levenson argues that Lewis subverts the image of the isolated, bounded self by continually showing its integrity to be compromised by the flux of bodily experience. Levenson shows how in Lewis's *Tarr* "thoughts and emotions do not possess that intimate *inwardness* which the realist tradition had ascribed to them."[19] Instead, they seem like physical externalities, which means that "any attempt to pierce to the innermost thought, the central emotion, must expect to find, not an ineliminable sincerity, but more elaborate artifice."[20] In other words, for Lewis, identity itself is a form of artifice; it is a performance, and one that is continually being undermined by the "wild body" of involuntary physical responses.[21]

Paul Peppis also provides a highly valuable contribution to this antiegoistic conception of Lewis. He claims that *Tarr,* which appeared in serial form in *The Egoist* from 1916 to 1917, is in fact a literary critique of the philosophical and aesthetic Individualism espoused by that journal. Instead of the unique, Stirnerean individual, who struggles against external social constraints, Lewis depicts a "would-be Individualist" who is continually thwarted by his own "conflicted, porous, and shifting subjectivity."[22] And, like Levenson, Peppis suggests that the deeply unstable forms of identity in *Tarr* cause characters to "keep trying-on social identities... in hopes that by performing such pseudo-selves they might somehow acquire real ones."[23]

These analyses go a long way toward exposing Lewis's ambivalences about egoism, but there is one aspect of Lewis's antiegoism that invites even more critical attention. In much of his work, Lewis does not represent the ego as *beset* by extraegoic forces that overwhelm it. Instead, he often seems to recommend the active and deliberate suspension of egoic boundaries. For example, in "The Code of a Herdsman," Lewis writes, "*Never* fall into the vulgarity of being or assuming yourself to be one ego." Instead, "leave your front door one day as B.: the next march down the street as E. A variety of clothes, hats, especially, are of help in this wider dramatization of yourself."[24] This agrees nicely with Peppis's insight that in *Tarr* "self-realization... can consist only in the consummate performance of pseudo-selves."[25] But here it is clear that Lewis *recommends* that one venture among the "herd" of popular humanity in search of these pseudoselves. One must "borrow from all sides mannerisms of callings or classes" and "contradict [oneself], in order to live." And according to Lewis, "you must remain broken up" in order to fulfill this imperative.[26]

It is important to note that Lewis is not recommending a passive surrender to crowd-life here. Indeed, as in Lewis's vignette "An Experiment with a Crowd," this temporary excursion outside the ego is done in the interest of a peculiar kind of "research." In the vignette, which appears in Lewis's 1937 autobiography, *Blasting and Bombardiering,* Lewis's alter ego, Cantleman, resolves that he "would not only mix with the crowd, he would train himself *to act its mood,* so that he could persuade its emotion to enter him properly."[27] He then becomes an "entranced medium," "allow[ing] himself to be carried by the crowd" and "offer[ing] himself to its emotion."[28] But even amid this immersion, Cantleman "strain[s] for a distinct sensation" and "from time to time, hastens outside" the crowd, in order to "examine himself in the Crowd-mood" in isolation.[29]

What Lewis illustrates in this vignette is precisely the detachment-in-immersion that defines the spontaneity of willed intersubjective involvement, as opposed to the spontaneity of unconscious collective reflex. This kind of mediated spontaneity is central to Lewis's aesthetics, as he intimates in "The Objective of Art in Our Time," where he claims:

> In art we are in a sense playing at being what we designate as matter. We are entering the forms of the mighty phenomena around us, and seeing how near we can get to being a river or a star, without actually *becoming* that. Or we are placing ourselves somewhere behind the contradictions of matter and of mind, where an identity (such as the school of American realists, William James, for example, has fancied) may more primitively exist.[30]

This idea of temporary, experimental surrenders to realms of primal, collective, and material experience is not something we typically associate with Lewis. Much more familiar are his statements to the effect that "our only terra firma in a boiling and shifting world is... our 'self.'"[31] But in the late 1920s and early 1930s, Lewis was undergoing a crisis of faith in the agency of the individual ego, a crisis inextricably bound up with his ambivalences about individual political "heroes" and their relationship to the multitude.[32]

In many of Lewis's writings from this period, for example, fascist leaders are exemplary in their ability to avoid the reflexive "spontaneity" of the multitude, which consists in an unthinking voicing of the administered truths of bourgeois rule. Casting off the official egoism promoted by capitalist rule, fascist leaders embody a mediated spontaneity, which involves a journey outside the ideological reflexes of the self and a broad, many-sided contact with the multitude. According to this political narrative, the multitude's latent capacity for critical agency is reflected back upon them by the flexible, self-suspending attitude of the fascist leader, and this reciprocal dynamic allows the multitude to realize the responsible, public will that was buried in them.

At other times, however, Lewis is deeply suspicious of the narrative he evolves about the spontaneity of fascist leaders and of the extraegoic journeys they perform. In fact, works such as *Time and Western Man, The Art of Being Ruled, The Lion and the Fox*, and *Enemy of the Stars* tend to interrupt this narrative at the precise moment that the multitude begins reshaping its sense of public identity in response to the spontaneous social journeys of the fascist leader. This is because it is at this exact moment that the seemingly unprejudiced, public-minded commerce that the fascist conducts with the multitude begins to seem like a form of ideological indoctrination of its own. The new public identity of the multitude, emerging from a seemingly free exchange of critical opinion, suddenly seems as if it is being guided, in occult ways, by the phantom will of the fascist himself. Indeed, the very idea that fascists oppose the supersystems of capitalist finance through their spontaneous, self-suspending attitudes toward the multitude itself comes under suspicion. The mediated spontaneity of the fascist, with its seeming selflessness and solicitude for the multitude, now seems like a thinly disguised version of capitalism's own machinery of emotional compulsion. It appears to work by exactly the same methods as capitalist pseudodemocracy and to intend exactly the same result: an entranced multitude that believes itself to be choosing power systems that are in fact imposed upon it by a combination of stealth and force.[33]

The category of spontaneity therefore encodes some very concrete political anxieties in Lewis's work. Ideally, it represents the ability to step outside the self constituted by bourgeois ideology and involve oneself in the revolutionary ferment of the multitude. But any aspiring political leaders who actually perform this journey into the body of the multitude are suspected of deceit and exposed by Lewis as political charlatans. This is because, although he is attracted to fascism, Lewis suspects that the structure of fascist government, once established, would be impossible to distinguish from capitalist forms of mass control. The moment of political agency in which Lewis is most interested, then, is the one in which the multitude realizes the imposture of fascist leaders, exposes them as false men of the people, and ritualistically murders them.

This moment is, of course, semimythical. Lewis depicts it, in quintessentially modernist fashion, as a moment in which the undercurrents of collective political sentiment take on qualities associated with everything from pre-Christian fertility ritual to the customs surrounding regicide in Bantu cultures. But from out of this political myth, Lewis forges a third model of spontaneity that expresses his most ambitious political imagination: a collective spontaneity that activates the multitude's ability to improvise rituals of political association that allow it to organize its own activity in the absence of centralized rulers.

This third, collective, form of spontaneity could be viewed as the speculative frame against which Lewis's political figurations take shape in the late 1920s and 1930s. In the final analysis, no concrete political program corresponds exactly to the mechanisms of this collective spontaneity. More than anything it expresses two things: Lewis's utopian desire for a process of reciprocal social self-organization and the betrayal of that possibility by the pseudopopulism of European fascism. But his 1932 play *Enemy of the Stars*, which Lewis significantly expanded from a 1914 play of the same name, could be read as an experimental investigation of the kinds of social intercourse that might give rise to such collective spontaneity.[34] This text will therefore be at the center of my analysis of Lewis's models of spontaneity, along with two texts that could be read as expositions of the philosophical and political substance of the play, "Physics of the Not-Self" and *The Lion and the Fox*. In all of these texts, the multitude's capacity for spontaneous self-constitution serves as the backdrop against which various forms of individual agency are enacted, including the agency of the fascist leader, which fails dramatically in every instance. The literary experimentation on display in *Enemy of the Stars* thus allows Lewis to offer highly abstract visions of the relationship of the intellect to the multitude, all of which pose the following question: Must the intellect always be detached from the multitude and thus exert some form of dominion over it, or might the multitude evolve some principle of directive intelligence that could express its capacity for spontaneous self-organization?[35]

At stake in this question is what Giorgio Agamben calls "the problem of constituting power"—the question of whether the multitude can be imagined to possess a socially constitutive capacity separate from or prior to the apparatuses of sovereign power.[36] Contemporary political thinkers tend to stress the difficulty of distinguishing between such constituting power and the constituted power to which it is so often consigned.

Hence Agamben refers to the "spontaneous councils" of 1917 and 1919 that were progressively subsumed by the apparatuses of authoritarian party-states.[37] In a similar vein, Alain Badiou refers to "the great enigma of the century," namely, "Why do the most heroic popular uprisings, the most persistent wars of liberation, the most indisputable mobilisations in the name of justice and liberty end... in opaque statist constructions wherein none of the factors that gave meaning and possibility to their historical genesis is decipherable?"[38]

Like Lewis, Agamben and Badiou have no straightforward answers to this question. Instead, they create highly speculative constructs that hold the place, so to speak, of collective subjects whose capacity for spontaneous organization remains virtual, unfulfilled. For Agamben, this conceptual placeholder exists within the sphere of ontology; on this level, the prepolitical social body exists as a "raw power" whose internal structure "requires nothing less than a rethinking of the ontological categories of [actuality and potentiality] in their totality."[39] Similarly, Badiou's conceptual placeholder is the "mass movement," conceived ontologically as "a multiple on the edge of the void, a historical event site... being presented but not re-presentable (by the State)."[40] For both of these thinkers, then, the attempt to imagine the creative ontology of the multitude—its "constituent power"—involves a crisis of representation. At issue is the question of how to describe, imagine, and represent associative powers that have no place within the socially stratified regime of representational politics.

Lewis too has great difficulty representing a collective intelligence that could persist without some central, directive figure to organize it. For the most part, this potentiality is visible only in the cycles of mythic upheaval and quasi-anthropological speculation we find in works such as *The Lion and the Fox* and *The Art of Being Ruled*. For this reason, Lewis's work returns obsessively to the murder of the fascist leader as a concrete political moment that would ideally be permanentized, transposed into some mythic temporality in which the unmasking of "political magic" would be performed unremittingly and could thus serve as an impetus to new forms of spontaneous association, free of the fascist leader's political duplicity.

According to this temporality, constituent power would continually resist what Antonio Negri calls "constituted power": political power conceived as a "centralized mediation, starting from a 'space' that has become 'political' because totally invested by the process of 'representation.'"[41] The party and the state are the principal embodiments of constituted power, in that they constantly refer themselves to constituent power as their legitimating foundation but in reality function as "machine[s] predisposed not so much to exercising strength but, rather, to controlling its dynamics."[42] Constituted power thus controls the constitutive *potenza* of the multitude by masquerading as its practical fulfillment, by pretending to be a deputy of the multitude rather than a transcendent power operating according to its own imperatives and interests.

The concepts of constituent and constituted power will be useful in our analysis of Lewis since they refer to tendencies and forces that are active in the kinds of revolutionary situations Lewis constantly rescripts. What emerges from these situations is the image of an immense, collective potency that is chronically betrayed by centralized forces in the process of becoming hegemonic. Constituent power thus appears in highly abstract ways in Lewis's work and is never clearly associated with actual historical agents, such as Agamben's and Negri's workers' councils or the revolutionary workers Badiou analyzes in his *Polemics* and *The Communist Hypothesis*. Nevertheless, we can track the emergence of Lewis's idea of constituent power in his engagement with anarchist thinkers in *The Art of Being Ruled* —figures such as Pierre-Joseph Proudhon and Georges Sorel, whose models of spontaneity and collective action Lewis defines himself in relation to. As we will see in a moment, anarchism and anarcho-syndicalism provided Lewis with a language of constituent power and spontaneous organization that promised an outside to the endless cycle of revolution and co-optation to which Lewis so often returns. It is a political language that Lewis often critiques and lambastes, since it is difficult for him to imagine the multitude cohering in the absence of a centralized power of some sort. And yet Lewis's distrust of constituted power is so strong that he continually resurrects the image of a constituent power that could resist it. This image is always shadowy, strange and abstract, but it is one that emerges in *The Art of Being Ruled* and reappears repeatedly in Lewis's literary work. It is a figure that will exhibit Lewis as existing in a bizarre political universe, somewhere between anarchism and fascism, between constituent power and constituted power.

Let's examine Lewis's relationship to anarchism more closely, so we can understand how it relates to problems of spontaneity and constituent power that continue, even today, to obsess theorists of the multitude.

The "Massed, Organized, Facultative Personality"

To understand Lewis's relationship to anarcho-syndicalism and its models of constituent power, it is helpful to look at a surprising quote from *The Art of Being Ruled*. Lewis writes: "Syndicalism... is still the most well-marked and powerful endeavour of a constructive sort that the french revolutionary mind has made since Proudhon" (300). Not the fascism of *Action Française*, which briefly interested Lewis in the 1910s, not the Marxism of Lafargue or Jaurès, but syndicalism, in the tradition of Proudhon and Sorel, is what Lewis singles out. Why?

The answer to this question lies in Proudhon's hostility toward political centralization. Lewis explains: "Proudhon was against a centralized control on the capitalist model: whereas Marx was, of course, in favour of a great bureaucratic hegemony, which would result in a world-state on capitalist lines, but theoretically purged of capitalist oppression" (291). In *The Art of Being Ruled*, Lewis continually resurrects this idea of a massive state and industrial machine, which capitalism evolves, but into which Marxists believe "the will of the proletariat can be put" (300). By contrast, Proudhon believes that production and exchange must be coordinated from below, by a federation of workers' associations. Lewis quotes from *Du principe fédératif*, where Proudhon argues that only such self-managed cooperatives, and not centralized bureaucracies, can provide for true social equality: "Political centralization has for principal corollary... commercial anarchy—that is to say, the negation of all economic right, of all social guarantee" (301). Lewis applauds this critique and casts it in a contemporary light, suggesting that "the bitterest opponent of state-socialism could not state the case against it more forcibly than Proudhon" (301).

Lewis's engagement with Proudhon thus has the question of constituent power at its heart. Proudhon's self-managed workers' associations embody a constituent power that the constituted power of centralized rule continually threatens. Lewis even provides a sketch of how constituent power is continually in danger of lapsing into constituted power: "As soon as the last death-rattle of the last revolutionary fanatic at the last and most desperate barricade has ceased, the fanfare is sounded, and the dictator or emperor steps on to the scene once more, with the clockwork aplomb of the figures of a musical-box" (295). In this way, "the people, in their revolutions, have always, 'instead of a protector, provided themselves with a tyrant'" (295). At this point in his analysis, Lewis does not see this neutralization of constituent power as inevitable. He traces it to Proudhon's idea of the *préjugé gouvernemental*, "the fixed idea of the necessity for a government of some sort," which Proudhon ties to Lewis's most vilified object of critique: "the obsessing paradigm of the family" (295). But "*power, government, imperium,* ἀρχή" (296) are not the only available models of social organization. Proudhon offers us the model of a pact or contract that is opposed to government—one that has nothing to do with the "dead docility of Rousseau's system" but represents instead a "spontaneous dispersed exercise of power" (314).

Lewis thus provides us with an image of constituent power that is spontaneous, in that it arises from the associative patterns of the multitude, and yet capable of discipline and self-direction. This "associational or group life" may not "furnish the *intensest* life," since only individual life can provide this, but it nevertheless "mobilizes certain faculties of each of the members of the group—those they possess *in common*—and enables them to employ this massed, organized, facultative personality effectively" (316). Lewis thus provides a model of constituent power whose collective functionality promises to oppose the political designs of dictators and pseudodemocracies while at the same time liberating the energies of the individual for extrapolitical pursuits.

But every time Lewis approaches such an image of constituent power, it metamorphoses slowly and inexorably into its opposite, into an illusion promoted by a covert class of rulers, into a horrifying statist construction, merely masquerading as a force of the multitude—in short, into a constituted power pretending to offer freedom to the multitude while securing it ever more firmly to its governmental mechanisms. Hence, in the Proudhonian tradition, Georges Sorel's anarcho-syndicalism *seems* to liberate us from illusory democratic ideals, which, Lewis states, "hold up to the workman images of a life that is not his, and to which he can never belong" (30). But for this "pretended cosmos" (30) in which individuals only factor as bizarre abstractions, Sorel substitutes "a horizontal diversity" (30) in which individuals are trapped in "the narrow integral self-effaced unit of the syndic" (30). In this syndicalist world, most people would be "screwed down and locked up in their functions... the doctor smelling of drugs... the miner covered with coal-dust, the soldier stiff and martial," while "the only person who can be an 'all-round' man, *éclairé,* full of scepticism, wide general knowledge, and 'lights' is the ruler" (31).

Lewis repeatedly admits that this is not Sorel's political image but his own. It is, to be sure, what Sorel's model of constituent power *must become* in Lewis's political universe. It is an image that Lewis also grafts onto Proudhon's model of constituent power. The self-governing federative commune may seem free, but because of its small size, it would begin to resemble (yet again) a *family,* or a peasant village. Lewis elaborates: "In a village ruled by public opinion... there is little freedom of action or opinion—both are curtailed and held down by public opinion, more effectively than any police force could do it" (307). In this context, the individual would come to be regarded as "an insurgent, a breaker-up of homes, an indelicate interloper, a walking lie, a disturbing absurdity," which "a central specialized political authority" must look after (314). If possible, this is an even more bizarre political distortion than the one to which Lewis subjects Sorel. Proudhon's militantly anticentralist political philosophy, once it is imagined as a reality, must be made over into a centralist, authoritarian state, policing the promiscuous, unrestrained activities of individuals. Constituent power, it seems, must never identify itself with the functioning of actual social institutions. To believe that it could means being the victim of an ideological campaign—one that ensures that "the real executive must always elude you" (315).

The impasse Lewis faces could thus be described as that of "constituent governance" or, as Hardt and Negri put it in *Commonwealth,* "the institutional development of the powers of social cooperation."[43] The problem here is that of imagining social *institutions* that would not rigidify into centrally controlled bureaucracies and that could serve as "an open and socially generalized schema for social experimentation and democratic innovation" (374)—all without losing their institutional character. Hardt and Negri admit the difficulties that attend such a conception of flexible institutionality. They distance themselves from the kind of spontaneism that aims merely at the destruction of extant systems of power because of its naive trust that "the perfect human society already existing beneath the yoke of oppression" would under such circumstances "spontaneously flourish" (361). Against such political credulity, Hardt and Negri refer us to the Leninist critique of pure spontaneity—that "in their habits, routines, mentalities, and in the million capillary practices of everyday life, people are wedded to hierarchy, identity, segregation, and in general corrupt forms of the common" (362). Given this to be true, how can an institution of democracy come from anywhere other than an external vanguard, teaching the multitude to break with its habits? It is a question that Gramsci, Lukács, and even Marcuse will echo in their own critiques of spontaneity.

Hardt and Negri respond with the observation that "'transitional' dictatorships" have a habit of "stubbornly hold[ing] on to power" (362–63). Their dialectical procedure of negating democracy—in order to educate and direct the population—only then to negate dictatorship in favor of genuine democracy, tends to become arrested at the halfway point, constituting itself as a permanent dictatorship that merely masquerades as democracy. What is necessary, for Hardt and Negri, is a "positive, non-dialectical solution" (363) to this impasse, one that "relies entirely on the immanence of decision making within the multitude" (xiii). Hardt and Negri stress that this immanence is not the same thing as spontaneity, in the sense of an upwelling of a pregiven human nature; instead, it refers to "the capacities for self-organization and cooperation in people's daily lives, in their work, or more generally in social production" (176). It is thus closest to Marcuse's idea of "mediated spontaneity," with the multitude itself as the locus of this mediating activity, exercising what Hardt and Negri call the "constituent elements of human subjectivity" in its collective production of "ideas, codes, images, affects, and social relationships" (172).

Lewis clearly shares Hardt and Negri's distrust for so-called transitional dictatorships and their promises to reinscribe dialectically the multitude's powers of self-rule. But he also distrusts *any* institutionalization of the multitude's constituent power. In *The Art of Being Ruled*, Lewis argues that whenever "workers are promised under a collectivist régime the direction of their respective industries, they are being deceived" (303), since their collectivity would necessarily be represented by some functionary, from whom workers "would be obliged to solicit ... the use of [their] tools: in other words, [they] would be absolutely at the discretion of [their] (new) masters" (303). For this reason, Lewis continually returns us to the moment when the powers of the multitude are still preinstitutional, when they constitute not an established system of self-rule, with all of the pitfalls this confronts, but a complex play of social aptitudes.

Lewis calls this matrix of play and experimentation the "Not-Self" and describes it in *The Art of Being Ruled* (in a chapter that was not published in the book's first edition) as an "emotional mimetic" (386) in which individuals try on new attitudes, behavior patterns, and affective orientations.

According to Lewis, social life has become almost completely standardized. It is "held in place and revolves around a series of norms" for which one mistakes one's subjectivity: human "types" such as "the 'live wire,' the dreaded *mauvaise langue*, the 'charming boy,' or the nice 'unaffected girl,' the 'good sort' and so on" (387). In contrast to this artificial "personal machinery" (387) stands the Not-Self, "the great environment of an alien universal life" (387). To evoke this "universal life," which individuals can join only by becoming alien to themselves, Lewis borrows Sorel's image of the "abysses between which winds the path which the vulgar follow with the serenity of sleep walkers" (387). Lewis provides no citation for this quote, but it comes from Sorel's *Reflections on Violence*, precisely at the moment that Sorel is describing the way that metaphysical systems and political philosophies tend to become ossified into dogma. The Not-Self, in other words, is a zone of speculation in which social configurations are continually tested and revised, before they are in a position to attract disciples and become new orthodoxies. In the passage from which Lewis quotes, Sorel identifies this "spirit of invention" with what Marx's thought could have been, had he not been "transformed into the leader of a sect by his young enthusiasts."[44]

The Not-Self, then, refers to a world of unofficial social innovation, but also to the danger that its patterns of interaction could be dominated and controlled by leaders who might emerge from it. This is why Lewis describes two distinct models of self-othering that lay claim to the Not-Self. The first is the emotional mimetic described above; it is what Lewis calls "an instinctive exploiting of the rough material of [one's] personality" (387) and is at work in "the child pretending to be a locomotive or a horse" and in Madame Bovary's "fancying herself *the great lady*" (386). This kind of play tests the range of one's possible identifications and capacities and for this reason participates in the social inventiveness of the Not-Self. Its object is "to deceive *yourself*" and in doing so to discover relational capacities whose existence you had not suspected. The most complete expression of such play would be to "receive *all* [one's] stimulus from others and be quite impassible towards [oneself]" (387). Such an "expert" of the Not-Self would function as a kind of social capacitor, reflecting the multitude's capacity for innovation back upon it and regarding individuality as the locus of constant relational experiments.

This image of a professional imitator, however, brings up the other model of self-othering Lewis describes—that of dissimulators who take on new habits and roles to deceive others and control them. These figures deliberately make a show of divesting themselves of personality and move among the multitude, pretending to be nothing but a reflection of their movements. But they do this only to secure their rule over the multitude more surely. They are thus embodiments of Lewis's fears about constituted power: the dictators, juridical systems, and functionaries who co-opt and ultimately destroy the innovations of constituent power.

Lewis's hopes and fears about anarcho-syndicalism, constituent power, and constituted power are therefore all concentrated in the highly abstract figure of the Not-Self and the forms of spontaneity enacted with respect to it. The Not-Self is an intersubjective modality that opposes the false spontaneity of type-life, that is, people's effortless gravitation toward media images as surrogate egos. It is therefore the territory on which self-mediating forms of spontaneity could be awakened, where individuals could discover critical powers and affective dispositions that would allow for intersubjective forms of creation. And yet it is also on this territory that the duplicitous, self-suspending spontaneity of professional imitators is active—the "spontaneity" of those who prepare the multitude, by way of its own "emotional mimetic," for the rule that they mean to impose.

The Not-Self therefore returns us time and time again to the moment of the multitude's greatest strength and its greatest weakness, to the moment of constituent power, to the image of workers' associations, institutions in the process of forming themselves, individuals discovering within themselves the capacity for self-rule—but also to the forms of political deceit and dominion operative within this collective body. How is it possible to distinguish between the intersubjective mimesis of constituent power and the political deceptions of future rulers, especially since on this speculative terrain, most individuals are "mixed types" (386), deceiving themselves when they intend to deceive others, and vice versa? Who are the protagonists of this deception, and how might we begin to recognize their feints and ruses? These questions all concern the topography of constituent power, its resources and its limitations, and in "Physics of the Not-Self" Lewis begins to answer them in depth.

Spontaneity and the "Mixed Type"

"Physics of the Not-Self," which was originally titled "The Physics of Unselfishness," was published in 1932 and appended to *Enemy of the Stars* as what Lewis called a "metaphysical commentary" on the play.[45]

The essay creates a contrast between two human types who correspond to the different forms of spontaneity discussed above. The first type is Cato, the "mechanical egoist," and the second is a nonmechanical, oppositional figure who is "the enemy of all the constellations and universes" (198). The former type is perceived to be more truthful by institutional authorities because, when interrogated, he answers "without hesitation—frankly and freely" (197). By contrast, the "enemy" type "is apt to stammer, if not blush" and provide an answer "so beset with reservations that it remains a particularly offensive sort of lie for those who prefer the will's truth to that of the intellect" (196). The "will's truth" in this context is that of the mechanical egoist, a truth that, more than anything, affirms one's alignment with the interests of the ruling elite. Therefore, even though it is voiced "frankly and freely," it is spontaneous only in the sense that it unhesitatingly voices all of the truths that have been prepared for it in advance by the ruling elite. For Lewis, this kind of spontaneity is impossible to distinguish from complete ideological automation. It is an "official truth" that is repeated mechanically and that "obediently represents the man and his interests" (197).

The truth of the intellect, by contrast, belongs to a far more elusive principle, which Lewis refers to as the "Not-Self." The Not-Self is what Lewis calls an "oddity outside the machine" of ideological conditioning (195). It consists, most of all, in the ability to suspend one's habitual affirmations and explore alternative truths that are part of an "unofficial" landscape of intersubjective valuations. Thus, even though the Not-Self gives rise to stammering and blushing, it expresses a potent form of social spontaneity, since it allows one to break with the mental reflexes that bind the ego to ruling ideology. In doing so, the Not-Self finds itself involved in a collective world in which it participates. As Lewis writes: "The man who has formed the habit of consulting and adhering to the principle of the *not-self*... participates... in the life of others outside himself far more than does the contrary type of man, he who *refrains* from making any use at all of this speculative organ" (197–98). The adherent of the Not-Self is thus described as "a breaker-down of walls, a dissolvent of nations, factions, and protective freemasonries, a radio-active something in the midst of more conservative aggregations" (198). The spontaneity of the Not-Self, then, is a dissolvent principle, liquidating the settled social relations that artificially divide humanity.

From the perspective of the ruling elites, then, the Not-Self is an "enemy principle" which is "heartily disliked" (198). To demonstrate this,

Lewis parrots the ruling elite, voicing their petty objections to the principle of the Not-Self:

> We have *one* life, and we have *one* individuality. It is a ration, as it were. It is an "obligation"... to devote all our energies to that one self, and not to poach. We were not born twenty men, but one. It is our duty "to remain in our class." Equally it is our duty to remain in our self—our one and only. But if we *must* go out of our "class," then it is "a sacred duty" to get into a higher one at least. And if we *must* go outside our self—if we are so wrongheaded—then at least it is our "bounden duty" to see that we do not, at least, despoil ourselves for others. We must go outside in order to *take*, not to *give*. (198–99)

Those who adopt the principle of the Not-Self, then, appear to have many lives and many individualities; they venture outside their self and their class in order to give, not to take. All of this rouses the hostility of the ruling elite. And, as Lewis indicates, the Not-Self "by its very nature... awakens love," which from the perspective of these rulers is "not in its favor either."[46]

In *Enemy of the Stars*, Arghol represents the spontaneously disruptive, love-awakening principle of the Not-Self. His principal occupation is to make excursions outside his ego, into a common life Lewis represents in the form of violently tossing trees, which "*drive their leaf-flocks... propel[ling] them with jeering cry*" (146). From this external world, which is clearly meant to evoke the crowds, crowd-masters, and general ideological tumult of mass political movements, Arghol drags bits of raw material that he carves into stable, functional wheels. The function of the Not-Self, then, is not merely to combine itself with the multitude but also to remove the multitude, as much as possible, from the flux and confusion of mass political indoctrination. From the "wild nature" of political contention, Arghol isolates concrete particulars, to which he applies the shaping power of his intellect. In this way, Arghol hopes to lend stability to the intellects that constitute the multitude, to transform them from pieces of manipulable lumber into well-proportioned wheels, capable of thoughtful, independent movement.

The spontaneity of the Not-Self, then, is characterized by a certain doubleness. It is defined both by a flexible involvement in the patterns of collective existence and by an ability to exercise one's will and judgment so that one may calculate the lines of force that subtend the feverish atmosphere of the multitude.[47]

This image of the Not-Self as a mixture of collective involvement and analytic detachment is amplified by Lewis's suggestion that we should regard Arghol as a Socratic figure. In "Physics of the Not-Self," Lewis establishes a parallelism between Socrates and Arghol by depicting Socrates as a strangely modern man among the multitude—an intellectual *jongleur* immersed in the "promiscuous, sceptical, feverish atmosphere of post-periclean Athens" (203). Lewis stresses that Socrates was a "*popular* teacher," and cites Alcibiades's description of him as "always talking about great market-asses, and brass-founders, and leather-cutters, and skin-dressers"—the "raw material," Lewis points out, "of his famous 'induction'" (203). This human multiplicity, in other words, constitutes a social raw material out of which Socrates's philosophical postulates are distilled. They are the "rumbling stock-in-trade" of Socrates, who is framed as "'the ideal journalist' of his age" (204, 203).

And yet Socrates maintains a playful detachment-in-immersion that prevents him from being completely absorbed by the Bacchic "intoxication" (203) of his age. Like Arghol's quotidian labor of social stabilization, Socrates's "husbandry of goodness" is referred to as a "craft," which "can be taught, like a trade" (200). It therefore involves discipline and detachment. In fact, Lewis's account of the Socratic ethos reads like a manifesto of modernist impersonality: "You can only be just, moderate and beneficent if you are not involved in what you are called to act upon—if you are withdrawn from it and 'not interested in it'" (202). In other words, Socrates is simultaneously immersed in crowd-life and withdrawn from it. He represents a condition of doubleness; he is open to changing collective impulses, but he retains a principle of detached formal agency that allows him to evaluate and organize these impulses.[48]

This idea of spontaneity as a spiritual discipline may seem completely aporetic. After all, spontaneity is not supposed to require discipline. It is supposed to express the absence of all discipline, a relaxation of the will and a willingness to be guided by sheer impulse. But the profound paradox of Lewis's form of modernism is that in a totally administered environment, spontaneity is possible only as a consciously developed craft. Allowing oneself to be guided by impulse, in the absence of any analytic consciousness, will result only in one's expressing all the more swiftly the socially necessary illusions that have been naturalized by one's environment.

Spontaneity, in this context, is indistinguishable from ideology, in Adorno's sense, as "socially necessary semblance."[49] In *Minima Moralia*,

Adorno makes this clear: "The more immediate [a person's] response, the more deeply in reality mediation has advanced: in the prompt, unresistant reflexes the subject is entirely extinguished."[50] Lewis adumbrates a similar relationship between ideology and spontaneity in *The Art of Being Ruled*. He defines ideology as a "metaphysics of government" that consists in "the organizing and adapting of certain chosen *truths*, or discoveries, of philosophy or science, to an ultimately political end" (34). Through this process, "the ideology of a time," which is always "that of the contemporary ruling class," is subjectively naturalized, becomes "not an inhuman, objective bundle of pure scientific truth, but a personally edited bouquet or bundle, with a carefully blended odour to suit the destined palate" (34). In contrast to the kind of thought reflexes this conditioning produces, true spontaneity requires a complex double attitude—one that, for Lewis, does not come "spontaneously," in the sense that it must be practiced, as one would practice woodworking, waltzing, or meditation.[51]

For Lewis, the craft of spontaneity is the kind that artists practice when they open themselves to the raw material of their métier and are guided by the formal impulses that arise from their involvement with it. The spontaneity of this attitude lies in the fact that it allows formal impulses to pass through the artist, without the artist's involving his or her own ego in the process. Supposedly, all that is involved here is a nonpersonal organizational intelligence that lends these impulses order and significance. The resulting order thus arrives spontaneously in that it is an expression of tendencies that were latent in the artistic material, not prepared in advance by the personal will of the artist.[52]

At times, Lewis treats the Not-Self as the social equivalent of this artistic spontaneity. At these times, the Not-Self appears to allow individuals to open themselves to the collective impulses of their social environment while retaining an analytical poise that allows them to document these impulses with cool precision. The spontaneity of the Not-Self thus appears to allow collective impulses to achieve organization and intelligence in a way that is not distorted by the intervention of any individual, interested ego. This kind of spontaneity therefore traces a politically benevolent journey outside the "instinctive solipsism" of the individual ego. It abstracts the creative intelligence from the individual ego and puts it in the service of a collective process of social evolution.[53]

At other times, however, Lewis regards this model of spontaneous creation as a complex act of deception, one that is structurally similar to the political deceptions practiced upon the multitude by pseudopopulist leaders. In these moments, the Not-Self becomes one more tool that allows constituent power to be inscribed within the circle of constituted power, to be contained in what Alain Badiou calls the "space of placement."[54] This returns us to the problematic of constituted power and presents us with a very contemporary Lewis, one who sees revolutionary agency as perpetually in danger of co-optation by statist forces of the right and left. To combat this process, Lewis continually turns against the political saviors he most fervently desires to believe in, reimagining their social benevolence as just one tactic in an immense strategy of deception. And to the extent that artists mimic the populist masquerades of constituted power, they must be exposed and reviled as well.

The Artist as Seismograph

A passage from Lewis's 1925 essay "The Foxes' Case" presents us with a fascinating image of artists as social imposters. In posing as representatives of the spontaneity of the multitude, artists mimic the connivances of constituted power, its status not merely as a belated, unwieldy bureaucratic supplement but also as a supple presence at work in the processes of collective self-government:

> Since today life has to be humoured, and each act of the creative will has to pretend to rise spontaneously in the body of the world or of the crowd (since the democratic standards of western society... require that every act of government should appear to be the act of the governed), then, of course, there is nothing for it: the creator has to affect to be one of the herd.[55]

In other words, the spontaneously receptive aspect taken on by the creative intelligence may in fact be nothing more than a ruse, one of the "fox-like maneuvers of the creative intelligence" that allow the artist to disguise "his" role as a cultural "stud-bull" and instead to "pretend to be a cow... or at least... disguise his function so much that he could pass for one of the herd" (124).

Lewis, in other words, is extremely ambivalent about the category of spontaneity, at times attributing it to individuals who are capable of acting as genuinely detached "seismograph[s]" of collective forces,[56] at times exposing it as the alibi of would-be autocrats who secretly wish to "impose" their "canons directly upon the life around [them]."[57]

The political ambivalences that Lewis engages by way of the category of spontaneity can be seen clearly in his attitudes toward Hitler in the 1930s. In 1931, Lewis associated Hitler with the benevolent, populistic excursions of figures such as Arghol and Socrates, and thus with the principle of the Not-Self. Lewis describes Hitler as a "man of peace" and a "man of the people" who "enthusiastically embraces his typicalness."[58] And yet, before, during and after his book on Hitler, Lewis would denounce and unmask the imposture of any ruler who affected to be one of the ruled. In *The Art of Being Ruled,* Lewis writes: "*The ruler should be made to pay for ruling in every possible way. He should be prevented at all cost from sharing in the pastimes or simple advantages of his inferiors*" (93). His life should be "very unpleasant... full of the shock of the forces of outer vastness from which the masses are sheltered" (93). Lewis's political attitude here is thoroughly schizophrenic. At times he seems to identify himself with the heroic isolation of the ruler, at times with the anomie of the ruled. This makes it unclear whether we are to view rulers' commerce with the "outer vastness" of the universe as a protective, beneficent activity or merely an amplification of their selfishness.

In Lewis's 1932 *Enemy of the Stars* we are confronted with an almost identical undecidability. The protagonist, Arghol, is ritualistically battered by the "will of the universe" (153), but it is unclear whether he is acting as a persecuted, heroic intermediary between this outer force and the humanity it threatens to destroy or whether his serial beatings are a self-willed farce that only secure him more firmly within his own egoism. Hanp, for one, continually suspects Arghol's excursions into the multitude to be part of a self-willed charade. In fact, his accusation that Arghol's exercise of the Not-Self is a *sham* is what sets in motion the murderous scene that concludes the play. From this perspective, Arghol's Socratic wanderings outside the ego begin to seem like nothing more than cunning simulations of spontaneity. Similarly, it is unclear in "Physics of the Not-Self" whether Socrates's insinuation of himself into crowd-life expresses true spontaneity or only the cynical promulgation of an ideology of spontaneity. In fact, his status as the "supreme market-place performer" (204) at times seems to express merely a dexterous enchantment of the multitude.

Lewis's Socrates thus exhibits the same kind of doubleness that Gilles Deleuze sees in the ancient philosopher. As Deleuze points out in *The Logic of Sense,* Socratic irony is supposed to "tear the individual away from his or her immediate existence; to transcend the sensible particularity toward the Idea; and to establish laws of language corresponding to the model."[59] Socratic irony thus intends to assure "the coextensiveness of being and of the individual within the world of representation" (138). But because its method is that of comedy and derision, the Socratic encounter is always in danger of remaining at the level of semblance, which produces its effects by means of "ruse or subversion" (258). How can Socrates distinguish himself from the Sophists, Deleuze asks, if his principal mode is that of an "ironic encounter which takes the place of a mode of knowledge, an art of encounter that is outside knowledge and opinion" (258)?

For Lewis, it is precisely by way of such arts of encounter, and not simply through sheer force, that political hegemony is secured.[60] Socrates and Arghol, therefore, can be seen as subjective types who analogize the dynamics of political "benevolence" that Lewis seeks to explore. In the late 1920s and the 1930s, Lewis was drawn to the idea of political leaders who could impersonally absorb the shocks of the external world on behalf of the multitude. Accordingly, the model of the fascist leader that Lewis valorizes is that of a persecuted underdog, valiantly opposing forces of international finance capital that are far more powerful than he. Socrates and Arghol are local, aesthetic analogues of this idea. Socrates's "popular uncontrolled instruction" (203) is associated, in "Physics of the Not-Self," with "underground cults, such as the orphic, [which] were not the same thing as a widely accepted religion, with its machinery of emotional compulsion" (203). In other words, Socrates is part of a protopolitical underground, and he is an enemy of hegemonic institutions that are far more powerful than he. He undermines the class of "attic owners" (204) and their very modern-seeming "machinery" of popular indoctrination, and, as a consequence, his "popular teaching culminated in political execution" (203). Similarly, Arghol opposes the vast political universe of bourgeois rule and *its* machinery of emotional compulsion. And his individualist campaign, with its populistic overtones, results in his execution as well.

In these dynamics it is easy to recognize the *first* phase of what Fredric Jameson describes as a three-phase model of protofascist agency: "An initially strong populist and anticapitalist impulse [that] is gradually readapted to the ideological habits of a petty bourgeoisie, which can itself be displaced when, with the consolidation of the fascist state, effective power passes back into the hands of big business."[61] In characters such as Socrates and Arghol, Lewis seems to be continually returning to the initial, antihegemonic moment of fascist agency, in which the political leader can be depicted, like the artist, as a persecuted, wandering outcast, beset from above by a hostile ruling class and from below by a recalcitrant and undisciplined multitude. In this initial moment, the spontaneity of future fascist leaders seems real, in that they must move with the tides of collective sentiment, adapting their speech to these impulses and acting as a medium of the multitude's discontent with bourgeois rule.

Of course, a phantom will to dominate and control the multitude lies beneath these seemingly spontaneous encounters with collective life, which is why Lewis is compelled to destroy his enemy figures before they are able to consolidate any new hegemonic orders of their own. What Lewis replaces them with are the figures of the artist and the philosopher, who represent the spontaneous, antihegemonic, socially imbricated agency that Lewis valorizes, but who possess no real political power that they might consolidate at the multitude's expense. The artist and the philosopher may engage in cunning ruses in order to provoke the multitude into critical awareness, but their function is never to rule. Instead, it is to instruct the multitude—sometimes by exposing their own "spontaneous" excursions as masquerades—in how to resist the ruler's machinery of emotional compulsion.

Hence Arghol's spontaneous incursions into the multitude in *Enemy of the Stars* dramatize Lewis's ambivalences about fascist models of political agency, but they do so in a fairly oblique way. Arghol is not an actual leader. He does not shape mass processes, but isolates and immobilizes social "objectivity" so that it may be subjected to a process of ethical craftsmanship. And Hanp is not actually a hypnotized political indoctrinee. In fact, he subjects Arghol to caustic interrogations throughout the play and exhibits an extreme critical distance from Arghol's pronouncements. Lewis describes Hanp as a "disciple" of Arghol, but his discipleship seems to consist primarily of learning how to detach himself from his investment in Arghol's social machinations. Moreover, this seems precisely the craft that Arghol is attempting to impart to Hanp.[62]

In other words, even as Arghol's embattled relationships to the political elite and to the multitude reveal him to be an abstract template of fascist agency, his refusal to secure hypnotic emotional control over Hanp signals his opposition to the final two phases of protofascist hegemony that Jameson outlines. Arghol simultaneously enacts a model of fascist political agency and works deliberately to expose the groundlessness of his mastery, even going so far as to promote in Hanp a principle of political agency that is detached from and opposed to his own.

It is as if Lewis creates a character who embodies both his attraction to persecuted, protofascist political agents and his desire to expose and revile such figures. The result is a character—Arghol—who repeatedly performs the excursions into the multitude that define the spontaneity of the Not-Self, but who performs these excursions in a way that arouses suspicions about the "spontaneity" and "selflessness" they supposedly embody. Accordingly, as Hanp repeatedly witnesses these excursions, he begins to see that Arghol is not genuinely surrendering himself to collective impulses—that Arghol's spontaneity is in fact a ruse intended to secure his personal hegemony over Hanp and the multitude whom he represents. In this way, Hanp learns to distrust the political benevolence of individual leaders, to question it and subvert it at every opportunity. As a consequence, Arghol's ethical craftsmanship climaxes in his overseeing the ritualistic sacrifice of *himself*, a process that is intended to awaken a principle of genuinely spontaneous agency in the "crowd-mind" of Hanp.

In this way, Lewis dramatizes one of the central myths that attends twentieth-century theories of constituent power: that the revolutionary party could oversee its own abolition, could generalize the organizational instruments at its disposal and become nothing but an immanent process within the multitude itself. It is a myth that Alain Badiou stages in remarkably similar terms—indeed, in the form of a play he wrote in the 1960s titled *L'Incident d'Antioche,* from which he excerpts in *The Communist Hypothesis*. Similar to Arghol in his deliberate self-abnegation, a revolutionary leader in Badiou's play named Céphas, upon victory, "take[s] the unheard-of decision to renounce . . . power": "I will lie down in the ashes of states . . . The orderliness of my idea of disorder now stands in the way of the imperative to build. . . . May the rubble embedded in the restoration maintain its hold over you, and may the stink . . . Persist!"[63] As Badiou explains, Céphas's gesture is an attempt to evade the consolidation of constituted power, "the moment when we revert from revolution to state" (23). Instead, Paula, an advocate of "multiplicity" (28), takes center stage and argues with a newly emergent figure of revolutionary leadership: "Find the people that matter. Listen to what they say. Organize their consistency, and aim for equality. . . . Committees of the popular will in the estates and in the countryside. Let them transform that which exists, and let them be up to the generality of situations. Let their opposition to the state and the property-owning sharks be directly proportional to their immanent strength, and to the thought they wield" (29).

Find... listen... organize... aim... let: Paula's vocabulary testifies to her uncomfortable position between constituted power and constituent power. It is as if she is trying to effect a process of political tutelage that would fuse the organizational apparatus of the party with the constituent power of the multitude. But she does so from an impossible semantic position. She invokes a figure of constituent power similar to that which Hanp embodies in *Enemy of the Stars* but can imagine its evolution only as the function of an implausible act of self-abnegation she entreats party leadership to make.

The shadow of Lewis's Arghol—the leader who wills his own destruction, his dissolution into the multitude—is thus visible in Badiou's play, as are the political dilemmas he represents. How could a party ever be expected to abolish itself? And yet, how could the multitude organize itself in the absence of a party? These are the questions that frame the problematic of constituent power, and they are as active in contemporary political ontologies such as Badiou's as they were in Lewis's day. The impasse that Lewis confronted haunts us in the image of the "politically inexistent," or what Badiou calls "a new collective Subject in politics, of an organization composed of individual multiples"—in other words, a figure of constituent power not inscribed within the party-centered mediations Badiou's play narrativizes.[64]

By dramatizing this problem of constituent power in the interaction between two characters—between a leader who is not a leader and a multitude that is not a multitude—Lewis hoped to isolate and display the dynamics that might give rise to the kind of collective subject Badiou describes. But how does this process of political tutelage develop in Lewis's play? How are we to imagine the multitude's transition from a welter of ideological reflexes to a spontaneously self-regulating social body? A closer look at *Enemy of the Stars*, and particularly at the relation between Arghol, the abstract embodiment of directive agency, and Hanp, the collective persona of the multitude, will help answer these questions.

Rites of Sacrifice

In *Enemy of the Stars*, Hanp represents the sensationalistic, emotionally manipulable multitude, in contrast to Arghol, who represents the self-mediating poise of the intellect, which is the seat of the Not-Self. Accordingly, Hanp's emotional reactions exhibit the false spontaneity of those who unhesitatingly voice ideologically naturalized truths. Arghol, by contrast, represents the mediated spontaneity of the Not-Self, which allows one to distance oneself from these ideological reflexes and achieve contact with a broader human world. But what is the nature of this broader contact, and what kind of craft does Arghol work in this intersubjective space?

Arghol first emerges as a hero figure, struggling against social supersystems that seek to dominate humanity completely. Because these supersystems appear to be governed by inscrutable natural laws, Arghol is described as an enemy of the stars, that is, of vast power structures that work upon humanity with a seemingly unstoppable purpose. But Lewis makes it clear that it is not nature but a grouping of human wills that dominates the majority of humankind. In "Physics of the Not-Self," for example, he debunks the idea that events such as World War I are the work of natural laws, as opposed to human interests:

> Disguised as "nature," and taking on the impersonality and "inscrutableness" of natural laws, a small but picked number of men have put themselves at the head of the forces of nature, as it were, in their old struggle with Man. The results so far have been startling enough. But it is hoped, shortly, that nature will, with their assistance, achieve a really decisive and annihilating success—with regard to the human race a really *smashing* victory! (195)

Lewis italicizes the word "smashing" here in order to express a bitter irony: that the mechanical devastation of humankind could be viewed as a thrilling spectator sport, as a "smashing" success, from the perspective of a detached commentator. Arghol, then, is not exactly an enemy of nature; rather, he is an enemy of a ruling elite that masquerades as a force of nature in order to perpetrate its violence upon humanity with greater ease.

As a small, persecuted, individualistic enemy of these political forces, he undoubtedly embodies many of the characteristics of Jameson's protofascist model of agency. But from the outset, Lewis attributes behaviors and characteristics to Arghol that make his ideological position less easy to classify. For example, Arghol undergoes a bizarre ritual in which he leaves the safety of his wheelwright's yard and walks abroad, exposing himself to the shocks and depredations of the outer world. This is the moment at which Arghol practices a spontaneous openness to the flux of life, a sacrifice of his ego that allows him to achieve contact with the external social world. The purpose of this extraegoic excursion is to gather wild timber to shape into wheels when he returns to his yard, a task that requires him to half immerse himself in "life's swamp." In other words, he performs the Socratic gesture of half immersing himself in the multitude to gather raw material for his intellectual craft.

Lewis stresses Arghol's doubleness at this point. Like the detachment-in-immersion Socrates maintains, Arghol's position is somewhere in between the "terra firma" of the self and the fluid, blood-red tides of the outer world, under whose influence Arghol is continually "ROCKED AND TOSSED" (144). Accordingly, Arghol "LIES HALF HIDDEN" in a "TERRENE CLOUDLET" (147) with "*all but his trunk immersed in the miasma*" (146). In this ambivalent posture, Arghol waits obediently to be battered by a disembodied jackboot, which Arghol describes as a "sample" (155) of the universe's will.

What does all of this signify? In a remarkable display of narrative innovation, Lewis repeats this ritualistic battering in another context, where its significance becomes somewhat clearer. In this other scene, Arghol is involved in a street brawl with a force that is alternately described as Fate, the Police, and the Cossacks: all forces that oppose human agency, whether it be individual agency or collective revolutionary agency, as in the case of the Cossacks. Moreover, Arghol's ego is depicted here as a port town, half submerged in the "*aerian flood*" (164) of the sea, an image that perfectly parallels Arghol's half immersion in the "*opal mist*" (146) of the yard where he receives his beating by the shadowy boot of the universe. In other words, Arghol has a habit of partially immersing himself in the atmosphere of the multitude, not in order to impose his will on it but rather to receive its collective impulses and then be purged of them in a painful sacrificial ritual. In the brawl scene, Lewis creates an elaborate image of Arghol as a collector of social identities. The wild timber that Arghol collects from the "*mud-in-pond of the canal*" (140) is transformed into "*big timber boats ... nineteen nomad souls*" that float into an "*amphibious carcass*" (165) that clearly represents Arghol's half-immersed person.

In this context, Arghol's porousness, his willingness to "*have Humanity inside [him]*" (173), is clearly depicted as a socially benevolent attitude. It is Hanp, the "*son of the sensational masses*" (164), who is mechanically attracted to the forces of repression. He eggs them on against Arghol, who is represented as a "*big rebel*" who "*has a light of alien heroism in his eyes-that-speak-another-language—black and suspect, by no means a* true blue" (164). In other words, Arghol is a racially ambiguous outsider, the kind of person whom all philistines and "sports" regard as "unclean," "disreputable," and "irreparably un-pukka" (198). These "disreputable" attributes are the kind that Lewis aligns with the political altruism of the Not-Self and that correspond to Arghol's role as an "*adversary of Law and Order*" (164).

So, even though Arghol is "*in sympathy with the effects of a far-offness of long light years*" (148), he is not in a position to place himself at the head of this vast political power. He only establishes contact with these systems when he is half immersed in "life's swamp"—the river of the multitude that flows in the direction appointed it by the universe's will. Arghol walks against the tide of this will and, as Lewis makes clear in his 1932 revision of *Enemy of the Stars*, Arghol's "*place in this panorama of power is obscure*" (148). Rather than embodying the crowd-master's will to power, he seems to practice a spontaneous openness to the impulsions of the multitude in order to establish an ethical conduit between humanity and the inhuman political supersystems that threaten to crush it.

Arghol thus appears to be a medium of sorts. The nomadic souls he temporarily shepherds are "drunk up... upon the world's brink, by big stars, and returned [to Arghol] in the shape of thought, ponderous as a meteorite" (168). So, in a sense, Arghol represents humanity developing a spontaneous "feel" for the systems that oppress it and intellectually practicing the logic that will allow it to endure the world-historical shocks of political supersystems. In fact, through Arghol, the will of humanity even seems capable of reaching these powers in some way. Arghol indicates that as he ritually "dies" into "boiling starry cold... some guilty fire of friction, unspent in solitariness, will reach the utmost constellations" (160). In other words, some of the friction worked up by rubbing against the multitude will follow Arghol as he plunges headlong into the universe's power systems. Arghol's strange rites of sacrifice, then, seem to allow the multitude's faculties of intellection to be transported into the cosmic terrain of political supersystems.[65]

So, Arghol seems to be represented as a genuinely spontaneous figure here. He appears to serve as an egoless conduit through which the impulses of the multitude are communicated into the realm of large-scale political contention. And unlike the fascist leader, he does not even represent an underdog nation that can pride itself on its imaginary racial purity. He is "by no means *true blue*" and stands outside the forms of nationalist chauvinism that are part and parcel of fascist ideology. So, if his heroic, individualist opposition to capitalist supersystems is part of a protofascist form of agency, it is one that Lewis has attempted to strip of its self-interest and exclusivity. Arghol, *it seems,* is beyond these narrow identifications, and he labors to save all individuals from the crushing power of the political elite through his ritualized personal sacrifices.

So what are we to make of Hanp's suspicions that Arghol's egoic surrenders result in no real spontaneity, but are in fact part of a self-willed charade—that Arghol is not the unwitting victim of cosmic necessity but a trickster who has "done the whole thing to [himself] from start to finish" (167)? And how are we to interpret the fact that Hanp himself, as "*the rough stuff of the fecund horde of men*" (151), initially seems more like an experimental fringe of Arghol's own ego than an external matrix of social impulses? This suggests that Arghol is not rocked and tossed by a violent social world that threatens his ego from without. Instead, he seems to have cultivated a subservient egoic double that allows him to establish provisional, experimental contact with larger social realities. Arghol describes Hanp as a "poodle-parasite, a sort of mechanical bow-wow, to fetch and carry, for my inferior nature" (176). In other words, Hanp is a domestic representative of the multitude's social impulses, a proxy figure who allows Arghol to "walk abroad" (174) in the multitude and withdraw from it at will. In a sense, Hanp brings the raw material of the world to Arghol so that Arghol may perform experiments upon it.

All of this presents Arghol in a much more sinister light and suggests that the political narrative Lewis is evolving has less to do with individual benevolence than with Lewis's ambivalence about political "heroes" and their attempts to pass themselves off as conduits of the spontaneous energy of the multitude.

Destruction and Reorganization

A good way to approach Lewis's shifting representations of such political "heroes" and their gestures of self-sacrifice is in terms of Badiou's analysis of ascesis in *Deleuze: The Clamor of Being.* Here, Badiou critiques Deleuze's description of thought as an ascetic process that occurs only when "through the sustained renunciation of the obviousness of our needs and occupied positions [we] attain that empty place where, seized by impersonal powers, we are constrained to make thought exist through us."[66] This description of thought's itinerary corresponds closely to Lewis's ideal of the "Not-Self" as a practice of ascetic renunciation that transports one beyond one's narrow egoistic identifications and allows one to be claimed by preindividual currents. But for Badiou, this is a thoroughly "aristocratic" way to understand intellectual activity (12). It relies on the ideal of a hierarchically detached intellect, unusually expert in liberating itself from its immediate social context and immersing itself in the "world's play" (12). And according to Badiou, the fact that the "creative immanence of life" (9) appears to destine and guide this process makes it more aristocratic, not less. The fact that the "outside" of the self is represented as a cosmic Oneness that completes itself only in the "pure" and automatic intuitions of chosen individuals bypasses exactly the "reciprocal play of beings" (47) that for Badiou constitutes the actual matrix of Being.

Lewis expresses his reservations about the self-renunciation of the party, the leader, and the individual artist in quite similar terms. At first, Arghol's forays into the Not-Self appear to be precisely the kind of vitalist surrenders described by Deleuze: disinterested, creative sojourns into the flux of being. But soon they come to seem more like a conspiracy between a detached, aristocratic leader and cosmic social forces far removed from the collective agency of the multitude and, indeed, bent on their containment and subordination.

Admittedly, these kinds of qualms are surprising in an author who exhibited such sympathy for doctrinaire political leadership of both the right and the left in his political writings of the late 1920s and 1930s. For example, in *The Art of Being Ruled*, Lewis writes: "The present rulers of Russia or Italy, we must assume, are imbued with a 'creative,' compassionate emotion for the human being" (89). This is because they recognize that the spontaneous crowd-life of ordinary people leaves them will-less and irresponsible and that, as a consequence, "there must be a master" (89). But as soon as leaders actually achieve this mastery and begin attempting to naturalize their rule, Lewis tends to turn against them. This reversal is visible in *The Art of Being Ruled*, where Lewis initially asserts that "some one or other has to assume responsibility for the ignorant millions" (89) but then writes: "It often occurs... that the ruler becomes a confirmed practitioner of one of Haroun al Raschid's most objectionable habits, namely, that of spending his time disguised amongst his subjects as one of them.... such an arrangement should always be resented and resisted by the ruled" (93).[67]

In *Enemy of the Stars*, a reversal of this kind also occurs. Arghol at first appears to be filled with the political compassion that Lewis believes fascist and Soviet revolutionary leaders exhibit. He annexes to himself an "outcast *alter ego*"[68] in the form of Hanp and uses this dressed-down version of himself to make seemingly altruistic excursions into the spontaneity of the multitude. But near the end of the play, Lewis reveals the sinister and instrumental character of this annexation. Hanp, it turns out, as "a humble labourer," a "nobody," and one of "The Poor" (174), is of interest to Arghol only as a pawn in his fundamentally egoistic game of cosmic mediation. Ultimately, Arghol deprecates Hanp as "unclean" and "degenerate" (176), a strange development, since these are the qualities that wealthy "sports" attribute to "enemies" such as Arghol, who resist assimilation to the "group-spirit" (184). This leads to a fistfight, in which Arghol unexpectedly "*become[s] the soft, blunt paw of Nature—taken back to her bosom, as a matter of course—slowly and idly winning her battle!*" (180).

In other words, as soon as his fight with Hanp commences, Arghol is exhibited as an *instrument* of nature, not its enemy. In this surprising turn of events, Arghol seems to be in league with the political supersystems he once resisted. His self-mediating spontaneity, which opened him to the impulses of the multitude so that he might help them resist the tides of ideological training, has now become the immediacy of pure ideological reflex action. The jarring reversal this brings about is registered in a passage Lewis added to the 1932 version of his play: "*The Enemy of the Stars has of a sudden become solidary with the massive landscape. Its springs have become his springs, it is he who is at the heart now of its occult resistances*" (180). Some transition thus seems to have occurred, in which Arghol has abdicated his role as the stars' adversary and instead identifies himself with their occult power. In the process, Hanp seems intended to emerge as a new enemy figure—no longer a disciple of Arghol but rather an independent force that can consciously resist Arghol's controlling hegemony.[69]

This is a perplexing turn of events that opens up new vistas onto the politics of spontaneity in Lewis's work. At this point, Arghol is clearly no longer in spontaneous communion with the multitude. In fact, as soon as Hanp attacks Arghol, it becomes clear that this communion was never the unpremeditated openness to collective life that Arghol pretended it was. Instead, Arghol seems to have performed these excursions into the multitude so that he could covertly repattern the reactions of the multitude, shaping them according to his own individual will. Arghol's seeming spontaneity then, his openness to the multitude, his selfless adherence to the principle of the Not-Self, were in fact all part of a complex ruse, designed to insinuate Arghol into the vital existence of the multitude, the better to govern them, from the inside, by way of a sinister emotional magic.

Lewis clearly exposes the duplicity of Hanp's "Master" in this scene, then, but even this exposure does not seem to invalidate Arghol's earlier role as an authentic enemy of the stars. Lewis makes it clear that it is only "now" that Arghol has "of a sudden" become aligned with the political supersystems of the stars. This suggests that a new cycle of enmity and struggle is to begin, that Hanp is to inherit the oppositional role that Arghol once occupied. But Hanp is more of a collective persona than an individual character, so the form of agency that he inherits from Arghol seems destined to be a collective possession rather than an individual one. What happens, then, when spontaneity is no longer imagined as an individual practice, as a self-willed suspension of individual will, with all of the doubleness and deceit that such an attitude implies? What would a spontaneity of the multitude look like? What would its intellectual center be? And what would be the politics of this surprising role reversal?

One clue to this question about collective spontaneity can be found in *The Art of Being Ruled*, where Lewis writes, "Political revolution involves (1) destruction, and (2) reorganization: they are separate departments, but they necessarily work together, and sometimes get mixed up" (351). Seen in this light, Arghol's status as an adversary, a dissolvent figure, a breaker-down of social walls, represents the first department of revolutionary activity. Like Socrates, whom Lewis presents as the quintessential embodiment of the Not-Self, Arghol allows his intellect to walk amid the multitude as a destabilizing influence. And, also like Socrates, Arghol has a goal that is fundamentally negative. What he seeks to teach the crowd-mind is to acknowledge its essential nonentity: "*The more this Master cancelled in [Hanp] the satisfactory self-feelings, the more a contemptible matter showed itself, disfiguring the image of the Master—sunken mirror, that gave back Hanp's essential sickly silhouette*" (173). In other words, once the multitude learns to detach itself from the mechanical prejudices that are bound up with its ego formations, it will realize that it is not ruled by an external master but by its own emotional reflexes. This, presumably, will allow it to see through the deceptions of the ruler and develop an autonomous form of agency.

This is where the second department of revolutionary activity comes into play: the "impulse to new life" (351) and "reorganization" that Lewis describes in *The Art of Being Ruled*. *Enemy of the Stars* provides us with glimpses of this possibility for reorganization, primarily in the ways that Hanp, as a "*locum-tenens*" of the multitude (143), develops a critical capacity detached from the machinations of Arghol. Near the end of the play, Hanp begins to perceive Arghol's rituals of self-extinction as deceptions intended to secure his own egoic hegemony. Snoring loudly after his fistfight with Hanp, Arghol appears to him like a "*malodorous, bloody sink, emptying its water*," his snoring acting like a maddening tide that "*plunges into his mind with bestial regularity, in and out again, purblind and self-confident*" (187). Hanp's realization here is that Arghol's journeys into the multitude are not genuine moments of self-loss but rather self-confident and sexually aggressive penetrations into the collective body of which Hanp is a part. Hanp, by contrast, is a representative of the immanent life of the multitude, a "*port-prowler... like a strayed serf of Cosmopolis, serving the tongue and gait of the metropolitan gutter within the grasp and aroma of the convulsive bitter emptiness of the sea*" (164). Hanp thus exists at the meeting point of the sea, associated here with large-scale systems of commerce and political conflict, and the city's more local patterns of human interaction. The development of his powers of critique and organization thus represents the possibility of a multitude capable of reflective self-rule, the possibility that the multitude could mediate its own metabolic processes, without dialectically reinscribing the forms of mastery and deceit Arghol represents.

But something goes terribly wrong before this potentiality can be developed in *Enemy of the Stars*. Hanp successfully detaches himself from his master's control; "*all remaining bonds*" between him and Arghol are "*sever[ed]*" (177). And yet, instead of leaving Arghol's isolated yard and removing to Berlin, as Arghol suggests, Hanp attacks his master directly and murders him, in what Lewis describes as a "political assassination" (191). That this murder does not liberate Hanp, but instead leads immediately to his undramatic suicide, suggests that the revolutionary impulse to new life cannot, for Lewis, survive without a principle of intellectual coordination. And in most of his writings, Lewis cannot imagine this principle of coordination to be anything but the possession of a central, heroic personality. Accordingly, constituent power may seem like nothing more than a brief interlude in Lewis's work, continually reverting to either chaotic disunion or despotic institutional control.

And yet there exists a lengthy and somewhat neglected "exposition" of *Enemy of the Stars* that thoroughly disrupts this reading and acts, along with "Physics of the Not-Self," as a speculative extension of the play's action. I am referring to *The Lion and the Fox*, whose ostensible object of analysis is "the role of the hero in the plays of Shakespeare." Throughout this meditation on heroism, drama, and political agency, Shakespeare appears only intermittently, whereas the obsessions that inform *Enemy of the Stars*, as Lewis's own contribution to the genre of heroic drama, are everywhere present. For example, Lewis's description of the "'hegelian' contest" between "opposing forces" in Shakespeare's plays perfectly mirrors Anne Quéma's insight into the "agonic self-contradiction" that structures *Enemy of the Stars*.[70] And Lewis's contradictory comparisons of Shakespeare to Georges Sorel, the Bolsheviks, and modernist impersonality all suggest that *The Lion and the Fox* has as much to do with the politics of heroism in Lewis's own play as it does with Shakespearean drama.

To discover the elusive logic of collective spontaneity and its relationship to political heroes of all kinds, it is therefore necessary to see how Lewis scripts the individual and the multitude in his strange work of dramatic self-criticism.

The Public Vituperator

The first clue *The Lion and the Fox* provides about Lewis's models of individual and collective spontaneity resides in its astonishingly implausible account of kingship. According to Lewis, the king acted in the early modern period as an intermediary between the lordly oligarchy, which was the true possessor of political power, and the serfs whom the king ruled. "The king from age to age has been not only the scapegoat and villain, but the screen for oligarchical exploitation" (122), Lewis writes. So, much like Arghol, the king is essentially powerless, a "bold self-opinionated little speck defending itself against a circle of hostile forces" (124). And like Arghol, the king receives a ritualized form of punishment at the hands of this ruling elite. He is "constantly surrounded and threatened by an armed ring of great nobles who browbeat and threaten [him]" (124).

But the truly remarkable connection of Lewis's king to *Enemy of the Stars* lies in the king's proximity not merely to the *serf* but to the *modern proletariat*. For Lewis, the king "was an outcast of a sort... a strange, unchecked, dangerous element in life... on whose head the general tyranny must eventually be visited" (123). The king was indeed an egoist, but "behind his lonely, spectacularly egotistic, eminent figure a thousand equally intense, cosier, privileged egotisms could subsist" (123). Like the proletariat, then, the king is a victim of forces more powerful than he:

> How near [the king] is to the poor man . . . can be . . . demonstrated by considering a little closely one of the successors of the monarch, the modern "proletariat." The Proletariat—that fierce, pitiable, harassed abstraction—is in the same way a screen, but a far wider, better-built and more effective one. It can screen even more egotisms than can a king, and mask an even more powerful oligarchy than can coexist with a monarch. (123)

The proletariat, in other words, serves as a screen for autocratic Soviet officials in the same way that the king serves as a screen for the lordly oligarchy. Bizarrely, Lewis describes the proletariat as the "figurehead" of communist bureaucracy, just as he describes the king as the figurehead of the feudal aristocracy. Both are united in their role as scapegoats for what Lewis calls "oligarchical exploitation" (122).

In fact, Lewis does everything possible to represent the king and the "poor man" as kindred figures, united in their opposition to a repressive power structure that hovers over them both. The king here is thus a clear analogue of Lewis's populistic fascist leader, who unites the multitude to struggle against the "financial directorate" that supposedly oppresses both of them.[71] Lewis suggests that is "easy to see" how the king "liked 'his people' better than he liked his swarm of great feudatories—how, in short, the king and the poor man were 'drawn together,' and how it was possible, in a hostile world, for a considerable sympathy to exist between them" (128). To complete this implausible social portrait, Lewis invokes the bucolic habits of St. Louis, who was known to "dress[ ] in the plainest clothes" and "go and sit under the trees in the Bois and do justice" (128). By mixing with the multitude in this way, and by virtue of his sympathetic connection with them, the king reenacts the spontaneity of the Not-Self. This dressed-down king appears to be completely open to the entreaties of the multitude, adjudicating between them without personal interest or any preconceptions at all.

At this point in his exposition, Lewis is essentially still "on the side" of this populist king. Like Arghol, the king is an enemy figure, struggling heroically against oligarchical supersystems. He is in constant contact with the powers that oppress ordinary individuals, but the abuse he receives at the hands of these powers only brings the king closer to his subjects, just as the egoic despoilment that Arghol suffers allows him to coexist with a "son of the sensational masses." In both cases, the social altruism described in "Physics of the Not-Self" seems to be in play.

But then Lewis effects the reversal that we have seen him perform in *The Art of Being Ruled* and *Enemy of the Stars*. His description of the nobility's power in *The Lion and the Fox* becomes more and more abstract, until it is seems to be synonymous with the financial directorate of modern capitalism. The king, too, becomes much more closely aligned with this oppressive outer power and emerges as an enemy of people, not just of the power structure above him. In the person of the king,

> serfs had their *individual* stranger... quartered on them, giving a personal form to all the anonymous outer power of the universe, against which it was impossible to fight, but against which... on usurious terms... he agreed to protect them. He was their *enemy*, a representative of the outer hostile world, between whom and themselves the terms of propitiation and sacrifice had been systematized. (125)

Notice how in this passage the king is redefined as a possible object of the serfs' enmity. The focus is no longer on the king's enmity toward the oligarchical powers above him but on his status as a local representative of these powers, whom the multitude might choose to assail.

According to my analysis, this shift in perspective occurs because of Lewis's deeply ambivalent attitude toward the figure of persecuted, popular, fascist leaders and the spontaneous connections to the multitude that they feign. It is true that Lewis was strongly attracted to the fascist ideal of an underdog nationalist leader who could protect the multitude from the forces of international loan capital.[72] But as soon as the leader is actually *instituted* as a protector of the multitude—as soon as he begins insinuating himself into the local mythologies of the subject population in order to naturalize his rule—Lewis exhibits him as "the bull to be attacked and sacrificed if possible" (129). The king as a "rustic and democratic god" (127) is suddenly exhibited as a duplicitous opportunist who is to be ritually sacrificed by the multitude. Lewis compares this process to the dynamics of monarchical rule in Thongan society, in which, according to Lewis, Thongan kings are "severely criticized by the people, and may even be deposed" if their "actions run counter to received standards of propriety" (131). In fact, Lewis relates how this public criticism has been ritualized in Thongan society in the person of the herald, whose "duty it is to appear before the king's door every morning and to exalt the exploits of the ruler's ancestors, which is followed by vigorous disparagement of the present incumbent."[73] Lewis then links this ritualized abuse of the king to the sacrificial practices recorded in *The Golden Bough*, in which Sir James Frazer describes the treatment of the mock king of the Sacaea, who is seated upon the king's throne and mockingly exalted, only to be stripped, scourged, and crucified at the appointed time.

So, by the time he completes his exposition of the figure of the king, Lewis's sympathies are no longer with the ruler but with the "public vituperator" (132) who is on the side of the king's executioners. As we have seen, the turning point occurs when the king begins to "fit[ ] in with, [give] a name to, and reinforce[ ] . . . the field-magic and symbolic dances of the subject population" (127)—in other words, when his rule begins to pass as a spontaneous force of nature, to whose rhythms the multitude has become hypnotically attuned.

In this context, Arghol's status as an enemy takes on new significance. It is clear that he too practices "that admired method of insinuation whereby a particularly compendious pretended reality enables its creator to express himself as *though he were nature*, or a god" (286). In other words, Arghol represents "the artist [who] pretends to be nature" (286), and the metaphors Lewis uses to describe this pretense are almost identical to the ones he uses to describe the techniques used by rulers to "conceal the human mind" that manipulates the public.[74]

The Lion and the Fox's account of kingship thus illuminates the conclusion of *Enemy of the Stars* in some surprising ways. It suggests that Arghol's habit of making spontaneous excursions among the multitude is in fact a "genial bluff" similar to that in which "a man hunting a seal will cover himself with the skin of a dead seal, and, disguised in that way, stalk his prey" (286). And like *Enemy of the Stars*, its focus shifts away from the agent of this deadly masquerade and toward the ways in which public figures expose and vituperate such falsely spontaneous, falsely selfless agents. "To-day," Lewis writes, the "impersonal fallacy" is "no longer accepted" (286). Instead, like Hanp in *Enemy of the Stars*, the multitude has been "taught . . . to recognize the individual and his personal bias, at the heart of the philosopher's system: just as a seal by experience might learn eventually to recognize the hunter hidden beneath the skin in which it was being stalked" (286).

This process of collective enlightenment, and the way it is "liable to . . . explode[ ] at any moment" the "pretense of 'impersonality' " (287), becomes the focus of *Enemy of the Stars*. And by means of the parallel narrative Lewis constructs in *The Lion and the Fox*, it becomes clear that the short circuit that concludes *Enemy of the Stars* is by no means the only possible ending to Lewis's story of political unmasking and collective spontaneity.

"The Soul and Will of Man in the Machine"

Lewis's "alternate ending" to *Enemy of the Stars* comes in the form of a dramatic parallelism he establishes in *The Lion and the Fox:* Arghol and Hanp are "rewritten" in the figures of Prospero and Caliban. But, surprisingly, the play Lewis analyzes to illustrate this parallelism is not Shakespeare's *Tempest* but Ernest Renan's *Caliban*. In Renan's play, Caliban is a modern, proletarian character who overlaps in some obvious ways with Hanp of *Enemy of the Stars*. Prospero, by contrast, practices a pernicious "*government by magic*" (281) and, like Arghol, pretends to be "the instrument of a will that seeks expression" (280). In other words, he masquerades as a spontaneous agent who draws from "the great universal chaos" all of the "forces lost in nature" (280, 281). And as in *Enemy of the Stars*, the turning point in Renan's play occurs when "Caliban learns to 'see through' his master's magic, and through his master too" (281). Unlike Hanp, however, Caliban does not react with immediate, convulsive violence but instead repairs to the city, where he becomes "un clerc" in constant dialogue with "hommes du peuple."[75] Lewis quotes the tirade of this new, urban figure:

> When the people perceive that their rulers have led them by means of superstition, thou shalt see what a doom it will bring down upon their old-time masters. That hell, by which they terrified us, never existed. Those monsters on which Prospero's prestige rested were all imaginary, but they tormented me as greatly as if they had been real. (281–82)

For Lewis, these illusory torments correspond not merely to the otherworldly hell of Christianity but also to the *real* illusory torments to be found in the intimate realm of ideological regulation: the entire phantasmagoria of compulsions and prohibitions that are insinuated into humanity's most basic social instincts.

Thus, when Caliban "enlightens the populace ... pointing out to them the weaknesses of this tyrant, and indicating the sources of his power," when he "stirs up an insurrection, and is proclaimed reigning duke in place of Prospero" (282), what is at issue for Lewis is not just political practice, but rather the possibility that the emotional reflexes of social instinct, through political practice, could *themselves* be altered, as the social foundations of their existence were simultaneously altered. This idea, that the "childish machinery" (282) of emotional compulsion could be transformed into an evolving, adaptive, social logic, is at the heart of Lewis's conception of collective spontaneity. Lewis's narrative suggests that the transformation of one's basic patterns of social affect cannot be accomplished on an individual level, since variations of this kind must correspond to new lived patterns of social existence, a new "common world" that binds the multitude together. Individual spontaneity attempts, as thoroughly as possible, to dissolve established, restrictive patterns of social affect by combining itself with social potentialities glimpsed in the multitude. But without the reciprocal, self-creative spontaneity of the multitude itself, this individual spontaneity is little more than a masquerade, performed against the backdrop of a passive, undifferentiated multitude.

The difference between individual and collective spontaneity, then, is the difference between the "hero" who pretends to encapsulate the vital possibilities of the multitude in the course of his or her individual social excursions and the multitude that *transforms itself* in unpredictable ways by collectively transforming its conditions of existence. As Lewis writes, "Prospero remains to the end the hero of Shakespeare's imagination, but Caliban grows up and transforms himself" (282). Lewis stresses that this transformation is a collective one, and that it does not proceed from the "benevolent" process of self-othering embodied in the Not-Self. He writes, "As the representative of the proletariat, the great citizen, Caliban, is no longer a monster" (282). Lewis then quotes Renan to illustrate how "Caliban can become Ariel": "Take the butterfly which is less an animal of itself than it is the blossom of another animal... suddenly the crawling, stupid creature has become winged and ideal and possessed of a purely aerial life" (282–83). This is how Lewis represents the spontaneous social evolution of which the multitude is capable. Not a response to political benevolence of any kind, it is instead a reorganization of elements that already exist within its collective body. And crucially, it is the imposture of the political hero that rouses the multitude from its slumber. By "becoming Ariel," the multitude reclaims the spiritual forces that had been used to regulate its emotional reflexes and deploys them to realize the affective variability suppressed within them. Spontaneity in this context is not an individual excursion into the possibilities of the collective but a collective transformation of the grounds upon which what is possible and impossible is deduced.

The Lion and the Fox makes this idea of spontaneity visible through a highly complex symbolic apparatus, in which the ruler, walking abroad among the multitude, is envisioned as a mythic king whose populist masquerade is turned against him. Similarly, the Socrates of "Physics of the Not-Self" had begun by cultivating a comic or experimental principle in himself, a kind of double that allowed him to merge spontaneously with the creative energies of the multitude. But according to the mechanisms of Socratic irony, he always ensured that this principle of self-negation—the Not-Self, in Lewis's terminology—nevertheless "belonged to him" and could therefore be revoked at any moment.

In *The Lion and the Fox*, Lewis envisions a situation in which this process of negation becomes detached from the individual who gave rise to it. What was at first an intellectual game, an experimental fringe of the individual ego that allowed one to step outside oneself and into the multitude, suddenly takes on a deadly seriousness. The multitude *itself* becomes the locus of its own experimental activity, and since it has become a "revolutionary crowd" (135), it is intent on ordering itself without borrowing anything from the "altruistically" self-negating ruler. In fact, the social altruism of the ruler is at this point revealed for the absurd comedy that it is; only now the joke is decidedly at the ruler's expense. The king offering himself as the representative of cosmic social forces, the ruler aspiring to direct the social energies of the multitude—in other words, the "man masquerading as a god" (134)—is "suddenly confronted with powers superior to himself" (134) and is consequently "exposed to the vulgarest misfortune, disgraced, humiliated and killed" (133).

For Lewis, the political consequences of this exposure are indeterminate. As *The Lion and the Fox* suggests, such demystifications can lead to spontaneous forms of collective initiative, or they can lead, as in *Enemy of the Stars*, to a mechanical political nihilism. But, for Lewis, much more important than the result of this process is the "intermediate zone" (284) of conflict in which the ruse of individual spontaneity meets with an outraged, spontaneously self-organizing collective. In *Enemy of the Stars*, Arghol simultaneously enacts such a ruse and is a willing participant in its unraveling. He is, in a sense, Lewis's ideal ruler: a self-destructing apparatus that *simulates* the mechanisms of rule while at the same time violently prompting its audience to recognize, expose, and vituperate its deceptions.[76] The question of whether Arghol's excursions into the multitude are altruistic, love-awakening endeavors or duplicitous "conjuring trick[s]" (285) intended to secure personal rule is therefore undecidable.

This is because, in the final analysis, Arghol is less a self-consistent dramatic character than an emblem of spontaneous critical and synthetic powers Lewis hopes to awaken in the multitude.

Collective Ontologies

Lewis's critical and dramatic work thus revolves around a concept that has taken on particular urgency in many contemporary political ontologies: the concept of constituent power. Defined by Negri as the "motor or cardinal expression of democratic revolution,"[77] constitutive power refers to the *potenza* of the multitude, its capacity to organize itself outside the strictures of codified, hierarchical, constituted power. The central question of constituent power, therefore, is how the multitude might develop institutional structures to express its self-organizing capacity without reverting to the statist constructions of constituted power. This potentiality is repeatedly voiced by theorists such as Alain Badiou, but often in the form of an abstract emblem or image, for example, that of "a combination of a subjective capacity and an organization—totally independent of state—of the consequences of that capacity."[78]

The dynamic between Arghol and Hanp in *Enemy of the Stars* is another such emblem of the possibilities of constituent power. The fusion of individual intellect and collective *potenza* that these characters enact points toward the possibility of a multitude guided by self-suspending, critical powers typically imagined to be the sole possession of the individual mind. And as Lewis's critical extensions of the play suggest, Arghol's inability to oversee this process of intellectual tutelage to the end could be read not as a failure of constituent power but as its most hopeful moment. Hanp's violent break with Arghol evokes a figure of collective agency that does not dialectically reinscribe the transcendent structure of rule that Arghol embodies. Instead, it suggests that on some other scene, removed from the local action of the play, this spontaneous revolt might develop itself as a collective capacity for self-rule.

No doubt Lewis's figurations of this capacity emerge strangely and indirectly, as they do in all the modernists I consider in this book. Williams evokes the self-organizational powers of the multitude as an erogenous metabolism of the body politic, and, as we will see in the next chapter, Laura Riding depicts it in similarly abstract terms, as a "common potentiality" that precedes the divisions of society into private and public spheres.[79] In all of these cases, obscure and often bizarre images serve as conceptual placeholders for collective ontologies that do not yet exist—forms of spontaneous self-direction that remain dormant in the social body. To document these collective potentialities, Williams, Lewis, Riding, and Stevens must venture beyond the images of moronic or sadistic crowds that we associate more readily with the modernist imagination. They must attempt to discover, beneath the senilities of mob sentiment and commercial culture, something of almost unwarrantable beauty: what Riding calls the "common urgent life of spiritual experience."[80]

3   "AN INSTANTANEOUS SYMPATHY OF COMMUNICATION"

Laura Riding and the Politics of Spontaneity

OF ALL THE MODERNISTS I consider in this book, Laura Riding harbors the deepest and most explicit suspicions about the very category of artistic spontaneity. As we saw in the previous chapter, her closest rival in this respect, Wyndham Lewis, is quite ambivalent about artists and politicians who stage "spontaneous" mergers with the multitude. At times, Lewis energetically critiques these figures for attempting to pass themselves off as vessels of the multitude's will while they conceal the personal interests that truly motivate them. But at other times, he offers spontaneous contact with the multitude as an antidote to liberal democracy's powerful forces of ideological training and social control. This idea of spontaneity allows Lewis to imagine the artist as a wandering, disruptive figure, similar to the heroized image of the fascist leader we sometimes find in Lewis's political writings. And even when Lewis exposes this image of the fascist "man of the masses" as a repugnant myth, he attempts to redeem a certain artistic restaging of it, one in which the artist performs a similar populist masquerade while at the same time exposing it for the farce that it is, instructing the multitude in the methods of emotional manipulation he is practicing upon them and showing them how to recognize similar deceptions in the political realm.

Riding, by contrast, cannot abide even such a self-critical, self-sacrificing model of artistic spontaneity as Lewis's. In her incredibly acute critiques of Wyndham Lewis and other early twentieth-century artists and intellectuals, she points out that myths involving the collective exposure and sacrifice of the artist serve only to enhance the mystique of such artists, conferring on them the status of vanishing mediators or dying gods whose experimental, disembodied attitudes toward social life are all too easily naturalized in the multitude's attitude toward itself.[1] In her poetry and philosophical work, then, Riding interrogates the very metaphorics of surrender, merger, and depersonalization on which this idea of spontaneity depends.

In works such as *Anarchism Is Not Enough*, "The Word 'Woman,'" *The World and Ourselves*, and *The Telling*, she advances this project by arguing that the entire idea of artistic spontaneity as an experimental journey into social life is based on the mistaken conception that society is an "elsewhere," a "play-world" that can be visited in moments of speculative contemplation.[2] For Riding, this conception is rooted in the gendered division of social spheres, with the "outside world" being defined as a male region of experimental production and abstract debate and the "inside world" being defined as a female region of social accountability and reciprocal mediation. According to Riding, Lewis's brand of modernist spontaneity attempts to unite these spheres by discovering affectively charged relational patterns within the realm of public life. To do this, modernists such as Lewis liquidate all the rigid, habitual affective structures of their private existence and roam spontaneously in the public world, attempting to tune in to much more plastic modes of social valuation.[3]

For Riding, however, such social journeys reaffirm the split between the public and private spheres rather than heal it. By treating affective relationships as a matter of abstract experiment, modernists remand all embedded, reciprocally accountable forms of affect to a feminized private sphere. And by treating "the private" as an affective home to return to after their forays into the realm of virtuosic male exchange, they reaffirm the public sphere's status as a site of noncommittal, disembodied performances. The double attitude of modernist spontaneity, then, with its play of affective involvement and intellectual detachment, reproduces the actual, material split between a private sphere administered "behind the scenes" by women and a public sphere where "competitive cleverness" reigns.[4]

This split cannot be overcome by the technical acrobatics of literary spontaneity, according to Riding. But like all of the other modernists I analyze in this volume, Riding offers an alternative model of spontaneity to counterpose to the one that is being subjected to critique. Riding describes this alternative spontaneity as an intersubjective manifestation, rooted in concrete human existence and all the interpersonal associations from which one cannot extract oneself at will. This form of spontaneity evolves not in a zone of social free play but rather in a sphere of binding affective networks. It is a spontaneity of ongoing "mutual verifying" rather than a spontaneity of experimental assertion.[5] In other words, it is a spontaneity that is defined by interpersonal processes, not just individual ingenuity.

By identifying spontaneity with interpersonal affective processes, Riding adds something crucial to the narrative of modernism and the multitude that we have been tracing. Rather than approaching the multitude as an anonymous flux into which the modernist author migrates, she approaches it as a productive nexus that constitutes itself precisely in its resistance to such incursions. Riding's definition of spontaneity thus opens upon what Antonio Negri and Michael Hardt call "biopolitical production," that is, forms of living labor that "directly produce[ ] social relationships and forms of life."[6] For Hardt and Negri, "biopolitical production" refers, on one hand, to the set of communicative and organizational capacities activated in the social body when it is subsumed by capitalist relations of production and becomes a highly flexible, socialized, and cooperative ensemble of forces. On the other hand, "biopolitical production" refers to the reproduction of social life that occurs within the private sphere—to what feminist theorists have described as caring labor, kin work, and labor in the bodily mode. Equally important to both of these forms of biopower is "affective labor," which Hardt defines as "the processes whereby our laboring practices produce collective subjectivities, produce sociality, and ultimately produce society itself."[7] Affective labor therefore produces not commodities but knowledges, dispositions, and sensibilities. And most important, it is a power of self-organization that is embedded in the ordinary life processes that connect friends, families, and coworkers to each other.

Such a model of embedded social production will be crucial to our understanding of Riding, since one of her principal concerns is to imagine forms of political association that would not rely on external leadership figures of the kind that appear in Lewis's work. The forms of affective embeddedness and productivity Riding explores are meant to serve as antidotes to the kind of emotional magic performed by Lewis's leaders—vanguard figures who repattern the multitude's feelings and self-images in order to transform the multitude into an obedient political mass. Affect in Riding thus has less to do with personal feelings or attitudes than with what Patricia Ticineto Clough calls "capacities to affect and be affected or the augmentation or diminution of a body's capacity to act, to engage, and to connect."[8] This is a Spinozan definition of affect, which, as Brian

Massumi explains, involves the way "the body coincides with its own transitions."[9] In contemporary affect theory, this idea of affect as a self-relating emergence, or as an organism's "autopoetic" relation to its environment, has promoted a relational definition of affect. Affect is often seen less as an individual possession than as "pre-individual capacities to affect and to be affected" or even as a capacity for "self-organization" residing within matter itself.[10]

Riding anticipates this new way of theorizing affect and develops its political implications much further than what we sometimes see in even its most daring theorists. This is because for Riding affective relatedness is not something that can be experimentally advanced, nor is it something indeterminate and abstract. Instead, it inheres in interhuman exchanges that are governed by intuited rules of proportion that cannot be violated without interpersonal consequence. Affect in this context could be described as the sensuous measure of interpersonal exchanges that possess no external standard of valuation. This idea of affect is thus close to Negri's—that is, "a *power to act* that is singular and at the same time universal ... singular because it poses action beyond every measure that power does not contain in itself, in its own structure, and in the continuous restructurings that it constructs ... universal because the affects construct a commonality among subjects."[11] Affect, for Riding, is similarly a collective power to act and be acted upon, but unlike Negri, Riding worries incessantly about how to differentiate between this self-organizing dynamic and the process whereby interested parties insinuate their ideologies into collective life, naturalizing them as valuative standards.

In the works I examine in this chapter, Riding evolves a number of different affective economies, each of which proposes a different solution to this problem. At one moment, Riding will imagine a political utopia in which the compass of all individuals' political activities would be identical with the social spheres that have determining claims on their existence—a vision that embeds political life within interpersonal affective currents that cannot be suspended at will. At another moment, she likens political spontaneity to the affective modality of love, in which one submits oneself, at great risk, to binding and interpersonally negotiated laws of proportion and mutuality. As I will argue in this chapter, this idea of spontaneity as requiring internal limitation and correctives, requiring ceaseless vigilance on the part of social actors, is ultimately less in step with Negri's models of political *cupiditas* and *amor* than with the more cautious and self-correcting models of spontaneity put forward by anarchist and anarcho-syndicalist theorists. In the works of Anton Pannekoek, Rudolf Rocker, and Paul Mattick we find modes of political organization that are bound to "the praxis of daily life" and therefore serve as internal biopolitical correctives to the forms of political opportunism of which Riding is so wary.[12] Riding's affective economies are thus ways of redramatizing the early twentieth-century dream of a society that would be governed by council associations—organs of self-government coextensive with individuals' everyday interpersonal networks.

I use the term "multitude" in this chapter to refer to these interpersonal networks, since Hardt and Negri's term eloquently expresses Riding's vision of society as a matrix of mutually embedded singularities. Though Riding worries more than Hardt and Negri about the forms of opportunism and ideological deception that can be brought to bear on collective life, she provides an early vision of the kind of self-valorizing, affectively productive subject that is so central to the work of contemporary multitude theorists. This subject resides in what Riding calls the "spontaneous essence of humanness"[13]—a collective power that must always be betrayed by the politicians who pretend to express it, since it is composed not of anonymous, quantifiable masses but of personally binding points of social contact. Such an interpersonal continuum cannot, properly speaking, be represented by a power external to it, since this continuum *presents* itself in the form of reciprocal attachments that are constitutively excluded from the agents and mechanisms of public power. Much of Riding's work is thus an attempt to discover how the internal life and potentialities of this productive ensemble, this multitude, might be expressed, without partaking of the anonymity and "experimentalism" of the public sphere.

Of course, this association of Riding with the life of the multitude might come as a surprise, since much Riding criticism stresses her sense of the "unreality of the masses"[14] and her idea that the poet is "radically disjoined from the social and historical world."[15] Carla Billitteri, for example, is completely correct that Riding condemns "the ignorance of a 'miseducated' public and its 'tyrannical influence' on the conduct of literature,"[16] as is Ella Zohar Ophir when she describes Riding's arguments for "the autonomous authority of the individual mind as against the system-based authority of science."[17] But these critics also acknowledge that Riding's hostility to public order and knowledge systems never led her to "retreat[ ] to a notion of 'poetic' or 'personal' truth."[18] Instead, in Billitteri's account, Riding evolves forms of poetic agency that "bridge[ ] thought and things, poetry and the society of things, allowing the ontologically expatriate poet to operate in society."[19] Likewise, Ophir stresses the "deeply egalitarian" character of Riding's late philosophical work, which describes how "every individual's devotion to the speaking of being will eventually converge with every other individual's in an articulation of the indivisible whole, which is truth."[20]

In other words, Riding's despair about the masses, "dazed and spasmodically terrified" by "the hellish unhappiness forced upon their consciousness in these times,"[21] is rivaled only by her solicitude for some other interpersonal entity, one that has not yet assembled itself, but the processes of which Riding attempts to evoke in her creative and philosophical works. Luke Carson describes this interpersonal entity as "the community of language users";[22] Jerome J. McGann describes it as the "transparticular," or "human life in the whole";[23] and Lisa Samuels evokes it by describing Riding's "world-changing impulses," which "begin with the individual and move to other individuals through the medium of human language acts."[24] But however this interpersonal matrix is described, it always becomes palpable as something latent in collective life, present only when large groups can be identified as a network of locatable, speaking subjects—in other words, when they are not anonymous masses, but a *multitude:* a company of accountable, embedded singularities.

Imagining how such a network of singularities, such a multitude, could act on a massive scale without reverting to a condition of anonymity and disembeddedness is a project that guides Riding's creative and critical work from her early *Anarchism Is Not Enough* to her late philosophical work *The Telling*. In the readings that follow, I analyze the numerous and often bizarre images that Riding uses to evoke such large-scale organizational processes, from images of world-historical "hostesses" who will help "resolve the discrepancy between...personal consciousness... and the historical time of the multitudes"[25] to images of a "mutuality of testing" to be effected amid "large-scale communal diversity."[26]

But like so many of modernism's utopian visions, Riding's emerges out of a diagnostic attention to the alienated exchange processes and political agents of the present. To understand what Riding hoped spontaneous organization might achieve, then, we should first try to understand all of the failures and alibis that Riding lays at its door. And it is in early critical works such as *Contemporaries and Snobs* and *Anarchism Is Not Enough* that Riding pursues this indictment of current forms of poetic spontaneity most exactingly.

The Systematization of Impulses

In her 1928 *Contemporary and Snobs*, Riding levels some of her most explicit critiques of modernist spontaneity. Foremost among these is that modernist spontaneity aspires to present the writer not as "a person but the spokesman of his age, a mechanical recorder of time."[27] In this mode, the individual will of the writer is masked, since the writer is posing as a "mechanical soul" (21) in spontaneous harmony with the multitude. Masquerading in this way as a "mass-consciousness which contemporaneous facts seem to form automatically" (22), the writer tries to pass off his or her personal biases as the spontaneous expression of collective desires.

Riding develops this critique of modernist spontaneity in a work titled *Anarchism Is Not Enough*, also published in 1928. In this book, she offers Oswald Spengler, whom she describes as a "philosophical modernist," as the most egregious example of this tendency. Because he views individual consciousness as the expression of larger social systems, Riding brands him a "collective realist": someone who approaches the self as a mere "analogy" of collective processes. For Spengler, as for all "popularists," "culture is the large-scale, accumulative participation of everyman in progress; conduct is behaviourism, perfect social automatism," and the "idea of a non-social self outside the tradition and without reference to a cultural line of succession (a self rather, 'beginning again and again and again') would be equally foreign and repulsive" (121–22). Spengler, in other words, can view the spontaneity of the creative self only as an expression of a preexisting and hypnotically compulsive cultural system. Any original creation that might offer "a casual disorganized resistance to ordinary objects" (113) and thereby "free[ ] the self to self" (105) is absorbed within a cosmic determinism that insists that "all the values by which [the] self is organized are derivative values" (73).

Literary modernists such as Gertrude Stein, James Joyce, Virginia Woolf, and Wyndham Lewis belong to a slightly different camp, which Riding calls "individual-realism." Unlike Spengler, these writers give voice to the inner "unreality" of the self. They recognize that the self is not fused with its social environment and is therefore, in a sense, "unreal." But in their work, these modernists insist on "translat[ing] from the unreal into the real, the personal (inhuman) into the human (physically collective)" (63). In other words, they attempt to put the unreal powers of the self in the service of social systems of valuation. This means that their individualistic withdrawal from society is merely strategic. In fact, such withdrawal is merely a kind of cliquish exclusivity, maintained so that these modernists might revisit mass society and administer their refined standards of taste with the appropriate aura of superiority.

Riding labels this kind of elitist individualism "anarchism," not so much to associate it with the various forms of collectivist and syndicalist anarchism of the early twentieth century as to evoke, with a certain amount of irony, a "personal" anarchism that elevates the individual as an ideal to which the rest of society should aspire. Anarchism, in this idiosyncratic sense, refers not to a radical political program but rather to a "toryish" (67) affectation—a mental snobbism that proclaims its distance from the multitude only in order to legitimate its desire to impose enlightened ideals upon it. According to this logic, Wyndham Lewis's encomiums against mass society only secure him a provisional distance from collective realities. In fact, his haughty disdain for mass society requires its existence in order to sustain itself and belies his true intention, which is to systematize his irritated reactions into a universal program that he hopes to promulgate among the multitude itself. For this reason, Riding writes, "his solution is that the few strong individuals who object to loss of consciousness should benefit by an anarchistic dispensation that leaves them their consciousness intact in order that they may politically administer sociality to the unconscious" (122). In other words, Lewis's anarchism amounts only to a tactical individualism, which then devolves into a universal dogma to be imposed, by stealth if necessary, upon the many.

This idea of the artist as a double agent, craftily insinuating personal canons of conduct into a hypnotized multitude, is central to Riding's critique of modernist spontaneity. In *Anarchism Is Not Enough*, Riding argues that this model of spontaneity is based on the idea that artworks should "create, by a synthetic, material (non-personal) action of the senses, real things... a pattern of reality, an arrangement of elements" (97), with a view to "hypnotizing" the reader "into a rearrangement of the elements of which he is composed... a sensual recombination of personality" (98). In other words, artworks that are not absolutely "unreal" participate in a logic of emotional conditioning. And the action of this process upon the reader is comparable to the ideological conditioning of the multitude by the political elite.

At stake in this critique is not merely the specific aesthetic strategies of Lewis or Stein but the question of how any form of art could aspire to more general significance without obeying a logic derived from the operations of ideological interpellation. For Riding, the case is hopeless so long as we rely on the idea that art should be an expressive patterning of reality or a reflection of public standards of value. All talk of values is, for Riding, talk of Reason, in the Hegelian sense of an immanent and evolving historical logic. The idea of Reason thus presupposes that social reality consists of various causal relationships, rather than being a meaningless series of accidents, as Riding believes it to be. The idea that society possesses a structuring logic that can be intuited serves only as a pretext for the artist to masquerade as a universal mind that is capable of spontaneously reflecting society's inner laws. Since, in fact, no such structuring logic, Reason, or zeitgeist exists, the artist's claim to be intuiting society's logic is nothing more than an elaborate form of mesmerism, intended to accommodate the reader's sympathies to whatever arbitrary systems of valuation the artist may happen to hold.

Synthesizing Wyndham Lewis and I. A. Richards into a portrait of this mesmeric social operator, Riding sets out to argue that all "modernistic" forms of art and criticism try to accomplish exactly this kind of emotional manipulation. For both of these men, Reason represents a "magical intelligence" (102) or "inspired...literalness" (102) that corresponds to "man's participation in the patterns of reality" (103). And this myth of Reason, that is, "the mathematics of synthesis by which reality may be accurately apprehended" (103), is then offered as a tool for "turning the human world into a world of values: making conduct (communication, relation) achieve significant pattern" (103). The ethos of modernism, in other words, is organized around a covert "recombination" of conduct. It amounts to "the training of the community as a whole in the traffic in reality, with the artist as band-master" (103). The fiction that the artist is able to discover objective laws makes possible a "'systemization of impulses'" (103), which is intended to produce the social analogue of "instinct" (103) and the "civilized substitute for magic" (103).

As far as Riding is concerned, this entire dialectic of spontaneous merger and emotional repatterning depends on the idea that reality is something separate from the individual mind, but able to be penetrated at will by the artist. Reality therefore becomes a "play-world" for the artist,[28] in which various systems of valuation can be experimentally tested. One crucial key to understanding Riding's critique of this kind of spontaneity, and the forms of agency she develops in opposition to it, is that she sees this dialectic of separation, penetration, and mesmerism as a fundamentally "male" phenomenon. Numerous female authors, such as Virginia Woolf and Gertrude Stein, are critiqued under the rubric of this "individual-realist" dialectic, which is one reason why we should view its "maleness" as a heuristic structure of feeling and action, as opposed to a physiological compulsion. Nevertheless, the tropes Riding employs to describe individual-realism are gendered in a completely unambiguous way. The artist's attempts to achieve a spontaneous immersion of the self in society are depicted as the "lascivious, masculine, Oedipan embrace of the real mother-body by the unreal son-mind" (70). The individual mind, discontent in its asocial isolation, posits a vast, fictitious social body as both its origin and field of intuitional dalliance. For a collective-realist such as Spengler, this represents the mind's attempt to

> overcome[ ] its perpetual temporariness by a perpetual give-and-take between itself and the Great Mother reality, whom it honours with its philosophical erections (what Herr Spengler calls third-dimensional extension) and from whom it receives sensations of infinity—the Great Mother's gratitude for this masculine 'conquest' of herself. (70)

Individual-realists, such as Lewis, do not make out much better in this sexual economy. For them, this "masculine extension" (71) of the self into the matrix of being is "actual and personal, rather than metaphorical and collective" (71). Nevertheless, the individual-realist operates according to a similar "sexual fantasia" (71), in which intercourse with the Great Mother reality is achieved through spontaneous intuition: "through *his* experience *now*" (71). The great modernist ambition of fusing mind and reality, in the stream of consciousness or the vortex of perceptual immediacy, is held up here as an infantile attempt to escape from the unreality and isolation of the self.

What is worse is that this form of spontaneity, with its fictitious processes of penetration and merger, perfectly replicates the very real structure of ideological conditioning Riding condemns. The adjective "male," in other words, comes to stand for the private tendency to project reality as a maternal body to be simultaneously propitiated and dominated. In this process, a strictly infantile experience of omnipotence is replicated, which rests upon the sense of complete dependence on, and complete mastery over, the maternal form. But this "male" dialectic also holds sway in the adult worlds of political life and aesthetic production. According to Riding, modernist art and official political activity both belong to a public sphere that is sustained by mechanisms of ideological compulsion. By making their own interests and values appear to be spontaneous reflections of collective need, actors within the public sphere are able to impose these interests and values with ever greater efficiency. And they are able to do so because these displays of spontaneous union with the multitude simultaneously propitiate them and provide for their actual domination.

Some of Riding's best critics have analyzed this dynamic in the context of her abandonment of poetry.[29] By the time she wrote *The Telling*, Riding had come to feel that even her own poetry could not escape what Jerome McGann calls poetry's "aesthetic (formal and apparitional) pretensions to power and completeness."[30] Thus Michael A. Masopust correctly views Riding's renunciation of poetry in 1939 as a repudiation of "the notion that linguistic authority lies with a priestly elite who act as intermediaries between the 'laity' and the 'Subject'—the role she had formerly assumed as a poet."[31] And yet some of Riding's most powerful indictments of the "congenital authoritarianism" (65) of poetry are to be found in her poetry itself, where she is able to walk the reader through the armory of "power-using... devices" (66) that are disguised in poetry's literary charms. One of the best examples of this negative pedagogy is Riding's poem "I Am," which provides an extremely detailed description of what can happen when an order-imposing will pretends to walk spontaneously among the multitude.

A Common Measure

"I Am" begins with the seemingly sympathetic image of the poet as a "presence" among the multitude—as an agent who has suspended her own ego so that she may effect a spontaneous involvement with "the common mind":

> I am an indicated other:
> Witness this common presence
> Intelligible to the common mind,
> The daylight census.[32]

In this passage, the speaker stages a process of self-othering, the kind that poets believe themselves to be performing when they achieve intuitive fusion with the multitude. She appears to surrender over her private being to a shared existence, so that her subjectivity can be counted as part of a census that occurs in the "daylight" of collective habits. In doing so, the speaker seems to surrender the narrow, "self-claiming self" that Riding reviles,[33] and to forge a spontaneous union with the multitude. But

Riding's point here is that the speaker's grandiose show of self-othering garners her no true alterity from herself, only an ostensible, "indicated" alterity that occurs as part of a self-willed, self-announcing merger with the multitude. The ambiguity of voice and modification surrounding the word "witness" suggests that what appears to be a disavowal of self may in fact be an attempt to absorb all alterity into the speaker's subterranean will. Is the "I" here merely *witness to* the common presence of the multitude or has it in fact *become* this common presence? It seems to be both, with the reader occupying the position of witness to the fusion. This makes sense, since for Riding the rhythms and sonic felicities of poetry itself are the site of a complex masquerade, in which the poet dresses down her complex intention, providing it with a common measure so that it may seem to partake spontaneously in the purely numerical existence of the multitude. But this would mean that the poet's spontaneous merger with the multitude is in fact engineered, that it is part of a scheme to penetrate and repattern the multitude.

This is precisely what Riding suggests in the rest of the poem. In its second and third stanzas, the spontaneity of the "I" is exhibited as a deceptive double phenomenon. On one hand, it represents the "I"'s abandonment to the multitude, its circulation among them, its passage from hand to hand as a pliable, fungible medium. On the other hand, it represents a principle of will that lies beyond this common circulation, sustaining and directing it from some invisible location. Riding provides an example of the first kind of spontaneity when she writes: "I am a such-and-such appearance / Listed among the furnitures / Of the proprietary epoch" (209). Here, the "I," in surrendering itself to the multitude, is transformed into a mere object of exchange. The multitude does receive an "inheritance" (209) from this transformation, since in a shadowy, "death-dim" (209) way, the commodified expressions of the "I" still evoke its powers of flexible, nonproprietary mediation. Nevertheless, the qualitative agency of the "I" is "unseeable" (209) from within the "spent kingdom of the senses" (209). So the life of the multitude, which is defined by this sensuous, commercial kingdom, is destined to remain "a population of names only / inhabiting... hypothetic streets" (209).

At first, Riding seems to be staging here the kind of quintessentially modernist failure that we encounter in works such as Williams's *Paterson* and Lewis's *Enemy of the Stars*. Approached according to this rubric, Riding's poem might seem to stage an earnest migration into the life of the multitude, where the poet then hopes to search for redeemable capacities latent in its collective body. This reading would align the speaker of "I Am" with *Paterson*'s speaker and *Enemy of the Stars*'s Arghol: figures who attempt to heal the social body through spontaneous spiritual commerce with it, but whose efforts turn out to be premature or foredoomed.

What actually occurs in Riding's poem, however, is very different from this. To begin with, the speaker of "I Am" is much more sinister than the figures of spontaneous agency we encounter in *Paterson* and *Enemy of the Stars*. It is not at all clear, for example, that the speaker's communion with the multitude was ever intended to heal it. In fact, this spontaneous fusion with the multitude actually exacerbates its collective malaise. This becomes clear when the poem's speaker asks herself why the multitude is condemned to exist as a series of standardized, interchangeable attributes. She answers herself:

> That I with you did lie
> In the same love-bed, same planet
> Of thinking bright against
> The black pervasion...
> ....
> That I thus to you am like,
> That I walk beside and straight
> On your same circle of argument (210)

Riding represents the poet's sexualized merger with the multitude here as a sinister escapade that binds its affections even more firmly to the standardized world in which it is forced to exist. This happens because the poet, instead of rejecting the multitude's commodified social world wholesale, mixes with it, enters into its logic in an attempt to modify its terms. But all this accomplishes is to help the multitude reconcile itself to a social system that should be rejected without precondition. By creating the impression that a new "measure" could be introduced into commodified social relations, that forms of agency could be discovered that might adapt the multitude's sensibilities to this alienated regime, the poet merely reaffirms the "circle of argument" that limits the multitude's sense of the possible.

What the poet should be doing instead is testifying to the "black pervasion" that stands in unmitigated opposition to the world of commodified existence. To the conventionally minded, this "pervasion" will appear as a dangerous "perversion"—literally a "steering-away" from the known and accepted. But to Riding, this pervasion is a beneficent realm of "sleep / That gives not back if none makes argument / That yesterday is self still" (210). In other words, the "black pervasion" is a power that allows yesterday's sense of order to be destroyed before it can reassert its hegemony over today's selves. For Riding, this power of negativity is the true provenance of poetic activity. It is completely irreconcilable with the commercialized rhythms of public life and can manifest itself only as a comprehensive rejection of this commodified world. Its negativity cannot, therefore, be leased out to this realm of everyday circulation, cannot take up a second life amid the multitude, stealthily severing their sensibility from the order of things. It cannot, in other words, be the engine of poetic spontaneity, injecting the poet into the social patterns of the multitude and helping her retrain its sensibility by means of poetry's artful recombinations.

It is exactly to this use, however, that the speaker of "I Am" tries to put the power of poetic negativity. The speaker, with true perversity, transports the "not-here" (210) of the "black pervasion" into the world of everyday circulation, disguising it in everyday speech so that it will be accepted by the multitude and become a habitual, patterned negativity. This fusion of the poet's negativity and the multitude continues until "you tire of the possession / And, falling prone, relinquish / The stale breath of stubbornness" (210). At this point, the poet has succeeded in severing the multitude's attachment to its commodified existence, and the multitude consequently undergoes a form of spiritual death. This death, however, is only a transitional state, since the "proved not-here" (210) of the poet's negativity outlives this collective death. Since this negativity has "proved itself," in Hegelian fashion, as a practical, worldly power, the poet is now in a position to re-create the multitude from scratch, to create a multitude free from the petty world of "possession" and inculcated with the poet's own powers of negativity and critique.

Something chilling happens, though, as the poet breathes new life into the multitude. She announces:

> And I will then stand you up,
> To count you mine, since dying frenzy
> Makes new dwelling-charm,
> O entranced wizards of place-magic.
> I, in the over-reaching moment,
> In the reign one-too-many,
> Dynasty too-long of time-kind—

> I, created time-kind by commingling
> Of the jealous substance with
> The different way to be—(211)

What has happened to the multitude here? Notice how upon being resurrected they are no longer simply "entranced." Rather, they are "entranced wizards." That is, they are both the subjects and the objects of entrancement; they possess the ability to entrance, but seem to be using it against themselves. This is because the poet, in granting them the power to transform themselves and repattern existence, has also assimilated them to her particular way of exercising this repatterning power. Instead of a genuine historical rupture, then, in which the multitude could break with commodity society and re-create itself on its own initiative, Riding depicts a pseudorupture, which is presided over by a frighteningly proprietary poetic will. It turns out that the extinction and rebirth of the multitude were in fact orchestrated by this will all along, so that the new sensibility of the multitude, its new "dwelling-charm," would be perfectly calibrated to the poet's occult rule.

Accordingly, in the final stanza, the poet is represented as a terrifying autocrat who "spin[s] round continuity" (211) in order to prevent the multitude from developing any true, independent critical power. Worse yet, the poet spins this continuity "out of your stopped mouth, our mouth" (211), while the multitude

>   haunt[s]
> The windows that might be here,
> Looking for sign of elsewhere—
> If I perhaps such same fatality
> As before fast was magicked
> Into the this-year dialects. (211)

In other words, the multitude now suspects that there might be an alternative to the ideologically insular world that the poet-autocrat has created for them. In effect, they are attempting to make independent use of their fledgling critical faculties, but, since the poet has taught them that change only comes as a visitation from on high, they wait for her to bring it about. They look for signs that their current beliefs, speech, and social relations might soon be liquidated by the same kind of "fatality" that the poet once visited upon their old "dialects." But the poet has no intention of freeing the multitude from her grasp. Her seemingly benevolent, spontaneous mixing with the multitude now stands revealed for what it really was: a form of social magic that cripples the multitude's powers of independent judgment and assimilates them to the social experiments of individual rulers.

The speaker of "I Am," then, embodies everything perverse, corrupt, and dangerous about modernist spontaneity. Instead of opposing the commercialized public sphere unconditionally, the speaker enters into its logic, hoping to repattern it from within. It turns out, however, that the multitude is not liberated in this way, but rather is rendered hypnotically responsive to the suggestions of strong, central wills. The cogito on display in Riding's "I Am" is thus the agent of the kind of ideological mediation Negri describes in his own analysis of the Cartesian "I think." In Descartes's cogito, Negri hears resonate the profound separation of the bourgeois subject from the Renaissance dream of an integral world of scientific endeavor and individual freedom, overseen by the bourgeoisie as the hegemonic political class. With the virulent assertion of monarchical absolutism and the increasing need to forge alliances with the ancien régime against an increasingly revolutionary peasant and artisan multitude, this dream of uncontradictory bourgeois self-development terminates in crisis: the crisis of a cogito irreducibly separated from the external world. The transcendence of the cogito with respect to this external world thus signals the workings of an ideological compromise, a tactical doubleness according to which the bourgeoisie might "broaden its hegemony within the new structures of the Absolutist state" while at the same time announcing its absolute autonomy from these structures.[34] Negri even goes so far as to suggest that the current analogue to this process would be the attempt of the contemporary bourgeoisie to effect an ideological fusion between itself and the multitude: a "reasonable alliance" employing the same kinds of deceit Riding evokes in "I Am."[35]

Clearly, Riding rejects this process of ideological fusion, both as a model of artistic intuition and as a model of political coordination. But if all claims to represent social reality participate in this process of ideological manipulation, what alternatives exist for artworks other than pure silence? Furthermore, what are the larger stakes of the critique that Riding levels in the poem? Surely, Riding does not believe that poets are actually in a position to exercise the kind of political dominance over the multitude that the speaker of "I Am" exercises. So why does she represent the poetic imagination in terms more suited to the career of a political operator?

Some of Riding's later critical works address themselves to these questions explicitly. And contrary to what one might expect, "The Word 'Woman,'" *The World and Ourselves,* and *The Telling* all reject the easy alternatives that might seem to proceed most obviously from her critique. Riding rejects, for example, the idea that artists must limit themselves to purely personal forms of valuation and turn their backs on intersubjective processes. In fact, in *The Telling* she condemns "the abnormal tendency in a human self to withdraw into an unreal 'world of its own'" (171). The individualistic doctrines that promote such a "disintegration of the human identity into personal particles, each its own story or part of an isolated story" (171) also meet with her condemnation. Similarly, Riding does not reject the ideal of spontaneity at all, only the ersatz "male" disposition that identifies spontaneity with a temporary, ludic suspension of self-interest. And finally, Riding does not believe that artists must forsake all ordering roles in society. In fact, she will outdo many other modernists in her claims for the role that artists should have in the material reorganization of human relations. In Riding's vision, people of "inner" sensibilities—artists and women—should be responsible not merely for anticipating possible future orders but also for assuming executive functions in the self-governing utopia she foresees.

The main difference between the form of spontaneity she critiques and her own models of agency is that in Riding's narrative, "inside people" are not to reorder reality through acts of willed self-suspension. Such acts seem to provide for a spontaneous fusion of the self and the multitude, but this fusion can be annulled at any time, since social life is being treated as a "play-world" to be visited experimentally. What Riding opposes to this is a form of social organization that originates in reciprocal human connections that cannot be suspended at will, since one is embedded in them as part of one's ordinary life processes.

The object of her critique, then, is not the general idea that society should be fundamentally restructured, nor is it the idea that "inside people" should play a role in this restructuring. Instead, Riding critiques modernism's idea that social change should be the work of detached, experimental agents. It is the notion that ordinary existence should be repatterned from above, according to the intuitions of abstract, disembedded intellects, that Riding rejects. What she proposes instead is a process of social change that stems from the forms of affective labor that develop within and actively transform the concrete realities of interpersonal existence. According to her perspective, there is a collective spontaneity to this interpersonal dynamic that is diametrically opposed to more opportunistic forms of literary spontaneity. Interpersonal spontaneity thus represents a threat to the individualism and experimentalism of the modernist spontaneity Riding critiques—a threat Riding genders "woman."

The Production of Interiority

In her essay on Riding's gendered approach to language and truth, Jane Malcolm lucidly explains Riding's objection to the process of self-erasure on display in "I Am." Malcolm argues that Riding genders this dynamic "male" and repudiates it, since "despite its best intentions, this anti-Romantic self-erasure unwittingly champions a romanticized poetic mode, by obscuring the human agent behind the writing."[36] As we have just seen, the political consequences of this obscurantism are made quite clear in "I Am." But accounting for Riding's alternative to this self-erasing, "male" poetic mode presents us with some new difficulties. As Susan M. Schultz explains, this alternative is gendered "woman," which broaches the question of whether Riding's is an "essentialist poetics."[37] Schultz answers in the affirmative, arguing that "if masculine poets dress up for an audience, then Riding's feminine verse is stripped to the bone: she describes the idea itself."[38] This means, however, that Riding's "feminist poetics... is not professionalized or worldly," which results in a disturbing "equation of feminine power with silence."[39] With greater optimism, Malcolm argues that Riding entertains an idea of "generative femininity," in which "the 'feminine'... can be traced to the origins of *language* rather than *writing*—to the moment of creation as opposed to the moment of production."[40] This suggests that Riding opposes some gendered form of *spontaneity* to the public performances of "male" modernism. But does that mean that Riding's model of creative agency is strictly private, personal, socially disengaged?

To answer this question, we should determine what kinds of social roles Riding attributes to "woman" in works such as "The Word 'Woman'" and *The World and Ourselves*. What we will find is that in these works, "woman" comes to be associated with forms of social regulation and measure that have no place in the competition-based realm of public life, but that express forms of exchange and valuation that are implicit in the life of the multitude and must ultimately govern their public as well as their private forms of interaction. In other words, "woman" emblematizes what Luke Carson describes as "the protopolitical forms of personal experience at the heart of modernity... that make possible different forms of community and exchange."[41]

Take, for example, Riding's claim in "The Word 'Woman'" that "[woman's] personality is not a matter of will but of law: she is a law—the law of universal proportion."[42] By contrast, "man" must "suspend[ ] his personality" (75) in order to discover such universal laws. At stake in this gendered division is Riding's distinction between experimental, individualist spontaneity and the spontaneity of "interlaced responsibleness."[43] Experimental spontaneity Riding genders male, and "interlaced" spontaneity she genders female. But why?

The first reason is that Riding is using the term "woman" to represent the private sphere as a whole—a sphere in which the self is embedded in a shared social world that conditions the self's capacity to act and feel. Unlike the self of "male" modernism, which regards sociality as an elsewhere in which it might immerse itself experimentally, the self of Riding's "woman" is consciously embedded in concrete practical and affective relationships. The spontaneity of the private sphere is thus the spontaneity of reciprocal counsel and proportional give-and-take: a social dynamic from which one cannot extricate oneself at will, since one's personal existence is defined by its processes. By contrast, the spontaneity of the modernist public sphere is based on the illusion that one can abstract oneself from these concrete dependencies and treat social life as a matter of experimental debate. Of this tendency, Riding writes:

> A "clear statement of attitude" generally means an experimental statement of opinion; and men reserve this kind of statement for their expansive leisure-time. Women are not given to opinionatedness or to dividing work-time and leisure-time. All time is equally work-time to them; and views do not exist for them apart from actualities—the actuality is the view. (75)

Riding suggests here that the gendered division of labor, and the separation of private from public experience that is its modern corollary, produces an analogous division at the level of "male" thought and aesthetic intuition. For Riding, "male" forms of psychological interiority are structured according to the models of social interiority provided by the domestic sphere; a private place is constituted where publicly binding commitments are relaxed, where a range of possible attitudes can be experimentally surveyed without personal consequences attaching to any of them, and where one's official personality can safely be suspended, since a private home for its speculations is continually administered by women. This sense that one's intellectual experiments are underwritten by a private, femininely nourished vitality is thus at the core of "male" modernism's definitions of spontaneity. It is a spontaneity that strays, experimentally, from known social bonds, since it can trust that these bonds are "being seen to" all along.

According to Riding, the institutional roles of women do not typically admit of such a clean distinction between public and private, which is why women are less given to "experimental statements of opinion." Within the private sphere, which for Riding is governed by mutually recognized standards of proportion and fittingness, it is not as easy to separate one's statements of opinion from one's socially accountable status as friend, confidante, or guest. This is why for Riding's "woman," the interior—again, in both the psychological and the social sense—is not a place of relaxation and play but of intense organizational activity. The spontaneity of this realm does not consist of a suspension of the everyday relationships that define one's private self, but rather a reciprocal confirmation of their inner dynamism.

"Woman," in this sense, must take responsibility for all the ludic determinations tried out from the position of male experimentalism. Her activity *constitutes* the very interiority that provides a place for such speculation and, as such, could be said to *be* the actuality that is foreclosed when social values are treated as a matter of ludic speculation. For Riding's "woman," social values possess all the gravity that "man" attributes to his public affairs. What is different about the realm she defines is that her personality is broadly and seriously identified with the sociality that forms the basis of her exchanges. Riding's "woman," in other words, is defined by her lived sense of inseparability from the consequences of her organizational activity.

It is not a surprise, therefore, that in contemporary discussions about the spontaneity of the multitude and the forms of affective labor that compose it, the questions of gender Riding brings up are never far behind. For example, in *Empire*, Hardt and Negri explain that "what affective labor produces are social networks, forms of community, biopower" and that this union of "economic production . . . with the communicative action of human relations" does not impoverish production but rather enriches it "to the level of complexity of human interaction."[44] In this connection, they cite Dorothy E. Smith, who argues that when women "keep house, bear and care for children, look after men when they are sick, and in general provide for the logistics of their bodily existence," they produce "the basic organization that... the abstracted conceptual mode of ruling exists in and depends upon."[45] This means that this kind of gendered production is not just one form of affective labor among others. Instead, "women's work," both in the home and in the market, is the foundation of all other forms of interpersonal mediation, since "at almost every point women mediate for men the relation between the conceptual mode of action and the actual concrete forms on which it depends."[46]

In Smith's work, as in that of Nancy Hartsock, this elevates woman to a privileged epistemological position, since women's lives are "institutionally defined by their production of use values in the home," which means that women's "immersion in the world of use—in concrete, many-qualitied, changing material processes—is more complete" than the male worker's.[47] This is far from being an unproblematic advantage, however, since even under the best circumstances, women must struggle within larger class-based conflicts to transform their own conditions of work, rather than simply carrying them over unchanged into a new social order. Analysis of internal, gendered struggles of this kind is something Hardt and Negri are often accused of ignoring; Susanne Schultz, for example, argues that "in the last analysis, Hardt and Negri's vague attempts to locate utopian potential in the new forces of production stand in a long left tradition of idealizing women's and reproductive work as spheres free from alienation and domination."[48] And even if we recognize that affective labor is both "a locus of exploitation and... a site from which resistant subjects and alternative visions might emerge,"[49] we are left with the difficulty of sorting out the emancipatory from the oppressive in a sphere—that of affect itself—that notoriously mixes the positive and the negative, with few differentiating markers.

Riding offers a refreshing approach to these problems, since she sees in the affective labor of women forms of mediation that should be developed as part of a general logic of social self-organization, not qualities that should be eternalized in their current form within the confines of the private sphere. Of course, Riding continues to elevate "woman" as the embodiment of these forms of affective production, a strategy that has both an ideological and a critical edge. In *The Gender of Modernity*, Rita Felski writes that with the development of capitalist relations of production, "the nineteenth century saw the establishment of increasingly rigid boundaries between private and public selves, so that gender differences solidified into apparently natural and immutable traits."[50] It is during this historical period that "woman," "by being positioned outside the dehumanizing structures of the capitalist economy as well as the rigorous demands of public life" (18), comes to represent "a mythic plenitude, against which is etched an overarching narrative of masculine development as self-division and existential loss" (38). At times, Riding clearly recapitulates this idea of "woman" as a "mythic referent untouched by the strictures of social and symbolic mediation" (38), evolving an idea that a spontaneous relational sense is part of woman's "timeless nature."

And as Felski's critique implies, Riding's generalizations about "woman" and the private sphere are gauged most closely to the experiences of middle-class white women in industrially developed nations. Claiming the word "woman" exclusively for them silences the diverse ways in which sex and gender are constructed in other social contexts. Therefore, the cultural specificity of Riding's critique and of her myth of "woman" must be foregrounded if they are to be fruitful in any way. It is primarily in social contexts where industrialization has radically nuclearized the conjugal unit and defined the intimate sphere as one of atomized "women's work" that Riding's critique is most useful. As Seyla Benhabib shows, however, if the cultural specificity of such gender critiques of the public sphere is acknowledged, these critiques can provide a great deal of insight into epistemological binarisms that are central to the constitution of modern philosophical and social thought.[51] What Riding shows is that they can also help us understand how the category of "spontaneity" has been used to imagine alternatives to the public/private split that is at the heart of capitalist modernity.

Take, for example, Riding's claim that "woman" is a "universal law of proportion." If we are to take Benhabib's suggestions seriously, we must read into Riding's definition of "woman" as a "universal law of proportion" a long history of U.S. socioeconomic development, which for Riding dead-ends in the acute crisis of overproduction that obtained as she wrote those lines. For Riding, "maleness," capitalist production, and literary modernism all belong to this overproductive sphere, which is governed by experimental exchange and gratuitous innovation. Because of this depersonalized, unbalanced regime, the outside world is glutted with commodities for which no one is willing to take responsibility. In *The World and Ourselves*, Riding writes:

> Emphatically: we do not want "more"; we suffer not so much from the lack of good things as from the production of a reasonless more. We suffer from an excess of means—things produced with no foreseen end of good service and which remain, therefore, mere means. (420–21)

For Riding, the external world is governed by an irresponsible model of production for production's sake, a model that includes no qualitative mechanisms for the absorption and diffusion of increasingly large quantities of goods. Riding writes, "Industrialization has overwhelmed us with matter in quantity, to which we have as yet evolved no qualitative response" (388). For Riding, commodities themselves come to represent a proliferation of disowned, purposelessly conceived values. She therefore recommends a process of reclamation to counteract the economic threat these superabundant commodities represent, a process that would allow for the spontaneous reintegration of experimentally conceived values. Riding even goes so far as to refer to an "emancipation of possessions" (388), which would represent "an emancipation of ourselves from the dead-weight upon society that the modern clutter of commodities has become" (388). In such an emancipation, "we should be weaving otherwise extraneous and dead material into the personal texture of life" (388).

Notice, however, how these passages couch the solution to overproduction in highly gendered terms. Overproduced commodities represent not just a mass but a "clutter"; emancipating commodities is a matter not so much of freeing them from the stagnant morass of unproductive economic activity (as, e.g., Ezra Pound would have it) but of "weaving" them into the "personal texture of life." In other words, Riding confronts the "male" realm of experimental, disembodied, irresponsible production with a crisis it cannot resolve on its own terms. All the countervailing values that have been relegated to the realm of the interior, the domestic and the decorative, suddenly appear as qualitative forces without which society will collapse under its own dead weight. Accordingly, commodities must be not simply mechanically redistributed but uncluttered and decently rearranged; possession must be not simply legislatively expanded but saturated with a sense of "proportion" and "grace."[52]

"Woman" thus emerges as a "universal law of proportion" under severe and historically specific conditions of economic disproportion. As such, "she" comes to represent all the ordinary human faculties for achieving balance and agreement in the private sphere, faculties that are structurally excluded from exercising themselves publicly. Her spontaneity, then, represents the immediate referral of social production to the organizational mechanisms of reciprocally accountable social groups.

Seen in this light, even Riding's most crudely biological arguments for women's "domain making faculty" can be seen also as political allegories belonging to a specific historical milieu. Compare the following passage to the one concerning commodity production above:

> For the male the reproductive principle is the abstract one that there exist possibilities of reproduction; and reproductive action begins and ends in the single, so to speak, *experimental assertion* that reproduction is possible. The female, on the other hand, is concerned with ... the actual problem of *embodied existence*—this is a concrete bodily attitude before the reproductive incident occurs, and for a long time afterwards. (461, my emphasis)

Notice how in the technological as in the sexual domain, it is the assertion of the *abstract possibility of production* that Riding attacks. For Riding, producing commodities with no plan for their economic integration carries a very "male" significance. Riding likens it to those who reproduce offspring without any concrete and abiding commitment to their nurturance. And she strengthens this association between industrial production and male sexuality when she writes: "When the object in producing an instrument is only the technical satisfaction of producing it," the result is an empty pursuit of "change" for change's sake (421). In other words, Riding aligns the "satisfaction" that is born of technological innovation with the "experimental" pleasures of both male sexuality and male modernism. In both, investments of productive energy are considered to be separable from real, embodied existence. In fact, the very idea that socially responsible existence can or should have any claim on the products of the imagination belongs, in Riding's view, to typically "female" forms of valuation. Riding's pressurization of "woman" here is thus part of her attempt to develop a credible model of continuity and communication that could serve as an organizing force in a social landscape that appears to lack a principle of political cohesion.

In sum, "woman" is Riding's name for a form of agency that does not approach actuality as a field of play, as a place where experimental forms of valuation are tested in a disinterested way. Instead, "she" represents a private sphere where human agents are situated in an intersubjective continuum from which they cannot extricate themselves at will. For Riding, this intersubjective continuum is the only credible source of social organization, since it represents a spontaneous process of mutual verification rather than an experimental assertion of order.

The next question to answer, then, is *how* Riding imagines that such spontaneous processes could lend their organizational logic to society as a whole. Riding is not content that these spontaneous verifying processes should remain within a sequestered countersphere, leaving people's public interactions to be defined by competition-oriented, opportunistic systems of political rule. Instead, she insists that individuals must, from the position of this spontaneous "inside" knowledge, "administer the supra-social principles that are so far only implicit rules in the minds of those sensitive to supra-social realities" (117). In Riding's imagination, this would result in a wholesale transformation of external reality, such that inside values of local accountability, proportionality, and equitable exchange would dictate both the productive relations and the affective exchange processes of society. Indeed, under these circumstances, hard-and-fast distinctions between productive and affective relations would disappear, along with distinctions between the public and the private spheres. In their place would be self-governing companies of individuals, engaged in reciprocal counsel and connected to each other by female sponsors who would be responsible for coordinating public knowledge and sentiment.

According to this idea, governance would not be administered from above, but would be "spontaneously generated within the social substance" (455). But how does one distinguish this kind of collective spontaneity from the manufactured self-abandon of "male" experimenters intent on emotionally repatterning society? And, on a concrete level, how does Riding imagine this process of spontaneous self-organization? Would not the subsumption of the public by the private sphere simply lead to some new form of autocracy, made all the more seamless because of the immense scope of its psychological influence?

These questions belong to a tradition of thought that extends from the anarcho-syndicalist theorists of the early twentieth century to multitude theorists such as Hardt and Negri. Their central problematic is what Hardt and Negri call the "institutional development of the powers of social cooperation," in other words, the "process of the multitude learning the art of self-rule and inventing lasting democratic forms of social organization."[53] The unique features of this intellectual tradition are its hostility to what Rudolf Rocker calls "bureaucratic ossification"—including that of Bolshevik Russia—and its belief that the regulative apparatuses of the state could be replaced with "the administration of public affairs on the basis of free agreement."[54] Of course, imagining administrative organs that would be porous, changeable, and participatory enough that they would not harden into bureaucratic fixtures is the central problem of this tendency in political theory. It is a problem around which contemporary theories of affective labor and self-rule are constellated, and that modernists such as Riding took up in their models of affective exchange and social reproduction. At its heart, it is a question about what Riding calls "the spontaneous essence of humanness"—about whether this spontaneity could organize itself institutionally, and, if so, what kinds of institutions could provide it concrete expression.

Riding attempts to answer these questions in her 1938 book *The World and Ourselves*, a work of philosophy, political theory, and speculative sociology that attempts to bridge the gap between the personal realm of mutual verification and the public realm of disinterested production. It is a work that tries to define a condition of collective spontaneity that could be opposed to the forms of poetic spontaneity that she critiques in her own poetry and earlier philosophical works. Because of this, it stands as her most robust attempt to imagine a departure from the "congenital authoritarianism" of poetic spontaneity, along with the social authoritarianisms that are their corollary.

"A Co-operative Articulation of Existence as a Whole"

In *The World and Ourselves*, Riding insists that "any collection of inside forces must take place spontaneously" and "not as a result of organizing pressure" (289). But what does "spontaneity" mean in this context, and from what source does she imagine "organizing pressure" might issue? Several scholars have noted the critical importance of the idea of spontaneity to Riding, notably Michael A. Masopust, who defines Riding's "linguistic ideal" as "a spontaneous method of speaking from one's soul,"[55] and Carla Billitteri, who describes Riding's creative ideal as one of "pure generation," which is akin to the "spontaneous, inconsequential creativity of nature."[56] But in the quotation above, Riding clearly deploys spontaneity as a *political* concept, one that involves "inside forces" collecting themselves for "an immediate infiltration... into the present living substance of existence" (521). Spontaneity in this context refers not just to literary generation but also to the collective life of socially embedded groups who are attempting to "practis[e] a general and permanent intervention in existence as a whole" (343–44).

To understand Riding's unexpectedly activist language here, and the concept of political spontaneity that drives it, it is necessary to understand her critique of the democratic state as a political order based on "personal anonymity" (454). In *The World and Ourselves*, Riding stresses that "the State ... only pretends" to "fill[ ] in the large outline of society ... since people do not articulately identify themselves with the social parts to which they properly belong" (454). In other words, "people allow themselves to remain unknown factors, have as it were no domestic address at which they can be civically located" (454). Because of this, the modern democratic state "leaves large elements of life ungoverned—the real, personal elements" (454). And though these personal elements have been emancipated from feudal ties and are now capable of "self-government" (454), they possess "no new, constructive basis of concentration" (454). Politicians, as a consequence, must "always guess at [people's] state of mind—and, so easily succumb to the temptation of inventing states of mind on their behalf" (454–55).

In order to overcome the personal anonymity of this form of governance, communities need to develop some form of "internal self-organization (454)—a "social organization that correspond[s] with our natural and free social movements—an organization in motion" (453). According to Riding, such a spontaneous, self-organizing social force could have nothing in common with the "fixed technical form" of "conventional public activity" (277). This ossified public sphere "forces all inside energy put into it to disguise its nature in technicalities and thus prevents it from accomplishing anything more than tricks" (277). At best, an inside person could "smuggle certain improvements into public machinery" through "the pretence that a value is a technicality" (277). But Riding rejects this kind of duplicity, aligning it with the modernist ambition to repattern social reality by means of its technical virtuosities.

Instead, it is necessary to imagine a form of social organization that could absorb the administrative functions of the state without adopting its anonymity and bureaucratic rationality—a social process that would be spontaneous in the sense that its public functions could not become detached from the everyday practical and emotional realities of the private sphere. For Riding, the basis of such a process would be self-governing community companies that would no longer make a distinction between public administration and private commitment. This is because these social units would be modeled on the "company of friends," and in such a mode of organization, "every kind of association... ought to have in it a quality of adult friendship—work and community associations as well as the private ones" (452). In other words, the realm of work and community associations currently lacks the reciprocity and proportion evinced in the private sphere, because it has been severed from the regulative laws of inside existence. Riding proposes to bridge this gap between public administration and private reciprocity through self-governing companies that would integrate material production and affective exchange.

Observing that "the company of friends is the natural successor to the historical family" (454), Riding asserts that "such companies are the real civic units, which if fully adult do not need a political parent—the State—to administer their personal responsibilities" (454). Instead,

> if society were actively identical with the companies of friends that compose it, and between these companies there existed an instantaneous sympathy of communication, the State would be an organic power; it would be not the abstract conception that it is now, "society as a whole," but the internally impelled action of people in the public field of action. (455)

According to this political vision, public life would no longer be a detached sphere of activity, governed by a depersonalized logic of competition and experimental production. Instead, the social metabolism would be regulated by a network of personally accountable, mutually embedded community companies. Each company would possess counselors of health, economy, entertainment, taste, learning, strategy, and "scruples," serving as "'administrative' functionaries" (462) and helping to maintain a "constant intercourse between private living and State action" (463). These counselors, however, would not be the representatives of any central governmental agency, and their counsels would have no legal status. In "company government," Riding indicates, "laws are not enforced, but counsel given and asked" (462). Accordingly, a process of spontaneous self-government would replace enforceable laws and "government resting on power" (461).

In formulations like these, Riding speaks to one of the greatest dilemmas that theorists of spontaneous self-government have faced, namely, how the activities of small, cooperative associations could be coordinated on a large scale without being subjected to the authority of some external bureaucratic power. In the anarcho-syndicalist tradition, Anton Pannekoek addresses this problem by envisioning rank-and-file delegates who would be elected by local workplace assemblies and would be immediately recallable by them. Such delegates would convene in large workers' councils but would be "no politicians, no government," instead serving as "messengers, carrying and interchanging the opinions, the intentions, the will of the groups of workers," making possible a "unity of general regulation and practical productive labor."[57] Rudolf Rocker imagines similar large-scale federations of "labor cartels," which would have no independent executive power but would instead "maintain the permanent connection between the local bodies, arrange[ ] for free adjustment of the productive labour of the members of the different organisations on co-operative lines, provide for the necessary co-ordination in the work of education...and in general support the local groups with council and guidance."[58]

At this point in Riding's analysis, she offers few political recommendations on this level of concreteness. Instead, she paints a picture of what everyday life might look like in a society whose productive and affective relations were organized by the kinds of mutually embedded councils envisioned by anarcho-syndicalist authors. In Riding's vision of such a society, the forms of proportion and affective mediation that were once sequestered in the private sphere would become mechanisms of large-scale public organization. This is why Riding suggests that in such a society, "every instrument of life that [has] a public use" should be "personally owned (roads, streets, railways, dispensing institutions)...with emphasis on the hospitality aspect of proprietorship" (378). In practice, this would mean that "the driver would own his engine, and the carriage attendant his carriages, and the station-master his station" (378), because these figures have personal relationships to the goods and services they offer and are thus best able to see that the various aspects of their trades are "good things well cared for and graciously shared in" (378). As for the railway directors, they would not exactly be "dispossessed" (378); instead, they would retain possession of the railways only in proportion to their ability to "cultivate the general graces of which railways are capable—as against the details of hospitality of which each carriage, etc., is capable" (378–79). As for shareholding, however, it should be permitted only to express one's "possession in some contribution of physical labour or of thought to the company's problems" (385). "The person who owns shares in Cuban Railways," for instance, and all those who "hold[ ] no fertilizing communication" with the actual personnel of a company, should no longer be entitled to ownership of that company, or any part of it. Money, in this scenario, may no longer "represent . . . the power of seizure from others" (378); instead, it must represent "the power of receiving and appreciating the gifts of hospitality, which is of equal grace with that of giving it" (378).

In Riding's vision, then, inside values are to saturate the social texture so completely that inside elements and outside elements become indistinguishable. Hers is thus not so much a vision of the precise political mechanics of self-government as an image of its affective distributions and regulations. It is an image of what Negri calls the "omnilateral diffusion" of affect: affect imagined as "a power of transformation, a force of self-valorization."[59] In the excerpts above, Riding is concerned primarily with imagining the forms of measure that would come to govern the production and reproduction of life in her social utopia. These forms of measure have nothing to do with labor time or any other empirical measure. What they gauge, instead, is the ability of individuals to mediate, with grace, their socially productive activity. In other words, the measure of the shaping influence one might have in a given productive context is the extent to which one would be materially and affectively embedded in it and directly engaged in the fertilizing communication that nourishes it.

This idea of measure is extended in *The World and Ourselves* to the operations of money, as a representation of "gifts of hospitality." Riding's gift economy thus seems similar in some ways to that of Marcel Mauss, in that it inserts one into a total system of social reciprocities. Her idea of *money* as a signifier of gift exchange, however, is as distant from Mauss's formulations as it is from Derrida's idea of the gift as an utterly unreciprocatable interruption of ordinary exchange economies. Riding proposes that money represent gifts of hospitality: a function that cannot be overproduced or underconsumed since it equals itself as a consequence of qualitative social interactions, not quantitative relations organized around production for production's sake. The gift of hospitality in Riding thus has little in common with Derrida's infinite openness to the other or Mauss's model of the gift as a spiritual bearer of personal prestige. Instead, it is a way of imagining forms of production that would bear within them the internal correctives and transpersonal negotiations that anarcho-syndicalist authors describe in the political realm. It is meant to represent the kind of accountability or "recallability" that is visited upon friends when they open their houses to one another: an inescapable but at the same time utterly quotidian form of affective reciprocity that Riding would like to see circulate with the kind of breadth and omnilaterality money has.[60]

It is essential to point out, however, that Riding is not imagining that the public sphere's forms of debate and exchange could somehow include or be tempered by the forms of affective production proper to the private sphere. In this, she differs dramatically from important feminist theorists of the private sphere such as Seyla Benhabib and Iris Young. Benhabib stresses the need to create space for "responsibility, bonding and sharing"[61] within the realm of public rationality, and Young argues that "an emancipatory ethics must develop a conception of normative reason that does not oppose reason to desire and affectivity."[62] According to the perspectives of these authors, the public sphere must be supplemented and enhanced by the affective structures of the private sphere. For them, it is only through the broadening of the conception of discursive action to include these intimate realms of experience that the social ideal of transparent, noncoercive communicative rationality can be realized.

For Riding, however, public rationality cannot be enriched by private experience, since the very structure of public rationality necessarily excludes the forms of bonding and solidarity that define the private sphere. As in the Habermasian model that Benhabib and Young take as their starting point, Riding's idea of lived experience has to do with patterns of sensed rightness that organically govern interpersonal exchange, but for Riding, lived experience is constituted and impacted in a way that renders it completely incompatible with the forms of public rationality they endorse. For her, the idea of lived experience refers to the local, embedded social positions one occupies; it does not extend into the realm of disembedded, abstract debate. In fact, for Riding, this realm of disembedded, opinionizing agents derives its logic from, and is socially coextensive with, the systemic forces Habermas imagines it to oppose. The economic logic of capitalism, its official bureaucratic structure, and its public sphere of literary and ethical debate are for Riding merely different aspects of a unitary external world in which experimental attitudes and competitive virtuosities reign.

Note, for example, the literary inflection of Riding's description of "public order." It could just as well be a description of the aesthetic "career":

> The political career has increasingly attracted ambitious minds as a field of mental play. These have made the outer world an arbitrary reality of their own, a play-world at the mercy of their competitive cleverness. In this fictional realm no force is at work except individualistic mental strategy, devoid of any emotional or moral relevance to the actual reality, as life, of the situations concerned. (287)

In the literary and political realms, performances such as these pretend to speak for the practical experience of ordinary individuals. Indeed, most people assume there is "some necessary relevance between the movements of their political figureheads and their own private feelings—but no such relevance exists" (287). As a consequence, "ordinary people... feel utterly deprived—not only of outer tranquility, but of their very selves, which they have allowed to be used to fill out the politicians' fantasies" (287–88).

What is at issue, then, is the exclusion of everyday emotional and practical realities from the mechanisms of political and literary representation. The remedy for this exclusion is not to be found in the supplementation of public discourse with the private realities it structurally excludes. For Riding, the very *form* of abstract ethical debate involves a duplicitous suspension of the direct relations of social accountability that are the only true source of social cohesion. Her primary distinction therefore is not between the exercise of ethical reason and the exchange of money and commodities. As we have seen, the former offers no resistance to the tyranny of the latter for Riding. The two forms of exchange constitute a unitary realm, governed by the same laws of detachment, abstraction, and merely formal or discursive modes of reciprocity. Instead, it is the realm of concrete, socially embedded, and materially binding organizational activity that Riding opposes to communicative action of the Habermasian variety.

Riding's refusal to broker any compromises between the embeddedness of the private sphere and the individualism of public life thus leads to a surprising form of radicalism, which is echoed in many contemporary theorists of the public sphere. Warren Montag, for example, points out that Habermas's ideal of rational-critical debate, which depends upon "the ability of individuals to abstract themselves from their material circumstances," necessarily forecloses any form of collective speech oriented toward action, branding it an unreasoning "pressure of the street."[63] Similarly, Ted Stolze notes how "Habermas intentionally retains the term 'self-organization'" when referring to the legal communities of democracies, while "dismissing any notion of workers' 'self-management.'"[64] He therefore critiques Habermas for the belief that the very productivity of society depends on an "uncoupling of self-directed systems from the life-world."[65] This is why Hardt and Negri express such suspicion about the category of the public sphere and of "civil society," in particular, as a node of social transformation. If civil society could once be posited as "the adequate point of mediation between capital and sovereignty,"[66] it is now "subordinated in the repressive, necessary structure of monopolistic development," which means that it should not be "voluntaristically idealized as a possible site of conflict and antagonism."[67]

Riding's explorations beyond the public sphere are especially timely in this context. Her position is that *only* the self-directed systems of the life-world are able to prevent social production from terminal collapse, since only they are able to organize social production and consumption with a view to shared, qualitative requirements. This is why Riding refuses to valorize either the public sphere or the private sphere in its current form. Instead, she imagines a form of spontaneous self-government that would liquidate these separate, gendered spheres and overcome the "artificial time-barrier between the outside situation and all those whom it affect[s] either physically or nervously" (463). In *The World and Ourselves*, this would mean constantly referring collective action back to the locally embedded councils from which it springs. Spontaneity in Riding therefore has nothing to do with individual whims or experiments. Instead, it refers to this permanent process of referral, the reflection of social determinations back into the councils who provide the "initial impulse of government" (462). Spontaneity is therefore meant to evoke not an unorganized push that is quickly diffused but a permanent process of autoreflection, in which public action is immediately reabsorbed and reevaluated by the locally embedded communities that constitute the basis of public action.

Nowhere does Riding define this ideal of spontaneous self-government more concretely than in *The World and Ourselves*. Indeed, Riding's process of authoring the book is intended to model the very forms of spontaneous organization the book recommends. To begin the book, Riding sent about four hundred letters to people of "inside sensibilities," that is, people devoted to "intensive communication between persons joined in local intimacy" as opposed to "the extensive, mechanical intercourse of peoples" (18). From these people, Riding requested written responses on the role of inside people with respect to the global economic and political crises developing in the late 1930s. The main body of *The World and Ourselves* consists of the letters Riding received, along with Riding's extensive commentary on them.

By authoring her book in this way, Riding sought to enact the kind of spontaneous, nonhierarchical mediation that she hoped would be implemented in the political realm. Attempting to efface her role as a central, authoritative writer, Riding draws together the unofficial political sentiments of her ordinary contacts in the private sphere and allows their contradictory propositions to collide and reverberate. Riding's commentary on the letters is thus supposed to model complex horizontal negotiation between political actors. Her contributions are not supposed to be authoritative judgments; rather, they are syntheses, mediations, compromises between differing viewpoints. Her voice, then, is meant to be the autoreflection of her contributor's voices. And the 148 pages of "recommendations" with which Riding concludes the book are offered as "deductions" from her contributor's letters.

In reality, however, Riding's utopian recommendations bear little resemblance to anything her contributors actually furnish her with, and her commentary is often used to refute contributors who do not share her biases. To a contributor who gently and colloquially suggests that "the 'outside' things of to-day may become the 'inside' things of to-morrow," recommending that we might use "inside" powers of intuition to educate "outer things" (162–63), Riding responds with a completely disproportionate rant against "the materialistic conception of history" (164) and a harsh close reading of the contributor's letter, focusing, with derision, on its use of "the magic word 'synthesis'" and the idea that "we are the agents of that mysterious process of internalization which takes place in matter" (164, 168). To a contributor who suggests that "outside" people—social rebels, politicians, strong partisans, men of action—might have an important role to play in addressing the social crises of the late 1930s, Riding responds, with strange impertinence, that Russia, as the highest example of "organized working-class response" has not been able to "mitigate the general madness" (72).

Riding's attempt to avoid "prophesy[ing] individualistically from the world platform" (x) thus meets with a peculiar form of failure in *The World and Ourselves,* as does the form of spontaneous mediation she attempts to model. At issue in this failure seems to be a question about who the *agent* of this process of spontaneous mediation is to be. And this question of how self-government might be organized on a large scale without the intervention of centralized, sponsoring agents is at the heart of Riding's anxieties about spontaneity in both the political and the poetic realms.

"I Am Not I"

A poem titled "Disclaimer of the Person" probably best expresses the anxieties about the politics and poetics of spontaneity that Riding voices in *The World and Ourselves*. It is a poem that appears to affirm the spontaneous agreement of particulars that Riding imagines in works such as *The World and Ourselves* and *The Telling*—a spontaneous agreement whose foundation Riding's critics have variously described as "the 'moral real' in common experience,"[68] "an authentic truth-impulsion of universal force,"[69] and "the common ground of human intercourse."[70] According to this vision of spontaneity, the subjectivity of the poet or sponsor is unproblematic; it need not be suspended, altered, or interrogated in any way, since at the level of intuition it is spontaneously fused with collective patterns of exchange and valuation. But this idea of implicit or preaccomplished spontaneity leaves us with the politically anxious image of benevolent centers of social exchange, administering truths that are supposedly implicit in the social life of the multitude. How is this different from the terrifying image of spiritual autocracy with which Riding concludes "I Am"?

At first, "Disclaimer of the Person" furnishes very little in the way of an answer to this question. The poem begins with an incantatory series of propositions that seek to align the "I" with a timeless "saying" that expresses "final agreement thing with thing."[71] In this context, the speaker indicates that "I am not I" (253), since Riding does not envision the "I" here as an individualistic enclave of private identity. Instead, she writes, "I am the one thing only / Which each thing is / When each as all is / In being each only" (253–54). In other words, the "I" at this point in the poem represents individual existence only insofar as individual existence expresses the totality of all individual existences. It is not identical with an individual "self," let alone with an individual "name." Instead, it bespeaks a relational agreement between individualities that can be expressed only when each individuality is most fully itself. And for Riding, this final individuality and this final agreement exist only at a level where individuality is free of the standardizing influence of the public world. The "I" thus represents a form of self-relation that could occur only if individuals were to find a relational ground outside the anonymous, abstract patterns imposed upon them by the world of commerce and bureaucracy. Under such conditions, the "I" would represent not just a compromise brokered between different viewpoints but a final agreement between internal life and external form—a spontaneous fusion of private feeling and public action.

Of course, the fact that Riding herself occupies the position of this spontaneous fusion—or at least attempts to—in *The World and Ourselves* is reason enough to view her concept of a timeless, integrative "I" with deep suspicion. Though she presents her recommendations in *The World and Ourselves* as the final agreement that is implicit in her contributors' positions, they are in fact virtuosic interventions that clearly bear the stamp of Riding's own extremely idiosyncratic personality. Nevertheless, Riding treats as unproblematic the fact that her presence is required for such final agreements to occur. In fact, this situation perfectly mirrors the kind of benign centralization that her political utopia envisions.

As Riding explains in *The World and Ourselves*, her political vision is not of atomized grouplets meeting and colliding as self-interest would dictate but rather of a spontaneous and binding self-relation of all social actors. According to this vision, the "common feeling developed in one company, or a benefit resulting from common counsel" would have to be in a position to "distribute itself spontaneously from company to company" (456). In this scenario, "we should not only be practicing co-operative development, but also giving society a pulse of opinion that could be felt at any and every point of contact" (456). In other words, a principle of social cohesion would spontaneously emerge that would prevent the various companies from splitting into factional rivalries.

And it is at just this moment—the moment when she is trying to imagine an organizational process that would transcend her self-governing councils—that Riding broaches the problem of centralization. She stresses that her model of centralization is unlike "any centralization enforced by men: that is always repressive centralization" (461). Women, by contrast, "do not 'enforce'—they sponsor" (461). She then goes on to explain that women's role in her political vision would be to

> teach people to know well what they may rightly possess, what they may not—to the controlled point of sufficiency; and always by the rule that those things would be more than sufficient which could not figure gracefully in the pattern of hospitality that the material range of each person's life should present to others. (379)

In this passage, Riding is obviously concerned with a historically specific kind of excess: the 1930s-era crisis of overproduction witnessed by the industrialized countries of the Global North—a crisis that is to be met with regulative principles of "sufficiency," "grace," and "hospitality" that Riding extrapolates from the private sphere. In such a situation, "woman" emerges again as an index of faculties, abilities, and sensibilities that, in the historical development of patriarchal kinship structures, have been forcibly excluded from social representation, along with the human beings said to possess them as a natural consequence of their sex.

So just as Riding serves as a centralizing node in her solicitation of the letters that would be included in *The World and Ourselves*, and just as she offers herself, and her deductions, as the "points of contact" out of which provisional consensuses are formed, so too should women generally, as the "collectors and accumulators of the company" (460), serve as the "natural sponsors" of "social intercourse" (460). In Riding's fully developed social vision, in which the distinction between private and public spheres has collapsed, this private role of women is fully identical with their public mandate to serve as forces of concrete political centralization. Indeed, Riding speaks in explicitly political terms about women constituting "an aspect of government, the executive aspect," that under transformed circumstances could easily be "translated into personal and lovable terms" (460).

Clearly, this idea of a "lovable executive" is an unsatisfying resolution to the problem of organization amid spontaneity. However robust Riding's social imagination is in its evocation of "woman's" qualitative powers of social mediation, this imagination often falters when it comes to imagining a society that could govern itself according to these principles, rather than relying on specialists entrusted with administering social life for the multitude.

Does this mean that Riding's model of spontaneity dead-ends in yet another modernist vision of central, benevolent political ordering? Not exactly. The second half of "Disclaimer of the Person" provides us with an image of spontaneity that inheres neither in a disorganized exchange of impulses nor in a centralized, regulative authority, however benevolent. It is a vision of spontaneity that is in many ways more radical than what we see in *The World and Ourselves*, because it proposes a form of intersubjective mediation that remains embedded and horizontally organized, even as it gestures toward the structural transformations that we see in Riding's philosophical work.

In the second half of "Disclaimer of the Person," Riding registers a number of anxieties about the totalizing "I" that, as we saw in the first half of the poem, was supposed to provide for a final agreement between particulars. This "I" was supposed to guarantee the spontaneous self-relation of particulars, just as "woman" is supposed to guarantee the spontaneity of Riding's political utopia in *The World and Ourselves*. But ultimately, this utopia is made possible only through the consignment of the complex temporal negotiations that define Riding's idea of spontaneity to a timeless "I" that is supposed to resolve them into a comprehensive and immediate identity. Such timeless immediacy is anathema to Riding's more complex imaginings of spontaneity as a permanent, collective process. The second half of "Disclaimer of the Person" explores this other idea of spontaneity, which occurs within a shared social world, not in a timeless enclave of authentic identity.

Riding begins by writing of an "I" that is trapped in the standardized time-world of commerce and bureaucracy, in "many solid miles of brain-rote" (255). Eventually, this "I" perceives the existence of the timeless, integrative "I" of the poem's first half. At this point, the timeless, integrative "I" presents itself as a primordial subjective power; in it, something "quivers new... which long loured archaic" (257). Now, however, Riding questions the origin of this seemingly timeless power. She asks:

> But is this I interior,
> The smothered whole that lurked unlive
> Till obvious fragment sought
> Its late entire and matching?
> Or the outer stranger, proofless,
> Come from stealth into defiance
> And with a heart incongruent—
> Suspicion's devilish shadow
> Which the lies are made of,
> For truth-proud reason to declare untrue? (257–58)

The question Riding asks here is essentially this: Is the integrative "I" that seems to embody a final agreement between particulars a purely "interior," "timeless," primordial function? Or has it developed as a "timely" response to a hostile historical environment—as an "incongruence" immanent to this historical environment that has, over time, come "into defiance" of it?

This question is central to Riding's anxieties about collective spontaneity and the ways in which it might express itself in concrete social contexts. At times, Riding believes that at our deepest, most primordial subjective layers, we all possess an identical, unchanging sense of mutuality and proportion, a final agreement that is distorted by current social relations, but that will achieve an automatic harmony of expression when it emerges into the daylight of collective existence. According to this line of thought, no complex social mediations are necessary in order to actualize this final agreement. In fact, this final agreement is already actual within our deepest recesses, where the "I" is integral with all other "I"s. At most, what is required are social facilitators, or sponsors, who could provide a neutral location where what is implicit in each "I" could become collectively explicit. Such sponsors represent no threat to this kind of spontaneity, because each sponsor's deep, primordial "I" is implicitly identical to those of the social actors they bring together; there is no danger of any sponsor substituting her own "kind" of finality for others'. Nevertheless, this image of a primordial "I" is subject to all of the political reservations Riding articulates with respect to the Cartesian cogito in "I Am," where what seemed like a neutral expression of collective desire was in fact revealed to be the most pernicious form of political hypnosis.

This is why Riding often suspects that the final agreement she seeks cannot be articulated by a single "I" as a primordial, unitary given. At these times, she describes the "I"'s sensed powers of human integration as a "self-postponed exactitude / An after-happening to happen come" (258). In other words, the final agreement intuited by the "I" is like an afterimage of the historical present, a possible order suspended within the details of social happenstance. Riding even describes this potential integration as a shadowy "other" that develops alongside social actuality as an "unnamed distance" (257). Riding sums up this state of affairs:

> Thus is reality divided
> Against itself, into domestic axiom
> And recondite surmise;
> And joins, when near to uttermost,
> When plain to covert leaps,
> In one extreme of here-to-here. (257)

In other words, the "I" is in two places at once. Part of it is mired in the comforting illusions provided by its social environment, feeling most at home with a standardized "domestic axiom." And part of it exists only as a "recondite surmise," as "a further" that "grows spatial / From lying next, in dark increase / Of the gregarious light with which / Compacting sense embraces straggling all" (257). In these passages, Riding stresses the mutual imbrication of commodified society and the covert "I" that resists it: the "I"'s covert sense of possibility is not timeless or unchanging, but in fact seems to "increase" in proportion to society's attempts to standardize experience. In the interest of its own survival, the "I" must "leap" from the "various neighbor-hearth" (257) of the known to a "bound of mystery" (257) where it will discover its own oppositional powers of human integration. In the course of this self-othering leap, the "I" joins its divided reality not by accommodating its sense of the possible to the limits of commodified existence but by imagining a process of mediation that could reconfigure the particulars of social existence to bring them into final agreement.

This sense of the "I"'s mediating function is very different from the static, atemporal "I" with which Riding opens "Disclaimer of the Person." By the end of the poem, the spontaneity of the "I" does not consist of a primordial oneness continually being realized on an atemporal plane of existence. Instead, it represents a temporal process in which the "I" experiences itself as "other" to the stultifying affirmations of standardized society, while at the same time relating itself to the particulars of this debased reality in an attempt to express the human possibilities that remain latent within them. This "I" thus lends itself to the contingent rhythms of collective existence in order to induct them, over time, into the "I"'s vision of final agreement. Of this process, Riding writes:

> So have I beat against my final ear
> Such whims and whirrings, stubborn echoes
> Whose lost persuasion I made my own,
> Whose dinning death. (258)

That is, Riding temporarily makes the chaotic way of the world her own so that she might take its "tremorless note to mouth" (258), transforming its silent need into articulate, final speech. Unlike the sponsors of *The World and Ourselves*, then, this "I" is not simply a logistical coordinator, providing a social space in which the automatic spontaneity of individuals might be made manifest. Instead, this "I" is an active agent in the external world, deliberately "approaching rhythms of old circumstance" (258) in order to awaken in the multitude new powers of spontaneous self-relation—powers that currently belong to "the perilous margin" (248) of society, but that Riding hopes will evolve into the means of collective self-governance.

All of this is quite surprising, since the forms of spontaneity that the "I" enacts in "Disclaimer of the Person" bear a close resemblance to the modernist forms of spontaneity Riding critiques. The idea of a self-suspending, self-othering "I" that temporarily takes on the rhythms of the multitude in order to repattern their sensibility is one that Riding vehemently rejects in all the works analyzed so far in this chapter. Is Riding simply contradicting herself here, offering an individualistic, experimental form of spontaneity that is basically indistinguishable from everything she most dislikes about modernist spontaneity? Or is she putting forward a new model of spontaneity, in which self-suspension can exist without becoming experimentation, and in which self-othering can occur even from within an affectively embedded, "civically locatable" position?

To my mind, Riding *is* putting forward such a new model of spontaneity, and, strangely, it is the very failings of *The World and Ourselves* that, examined through the lens of Riding's poetry, can best help us understand its significance. To make this connection, let us look at a final passage from "Disclaimer of the Person." For our purposes, it is the most important in the poem, since it attempts to lay out a form of spontaneity in which detached experiment is replaced with *personal risk*. This is essential, since it is in the nature of an experimenter to detach herself from the effects of her experiment. No risk to the experimenter's person is implied, since she has only temporarily identified herself with the raw material of the experiment. Whatever the outcome of the experiment, the experimenter escapes unscathed, since her personality has remained suspended in the interval and can be recalled at will. This is clearly not the case in Riding's model of spontaneity, in which the poet's "saying," though often strange and even disturbing, is enacted from a social address within a community of auditors with whom Riding's personal existence is inextricably interwoven.

This distinction between sociality as an elsewhere that one visits experimentally and sociality as a binding intersubjective continuum is central to the model of spontaneity Riding proposes in this passage:

> This is the latest all-risk:
> An I which mine is for the courage
> No other to be, if not danger's self.

> Nor did I other become, others,
> In braving all-risk with hushed step,
> Mind rattling veteran armouries.
> I did thus creep upon myself
> A player of two parts, as woman turns
> Between the lover and beloved,
> So it be well—she is herself and not,
> Herself and anxious love. (258–59)

In this passage, Riding distances herself from modernist forms of spontaneity in which the "I" "becomes others," disguising itself as a depersonalized force immanent in the world of social events. Instead, she displays a form of self-othering that never departs from its domestic address—a self-othering that occurs within affectively binding social relationships, and that Riding likens to what occurs when one finds oneself to be in love. In this context, the speaker does not creep upon the multitude as a stealthy force of emotional repatterning. Instead, she creeps upon *herself*, experiencing herself as "alter" at exactly the moment when she has become embedded in a new form of affective reciprocity. In other words, self-othering does not occur here as the product of an experimental will that allows one to suspend one's ties to the social world. Instead, the lover perceives herself as "other" precisely because she has been claimed by a form of mutuality that makes profound personal demands of her. Her alterity from herself is thus the index of her need to relate to herself by way of commitments that cannot be suspended at will. Nothing about the lover's predicament is experimental, and yet the lover finds herself in two places at once, is "both herself and not," since she has committed her being to a process that is both external to her and requiring of deeply personal forms of affective mediation.

In "Disclaimer of the Person," Riding makes it clear that this model of embedded self-othering does not just relate to private love relations but also contains the key to the forms of political spontaneity she is seeking to outline. She writes of a "thronging" (259), of a "world in me" (260) that she hopes to gather into a "taut community" (259) through her writing, and she compares this social romance to the "clasping" (259) that joins lover to beloved. In other words, Riding is trying to imagine a form of social mediation that would refer itself immediately to the communities upon which it is affectively and materially dependent. The agent of this mediation would undergo profound personal risk, since she would submit her social intuitions not in the way that a ruler "submits" herself to the abstract opinion of the ruled but in the way that a lover submits herself to a relationship governed by personally binding laws of proportion and mutuality. The risk one takes in such a situation is not the ersatz risk of modernist spontaneity, in which one experimentally opens oneself to the determinations of the socius. Rather, in the scenario Riding envisions, one is *already* open to the socius, because one has been embedded within it all along, practically and affectively intertwined with it in a condition of all-sided, reciprocal dependence. So the spontaneity appropriate to this scenario does not involve a specious suspension of personality; rather, it involves an anxious commitment of personal intuitions to a process of intersubjective verification—a process from which one's personal being is ultimately inseparable.

Of course, in the absence of concrete structural changes such as those Riding recommends in *The World and Ourselves*, this kind of spontaneous self-referral will really have a place only in the private sphere: in the reciprocal commitments of friends, coworkers, lovers, and families. But what "Disclaimer of the Person" helps us envision is the liberation of such reciprocal forms of social mediation from the cramped quarters of private society. In the social order that Riding imagines would follow upon this transformation, every individual would exist in a permanent state of risk, much as lovers set themselves at risk by submitting themselves to a process that is simultaneously an external dynamic and an internal impulsion. This union of external and internal is Riding's way of imagining the union of the public and the private spheres. In such a condition, individuals' economically productive activity would no longer be part of an anonymous, alienated, unaccountable process. Instead, it would be woven into a locally embedded social network whose everyday intimacies would be inseparable from large-scale processes of political self-government.

According to *The World and Ourselves*, this process would require centralized sponsors, embodying timeless human truths, who would "guarantee" the spontaneity of the multitude. In "Disclaimer of the Person," however, what Riding emphasizes is the temporal process of mutual verifying—a process in which each member of society would be structurally other to herself in that any social activity she might try on in the realm of public life would be immediately reviewable by a social network with whom she maintains inexorable everyday ties. In this context, "spontaneity" refers to the self-renewing fluidity with which this process of collective review would occur. This is a spontaneity, then, that can be guaranteed only through ceaseless collective effort, not through individual acts of will or the sponsorship of centralized agents. Spontaneity, in this sense, exists only as a permanent, collective leap from "here-to-here." It could be described as the arc of this collective leap—a *saltus mortalis* that continually refers public exchange back to the networks of personal verification that are their source.

Mutual Verification

In the final analysis, then, Riding's critique of modernism's spontaneous journeys into the multitude leads her to a robust, if highly idiosyncratic, political vision—one in which self-managing companies of friends would take over the functions once served by abstract, disembodied mechanisms of production and exchange. This allows her to evolve a very different idea of spontaneity—one that is defined not by the manufactured self-abandon of individual experimenters but by the self-relational processes of the multitude itself.

This model of spontaneity thus anticipates contemporary debates about the multitude and its powers of affective labor and internal organization. As we have seen, Hardt and Negri define affective labor as the ability to produce "social networks, forms of community, biopower."[72] The productivity of affect, then, is not sequestered in a sentimentalized private sphere, but is viewed as a socially organizing force of immense power. And like Riding, Hardt and Negri focus on love as a potent expression of this power. They define love as "a motor of association" active in "the production of affective networks, schemes of cooperation, and social subjectivities."[73] "Love" thus refers not merely to the romantic dalliance of couples but also to a large-scale, internal "training or *Bildung* of the multitude," in which new habits are "formed through the collective organization of our desires."[74]

Where Riding adds something unique to this narrative is in her insistence on the forms of personal risk and self-othering that love makes possible. Hardt and Negri insist that there is no room for negativity in the concept of love; the very idea of negativity denies one of the principal characteristics of love, which is "the power to generate *ex nihilo*."[75] According to Hardt and Negri, the concept of negativity inevitably and erroneously sets the creative power of the multitude in relation to some previous social condition, which is imagined to be conserved in a sublated form in the multitude's process of self-valorization, usually in the form of a transcendent power that oversees the process of transition. According to this analysis, the concept of negativity is closely related to the function of the bureaucratic-centralist party, which always maintains itself as strategically separate from the multitude and thus embodies a "corruption of... love," since "surreptitiously but implacably the party's determinations of norms and measures, its decisions (even the right to life and death) become separated from the experience of the movements and absorbed by the logic of capitalist alienation, turning bureaucratic and tyrannical."[76]

Riding's concept of love, by contrast, is animated by the negativity of self-othering and personal risk—functions that point to the forms of immanent accountability that would attend material and affective production in her social utopia. As I have suggested, this concern with reviewability, measure, recallability, and interpersonal vigilance in some ways places Riding in greater proximity to the anarcho-syndicalist tradition of the early twentieth century than to Hardt and Negri. Negri, for example, admits that syndicalism takes as its starting point "the social organization of diffuse webs of communication" but then claims that "this theory formulates the project of a process of re-centralization founded on the globally valid unit of (monetary, financial, etc.) measure."[77] Riding, by contrast, will insist that it is only through the discovery of forms of globally valid measure, proportion, and reciprocity that the tendency toward recentralization can be resisted. Her innovation, and what ultimately brings her clearly within the orbit of multitude theory, is her sense that such forms of measure can be determined only through qualitative interpersonal exchanges, not through empirical measures involving labor time or supply and demand. Ultimately, her ideal is one in which standards of social regulation would be inseparable from affectively embedded communities of production and exchange, so that their systems of reviewability and recall would be as flexible as their spontaneous powers of communication and creation.

Within the context of modernism, this represents a crucial contribution to the concept of spontaneity. Unlike the modernist spontaneities that approach the multitude as a foreign entity that the artistic imagination might relate to, work upon, and withdraw from at will, Riding uses the idea of spontaneity to denote the exact points where one is located in and by the multitude; it is a term that evokes the horizontal networks of association and exchange that lay a claim to one's social attention. In abandoning the idea of spontaneity as an experimental visitation of the multitude on the part of disembedded creative minds, Riding is therefore able to relocate spontaneity in the forms of social risk, improvisation, and negotiation that occur between agents who are situationally dependent on each other. This marks a dramatic departure from a tradition of early twentieth-century political thought that imagines collective spontaneity as a disorganized eruption of pulsions in need of external direction. For Riding, spontaneity is, definitionally, something that is highly organized: it *is* nothing more than the self-organizing processes of the multitude. In the absence of this collective self-organization, there is no spontaneity, only private emotional reflexes and standardized social interactions.

Riding's poetry and philosophical work are thus in large part devoted to imagining what these processes of collective affirmation, negation, and self-correction might look like—how they might emerge and sustain themselves in the absence of central direction. This is something that all the other modernists I examine in this book attempt as well, with varying degrees of concreteness and detail. As we have seen, Williams imagines these processes as the spontaneous self-regulation of productive and receptive energies in a libidinally charged social body. Lewis outlines a similar dynamic, in which the multitude discovers in itself the organizational powers once imagined to be the exclusive possession of heroized leadership figures. Stevens, as we will discover in chapter 4, also creates speculative social landscapes in which the attributes of spontaneous collective organization can be imagined. Like Williams's *Paterson* and Lewis's *Enemy of the Stars*, Stevens's "Owl's Clover" begins with the image that Riding critiques so vigorously—that of the disembedded, self-abnegating artist who tries to achieve "spontaneous" contact with an abstractly conceived and socially helpless multitude. By the end of the poem, however, Stevens too has frustratedly abandoned this idea of spontaneity and evolved a model of spontaneous collective organization as nuanced and suggestive as Riding's. Indeed, Stevens's reluctance to let go of the image of the "major man" as an organizational center causes him to speculate even more complexly than Riding does about the kinds of organizing nodes and discursive negotiations that could sustain such a collective process.

What Stevens adds to the story of modernist spontaneity, then, is an account of how mutual skepticism, political opportunism, and economic crisis can all be imagined as constitutive parts of a social body's spontaneous self-organization—how self-satisfied journeys into the multitude, such as the poet at first imagines himself to make, can be viewed not as lethal to the process of collective self-organization but as the very substance of this process. What this makes visible is the fact that modernism's utopian impulse, which Williams, Lewis, and Riding also express, has less to do with abolishing disagreement and conflict than with imagining collective sites in which this negativity could be taken up as a moment of the multitude's self-definition, where it could serve not as a terrifying external threat but rather as the motor of spontaneous *autogestion*.

"Owl's Clover" concludes with precisely such an image of agonic, polynodal spontaneity. Where it begins, however, is with an image of the solitary, "spontaneous" artistic genius whose social ontology, as Riding continually stresses, is predicated on the very social divisions it pretends to overcome.

4 RHAPSODIES OF CHANGE

The Location of the Multitude in Wallace Stevens's Poetry

IN THE PRECEDING CHAPTERS, we have seen that the ideas of spontaneity developed by William Carlos Williams, Wyndham Lewis, and Laura Riding all involve some form of negativity. For these authors, spontaneity cannot be conceived as a purely positive, affirmative act. On the contrary, many of their works suggest that affirming one's most immediate intuitions is the surest way to reproduce the ideological illusions of one's social environment. Spontaneity instead requires a critical, self-mediating attitude, whether in the form of Lewis's "Not-Self" or of Riding's "Individual-Unreal": emblems of the critical distance and negativity without which intersubjective creation and innovation are impossible. In this context, negativity is just the first moment of a process in which narrow subjective investments are challenged, expanded, and redefined.

Wallace Stevens, more than any other author I examine here, is associated with this kind of negativity—with what he refers to as "the purification that all of us undergo as we approach any central purity."[1] This process goes by many related names in the critical literature on Stevens. Gina Masucci Mackenzie and Daniel T. O'Hara describe it as Stevens's "poetics of destitution,"[2] William W. Bevis describes it as Stevens's "phenomenology of no-mind,"[3] and J. Hillis Miller describes it as Stevens's "willed disburdenment of all the ghosts of the past."[4] And as J. S. Leonard and C. E. Wharton stress, in much of Stevens's poetry this individual negativity makes available a world of interpersonal processes—"a multiplicity of relational perspectives" that "confounds our usual categories of objective, subjective and intersubjective."[5] Stevensian negativity thus finds a place in the forms of collective life that Stevens imagines. Critique, destructuration, and negation often propel and enrich collective subjects in Stevens's poetry, just as they propel and enrich the spontaneity of individual subjects.

In this book, I have been using the term "the multitude" to describe such collective subjects: interpersonal complexes whose immanent self-relation is defined by precisely the kinds of negativity and critique we find in Stevens. It may therefore be surprising to find that Michael Hardt and Antonio Negri, in their elaboration of the concept of the multitude, express profound reservations about the very concept of negativity. In *Empire*, for example, Hardt and Negri insist that the multitude acts "not as a negative that constructs a positive or any such dialectical resolution"; instead, "it acts as an absolutely positive force that pushes the dominating power toward an abstract and empty unification, to which it appears as the distinct alternative."[6] Likewise, in *The Savage Anomaly*, Negri makes it clear that one of his principal attractions to Spinozan thought is that "it does not know the negative," just as it "does not know the verticality of the mechanisms of sublimation and supersession (or, better, it knows them as temptations from which to liberate itself)."[7]

Does this mean that the multitude can be conceived only as a positivity, motivated strictly by the affirmative energy of "being, loving, transforming, creating"?[8] Or is it possible to imagine a multitude in which disagreement, critique, opportunism, and embarrassment are present—a multitude motivated as much by conflict and crisis as by *cupiditas* and *amor*?

The stakes of this question are high, for as Jacques Rancière points out, without a concept of "the negativity of political subjects," it is difficult to account for the ways that collectives "dispute the forms of visibility of the common and the identities, forms of belonging, partitions, etc., defined by these forms."[9] So to the extent that Hardt and Negri's concept of the multitude rejects negativity, it "denies the specificity of particular *dispositifs* or spheres of subjectivation" and ignores the ways that these social spheres combine and diverge in the process of political contestation.[10] Instead of internally ramified social subjects organizing themselves around "specific actions and utterances," the multitude presents us with an "unconscious will of Being that wills nothing."[11]

Stevens's poetics confronts a similar danger in its figurations of collective life. The interpersonal ontologies of Stevens's poetry rarely feature the kind of concrete political actors and utterances to which Rancière alludes. Instead, they tend to evoke the combined associative potential of a partly real, partly imaginary human matrix, a multitude whose *potenza* often seems so distant from everyday life that it can be invoked only as an elemental energetics—a primordial or not (yet) human presencing. And in much of Stevens's poetry, it is difficult to dissociate this interhuman matrix from "things as they are," that is, from the immanent givenness of phenomena, with the imagination of the poet standing as the lone source of negativity and mediation on the phenomenological scene.

Such scenarios not only threaten to reduce the multitude to the unmarked positivity to which Rancière objects, but they also represent negativity as precisely the transcendental abstraction that Hardt and Negri define the multitude against. In this context, negativity can be registered only as the distance staked out for itself by a transcendental agent vis-à-vis the multitude. The mind of the genius, the will of the party, the apparatus of the state—each of these agents separates itself from the immanence of the multitude, all the while promising to redeem the negativity of this gesture in a dialectical synthesis, a unitary construction in which the Many will be contained and represented. No wonder Negri rejects this form of negativity, seeing in it only "a frustrated will to recuperate the productive force of singularity."[12]

But is the negativity of transcendence, separation, and rule the only negativity imaginable? Are there not forms of negativity at work wherever collective subjects constitute themselves, in their disagreements, in their mutual critiques, even in their deceptions and crises? In Negri's work, the only constructive negativity that appears with any regularity is the outwardly directed negativity of violence and refusal that the multitude aims at the apparatuses of sovereign power. But what about the inwardly directed negativity of the multitude itself, the cognitive separations that make innovation possible, the ideas of order experimentally advanced and subjected to critique, the egoistic grandiosities masquerading as political thought and the mechanisms of their deflation?

It is difficult to imagine the multitude as an agent in the absence of these kinds of negativity. Without such internal separations and critical self-suspensions, political mediation really *can* be conceived only as an ominous outside of the multitude—as the power of a separate entity, removed from the immanence of the multitude and continually threatening it with domination.

Part of the immense critical purchase of a modernist such as Stevens resides in his imagination of the multitude as constituted and propelled by precisely the kinds of disagreements, self-suspensions, and experimental visions of the social whole that Negri has difficulty locating anywhere but in the alienated apparatuses of state power. No doubt Stevens often flirts with the idea of the poet or the political leader as a transcendent force, imaginatively configuring social reality from a remote position of mastery. But Stevens is extremely anxious about this image of the strong, central individual as the sole repository of negativity, and he develops a model of spontaneity in which critique, internal mediation, and intellectual poise can be imagined as constitutive elements of the multitude's collective life.

In this chapter, I focus on Stevens's uncollected 1936 long poem "Owl's Clover" as a limit case of this form of Stevensian spontaneity. It is the poem in which Stevens most closely allies the problem of poetic spontaneity to problems of collective organization, going so far as to frame the entire poem as a confrontation between the multitude, imagined as a potentially self-organizing force, and the poetic imagination, which is attempting to stake its own claims to organizational centrality. The poet, therefore, is consistently represented as an ordering presence who makes spontaneous journeys into scenes of collective life, either to channel the interpersonal processes of the multitude or to impose ideas of order upon them by way of stealth and cunning.

The poet's spontaneous journeys in "Owl's Clover," then, encode modalities of political desire and discomfort that we have seen at work in the writings of Williams, Lewis, and Riding. In "Owl's Clover," sometimes the poet's spontaneous commerce with the multitude is described as a benevolent openness to collective life, and sometimes it is exhibited as a potentially authoritarian masquerade. But just as Williams, Lewis, and Riding propose wildly divergent solutions to the problem of modernist spontaneity, Stevens tries to resolve the conflict between the artist and the multitude in a vision of collective spontaneity that is uniquely Stevensian and that proceeds directly from the antinomies we have long come to associate with Stevens's more canonical work.

This vision of collective spontaneity revolves around what Douglas Mao calls the "public objectification[ ] of a community's desires," a project "in which the demagogue and poet are linked" in "Owl's Clover."[13] According to Mao's account, Stevens's poetry of the 1930s expresses his fascination with the ways that "language can be used to order the masses by... embodying previously unarticulated desires."[14] However, in Mao's reading, the horrific political consequences of mass demagoguery eventually forced Stevens to abandon this interest in demagoguery and instead to explore "objectifications plausibly immune to demagogic manipulation," namely, those that can claim to be "'true' only to desire and not to the facts of Being or society prior to or apart from desire's appearance."[15]

In this chapter, I argue that all of the tendencies that Mao traces so rigorously are present "in miniature" in "Owl's Clover," and that the poem—sometimes celebrating the image of the poet as a central, ordering figure and at times attempting to evolve alternatives to it—serves as a vast, originary, and somewhat sloppy playbook of all the epistemological attitudes that Stevens would elaborate more carefully in the more canonical work that followed it.[16] More than this, however, "Owl's Clover" explores a proposition that often appears only as an absence or a dialectical impossibility in Stevens's later work, namely, that the multitude might possess the capacity to transform *itself* into a spontaneously self-mediating social body—that the multitude might, of itself, be both the raw material of society and its collective shaper. This proposition presents the multitude as the agent of the kind of performative negotiations that Mao tracks in Stevens's later epistemology. The multitude exists not as an outside that must be ordered by central individuals, but rather as a self-mediating network, possessed of a generalized capacity for negativity and revision.

Most surprising of all, "Owl's Clover" often imagines poets as participants in this generalized social process, not because they have performed dubious acts of self-extinction and merger but because these very acts now take place within an imagined realm of "universal deceit" in which the ruse of poetic merger has acquired such a quotidian, practical character that it is treated by its audience as a matter of permanent debate and contestation. This imagination of spontaneity is therefore at least as radical as anything we have yet encountered, because it enables us to see the organizational impulses of the multitude as part of a permanent, collective debate, shot through with negativity and possessing delicately counterbalanced forces and actors—something very different from the images of collective spontaneity as either a spasmodic reflex or a semimystical élan that I have analyzed here in reference to theorists such as Georg Lukács and Antonio Gramsci.

Stevens's poem thus allows us to appreciate collective forms of negativity that do not resolve into the kinds of static political syntheses that haunt Negri's writing. In Stevens's account, spontaneity names, more than anything, the process whereby potentially catastrophic separations, deceptions, and crises are reabsorbed within the social body as a "matter in hand" to be taken up in a spirit of critical inquiry and strategic readjustment. As I will argue at the end of this chapter, for Stevens it is this process alone that allows the multitude to "remember" itself as a constitutive network of powers and faculties: a productive matrix in which spontaneity and the capacity for critical negativity are indissociable.

In what follows, then, I will first identify the ways in which Stevens has deployed the idea of spontaneity at various times in his poetry and prose works, with a view to showing the political antinomies encoded in its conceptual structure. I will then turn to "Owl's Clover" in an attempt to demonstrate how Stevens uses the relationship of the artist to the multitude to evolve a model of collective spontaneity that aims to overcome the entrenched binarisms between subject and object, agent and substance, that we find in so much of Stevens's poetry. The argument that will guide this analysis of "Owl's Clover," therefore, is that this relatively unremembered, uncollected long poem can be read as a guide to the forms of political desire that recur, often in highly abstract ways, in Stevens's later formulations about poetic spontaneity.

A Chord between the Mass of Men

In "Stevens on the Genesis of a Poem," Frank Doggett provides an extremely incisive introduction to the status of "spontaneous creativity" in Stevens.[17] Quoting from Stevens's reflections on his own creative process—his method of "allow[ing] a thing to fill me up and then express[ing] it in the most slap-dash way"—Doggett observes that in Stevens "the freedom that is the element in which spontaneity exists is a condition of receptivity 'without understanding'"(467). This state of spontaneous creativity is not wholly involuntary, however; a principle of intentionality coexists with it, as if one were "awake / In the midst of sleep."[18] And in many of his writings, Stevens suggests that this dormant, unconscious condition is not simply a place of "personal memory" but rather one of "our inherited memory, the memory we have derived from those... whose lives have insensibly passed into our own and compose them."[19] From this, Doggett derives the observation that spontaneous creative powers are often linked in Stevens to "collective unconscious memory" (470).

There is a great deal of evidence to support this association, both in Stevens's poetry and in his critical writings. The idea that the poet's imagination "is not wholly his own but... may be a part of a much larger, much more potent imagination" recurs in "Chocorua to Its Neighbor," where Stevens evokes a "common self," a "collective being," which "rose because men wanted him to be": the "image, / But not the person, of their power."[20] And in "Notes toward a Supreme Fiction," Stevens refers to "the commonal" as "the major abstraction": "the idea of man," of whom "major man" is the "exponent," "abler / In the abstract than in his singular" (388). In both of these examples, collective forces are represented as giving rise to a "central mind" (298) that is supposed to serve as the forces' deputy. And Stevens stresses that to function properly, this central mind should not be embodied in any particular individual. In "Notes toward a Supreme Fiction" it is represented as "More fecund as principle than particle" (388), and in "Chocorua to Its Neighbor" it is supposed to exist as "thought / But not the thinker," "large" in the "largeness" of the collective self, "beyond their life, yet of themselves" (299). In other words, this central mind should not be imagined as an "external majesty" (299) imposing canons of conduct upon the collective being whom it is supposed to represent. Instead, Stevens tries to imagine an exponent that would be nothing but an expression of the collective self's own organizational powers.

This idea—that not just individuals but also collectivities could possess creative, organizational faculties—brings us to the topic of the multitude in Stevens's poetry. "The multitude," as it has been defined in this book, refers to the network of human minds and bodies that reproduces society in its current form and that possesses the virtual capacity to produce new forms of society. Thus, as Negri stresses, the multitude is "a class concept" insofar as it refers to the associative practices and creative powers of all those who labor under the domain of capitalist society.[21] But the term is also deliberately vague, since Negri does not limit the concept of the multitude to what has traditionally been conceived as the working class. Instead, he includes under its rubric all "social cooperation for production," including forms of intellectual, emotional, and otherwise "immaterial" labor that are part of society's ensemble of self-creative powers.[22]

In dealing with a poet such as Stevens, then, the term "multitude" is useful since it expresses one of modernism's central social fantasies: that of a collective body, physically and mentally stultified by the productive regimes of modernity but possessed of subterranean creative faculties to which the work of art can provide partial expression. This fantasy, like the idea of the multitude itself, must elide a host of social distinctions between artists such as Stevens and laborers whose social production is uniformly mechanical and ungratifying. But it is precisely because modernists often *do* seek to elide such distinctions, to bridge them with a variety of social cures or to negate them by imagining a spontaneous fusion of the artist and collective life, that the concept of the multitude is so useful. It provides us with a way to conceptualize the unstable negotiations that modernists stage between modernity's highly mobile, energized, and discontent populations and the forces of aesthetic and political order that continually offer themselves as their directive center. It is in this theater of negotiations, with all of its elisions, deceits, and outright betrayals, that Stevens seeks to intervene with his concept of the "central mind" of the multitude—a concept that he sometimes repudiates and sometimes attempts to accord an obliquely utopian potential.

Take, for example, the hope that Stevens expresses in "Extracts from Addresses to the Academy of Fine Ideas," that there might exist "a chord between the mass of men" and some "per-noble master"—a "central heart and mind of minds."[23] It seems plausible to Stevens to assert that in the new social worlds of modernity "all men are priests" who might "collect their thoughts together into one, / Into a single thought"—into what Stevens calls an "intercessor by innate rapport" (254). But in Stevens's poetry, this intercessor, this agent-principle spawned by the multitude, often turns against the multitude, passing off its own arbitrary orders as the will of all. In "Notes toward a Supreme Fiction," for example, Stevens offers us more egoists, opportunists, and outright frauds than he does credible images of "major man." "The President" who attempts to "ordain[ ]" (390) a permanent order out of the flux of historical experience; the poet-priest who, in a "facile exercise," "wear[s] the mane of the multitude ... to exult with its great throat" (398); and Canon Aspirin, who merely "imposes orders as he thinks of them" (403), rather than discovering them "out of nothing" (404) all suggest that no individual exponent could live up to Stevens's ideal of "major man." Each figure who is offered in the poem as a "spokesman at our bluntest barriers, / Exponent" of "the gibberish of the vulgate ... / The peculiar potency of the general" (397) turns out to be less interested in the spontaneous orders of collective life than in establishing himself as the arbiter of a new, static conception of humanity.

It is not surprising, then, that Stevens tends to locate the elements of spontaneity in collective patterns that have not yet been assimilated by institutional systems of valuation. In "Sketch of the Ultimate Politician," these collective patterns can be detected only as evanescent movements of feeling and thought, "words, in a storm, that beat around the shapes . . . Running in the rises of common speech."[24] One of the principal questions in Stevens's poetry is whether these spontaneities of feeling and thought really could unfold some organizing principle that would remain as plastic and many-sided as the multitude itself—that really could express in a concrete form the capacity for self-renewal that is part and parcel of the multitude's potential body.

Stevens approaches this problem in a highly abstract fashion, as a dilemma involving the multitude and the central mind, the latter term often seeming to refer to the poet himself, as if poetic spontaneity were the only medium plastic enough to encode the spontaneity of the multitude. In this context, the poet himself assumes the position of the exponent of the multitude, attempting to approximate its creative potentialities, but also representing the danger that the multitude's exponent could become detached from its interests, passing off individual hedonic exercises as expressions of collective necessity. This imaginative recasting of the author as a displaced directive will, which we have already analyzed in the work of Williams, Lewis, and Riding, allows Stevens to enact a process that these other modernists also enact, though in highly variable ways. It allows him to approach the multitude as a generative matrix possessing capacities for creation and synthesis typically considered possible only within the realm of the individual mind, and it allows him to stage and restage, at the level of individual poetic intuition, a dilemma that is central to the social life of the multitude, namely, that political order is almost always imagined in terms of an external representative lending order to society on its behalf—a dilemma that Stevens recasts in terms of the form-giving function of artists: their ability to shape, according to intuitively perceived requirements, the "raw material" of the multitude.

By constantly revisiting this tension between the multitude and the artist who is supposed to serve as its exponent, Stevens transforms poetic intuition itself into an experimental theater of activity in which nonhegemonic models of social agency can be tested. And yet, in all the poems from which I have quoted so far, these images of nondominative poetic ordering meet with some kind of failure. Moreover, each time Stevens tries to imagine the multitude themselves "gather[ing] their theses into one" (254), this process fails as well, lacking the central mind that would allow the multifarious impulses of the multitude to enter into sustained communication. The complementary failures of the multitude and the individual exponent thus seem to speak to some epistemological impasse that reappears with remarkable consistency throughout Stevens's poetic career. And since Stevens's ideas of exponency are so closely connected to early twentieth-century dilemmas surrounding spontaneity and political representation, this epistemological impasse must be a political impasse as well, involving some limit or horizon that Stevens's modernist imagination approaches only through the utmost exertions.

In the next section, I will attempt to trace the contours of this structuring absence in Stevens's poetry with reference to a poem that is itself something of a structuring absence with respect to his body of work. "Owl's Clover" is the longest poem Stevens ever wrote, the subject of one of the longest and densest exegeses to be found in Stevens's correspondence, and it is the poem in reference to which Stevens first broaches the idea of the "supreme fiction"—the proposition that "one's final belief must be in a fiction."[25] For reasons about which his letters provide little insight, Stevens decided to exclude "Owl's Clover" from his 1954 *Collected Poems*. As I will try to show, however, the poem is an indispensable clue to Stevens's work as a whole, specifically when it comes to sorting out the epistemological and political binarisms that constantly reappear in his poems.

Forms Formless in the Dark

The best critical treatments of "Owl's Clover" have already gone a long way toward exhibiting the poem's epistemological binarisms in terms of the interpersonal political object it confronts. Joseph Riddell describes this collective being as "a common self and a common need," which is defined by an "everchanging, fluid...rage for order,"[26] and Angus Cleghorn describes it as a "local and diasporic" network, whose "collectivity is composed out of differences constructed in rhetorical relation."[27] Cleghorn even goes so far as to demonstrate how this collective presence causes Stevens to abandon the image of the poet as an epistemologically central "visionary savior" and instead turn toward a "collective unconsciousness" in which the fictions of modernist individualism are unmasked.[28]

What I would like to contribute to this tradition of reading is an analysis of Stevens's hopes and fears about this collective ensemble and its potential modes of critical negativity and spontaneous organization. At times, the multitude appears in "Owl's Clover" as little more than a blind flux that the poet must shape from a position of imaginative mastery. This vision of the multitude sets in motion the processes of depersonalization that are familiar from Stevens's later long poems, and that revolve around the poet's attempts to become an adequate exponent of the multitude's necessities and potentialities. But at other times, this vision of the poet as a central mind is exposed as a myth, or an ontological placeholder, standing in for a process of social constitution that is in fact intersubjective, polynodal, and, above all, decentered. Stevens's attempts to imagine how such a process of reciprocal social ordering might be possible, and what position (if any) the poet might be imagined to occupy amid its horizontal currents of exchange, is the principal dilemma in "Owl's Clover."

It is a dilemma that will echo and reecho in the reality/imagination antinomy of Stevens's later work, a dilemma that sometimes seems to concern purely phenomenological or epistemological aporias. But in "Owl's Clover," the very thought categories that define these aporias are shown to be rooted in a social dilemma, namely, the "confrontation of reality (the depression) and the imagination (art),"[29] or the confrontation between "those who suffered during the depression" and the shaping powers of "poetic energy."[30] The possibility that this confrontation could be resolved into a "universal intercourse" or "a flow to and fro between reality and the imagination"[31] is the idea to which Stevens continually returns in "Owl's Clover," all the while enacting the varied forms of domination and subterfuge such a vision of utopic concord can so effectively mask.

Indeed, it is with precisely such an image of false social harmony that the poem begins—an ersatz utopia with which the apparatuses of artistic semblance are thoroughly complicit. At this point, the multitude is visible only in the pathetic, mute image of an old woman, who represents "those who suffered during the depression." In the first section of the poem, this old woman confronts a statue of winged horses that closely resembles a statue Stevens would describe in his 1941 essay "The Noble Rider and the Sound of Words." In the essay, Stevens describes the statue as evoking a "casual delight...in...nobility" to which "we cannot yield ourselves."[32] In "Owl's Clover," the statue is a "variable symbol," sometimes representing the "social aspect" of art, sometimes representing society more broadly: "a manifestation of the civilization of which it is a part...irrelevant, hence dead, a dead thing in a dead time."[33] As such, the statue fails to represent the realities of the indigent old woman. Its confident upward flight is out of touch with the economic decay and social antagonism of Depression-era America. The implication of the section, then, is that art should somehow open itself to the realities of the old woman and give them expression.

The idea that this kind of exponency might be necessary is buttressed by the fact that the indigent multitude symbolized by the woman has not yet learned to give organized expression to its negativity—that it lacks "an objective correlative in [its] environment," in Cleghorn's terms.[34] It is true that the old woman's negativity envelops the statue and blackens its form. Indeed, in her presence "the mass of stone collapsed to marble hulk" and "Stood stiffly, as if the black of what she thought / Conflicting with the moving colors there / Changed them, at last, to its triumphant hue."[35] But the old woman in incapable of reorganizing the statue in a way that gives expression to her suppressed social intelligence.

The closest the old woman comes to a state of spontaneous creative power is in her sense of the variable nature of social reality, a sense awakened in her by her ability to negate the statue on a cognitive level. Stevens evokes this double movement of negativity and sensed possibility like this:

> The clouds of bronze
> Slowly submerging in flatness disappeared.
> If the sky that followed, smaller than the night,
> Still eked out luminous wrinklings on the leaves,
> Whitened, again, forms formless in the dark,
> It was as if transparence touched her mind.
> The statue stood in stars like water-spheres,
> Washed over by their green, their flowing blue (77)

In this passage, the brilliant certainties that once lent vitality and intelligibility to the statue have "bronzed" in the autumnal sunset and disappeared altogether. This appears to liberate the woman's paralyzed intuition. Rather than being extinguished in an absolute void of being, her intuition now seems awakened as an active power, attempting to express itself in a social landscape that has become as changeable as itself. This is why a "luminescence" persists even when the statue's obsolete idea of order has been liquidated. On a literal level, this luminescence is a quality of the moon and stars. Figuratively, it represents the imagination, conceived not as a historical sedimentation but as a variable principle of formal coordination, existent even when night has descended upon outdated social forms.

Nevertheless, the old woman's sense of possibility is primarily unconscious. It is a "thing she felt but did not know" (77). And even this feeling is that of an extremely atomized individual. Her connection to all the others suffering in Depression-era America is achieved only in the form of a desolate testimony addressed, ultimately, to the poet himself, who will emerge heroically as the agent-principle they lack:

> Without her, evening like a budding yew
> Would soon be brilliant, as it was, before
> The harridan self and ever-maladive fate
> Went crying their desolate syllables, before
> Their voice and the voice of the tortured wind were one,
> Each voice within the other, seeming one,
> Crying against a need that pressed like cold,
> Deadly and deep (77)

Here, Stevens suggests that the superannuated imagination "[u]ntroubled by suffering" (78) might attempt to incorporate the reality of human misery into an unchanged social landscape by naturalizing its existence in the traditional symbol of the yew tree. Instead of this, however, an explicit negative synthesis occurs here, in which the woman's self and the collective "fate" of the multitude are combined in the socially transformative wind, which for Stevens is at the same time the force of poetic inspiration.

This is the point at which Stevens's heroic model of spontaneous poetic intuition takes over. By receiving the force of this social ferment as its own movement, and ultimately identifying itself with it, the poetic imagination establishes itself as the voice that spontaneously articulates the possibilities lying dormant in the social body. But already this identification is an uneasy one. The "desolate syllables" of this passage obviously evoke a common plight, but it is one that has not prompted overt forms of political organization. Instead, the exigency of the multitude appears as a sequence of disarticulated phonemes, which the poet must take up as the motive force and raw material of his imaginative activity. The credibility of this kind of spontaneous poetic exponency is immediately compromised, however, when Stevens suggests that the indeterminate voicings of the multitude and the poetic voice of the wind's historical movement constitute only a "seeming" unity. And this intimation that an element of semblance may exist at the level of the modernist's spontaneous mediations is only the first step in the anxious ritual through which Stevens attempts to purge himself of the dialectical deceit that shadows his imaginative acts.

Sequels without Thought

As if to dispel his own anxieties about the model of spontaneous mediation he has just put forward, Stevens abandons his delicate intercourse with the multitude of "Owl's Clover" I and at the beginning of "Owl's Clover" II declares, in the voice of heroic modernism:

> The thing is dead ... Everything is dead
> Except the future. Always everything
> That is is dead except what ought to be. (78)

The boldness of this statement has led many critics to believe that it is Stevens's way of ironically parroting Marxist orthodoxy. But a couple of critics have recognized its "ideas and rhetoric" to be "characteristically Stevensian"[36]—a plain statement of "Stevens' theory of flux" and artistic "exponency."[37] Indeed, Stevens's abolition of "the thing" here is quite similar to his more familiar attempts to negate stable thought systems and dead metaphors by assuming the "mind of winter" or attending to "the vulgate of experience."[38] In the above passage, then, Stevens appears to be trying on a rhetorical posture that will allow him to serve as an exponent of the multitude's negativity without committing himself to any positive forms of political investment.

Stevens continues this work of negativity by transforming the multitude's passive negativity toward the statue into an active aesthetic valuation:

> The statue seems a thing from Schwartz's, a thing
> Of the dank imagination, much below
> Our crusted outlines hot and huge with fact,
> Ugly as an idea, not beautiful
> As sequels without thought (78–79)

Here, Stevens announces his aesthetic challenge: the imagination must no longer embody a cheap, commodified "idea"; it must no longer be "a toy unworthy of its reality, incapable of unconsidered revelations." Instead, it must be capable of producing what Stevens calls "sequels without thought."[39]

But what does "sequels without thought" mean? This phrase, along with "unconsidered revelations," defines the mode of spontaneous social mediation to which Stevens aspires. But how does Stevens imagine the process whereby social facts communicate themselves spontaneously to the poet?

In an essay titled "The Irrational Element in Poetry," which Stevens wrote to accompany readings from "Owl's Clover," he offers some clues to the philosophical lineage of his ideas about spontaneity. In this essay, Stevens defines "the irrational" as "the transaction between reality and the sensibility of the poet."[40] In other words, Stevens's "irrational" has less to do with visionary experience or the phantasmagorias of the Freudian unconscious than with what he calls "the transposition of an objective reality to a subjective reality" (224). After describing this transposition as a "Hegelian process" (225), Stevens makes it clear that the "objective reality" he has in mind is a sociohistorical reality—a shared sense of the times, or what he calls "the pressure of contemporaneous" (230). So what Stevens describes as "irrational" is the process whereby this common historical experience encodes itself at the level of the poet's impulses and formal attunements. This process is irrational in that it occurs prior to the poet's conscious awareness. That is to say, it is "irrational in the sense that it takes place unaccountably" (225).

Stevensian spontaneity is therefore an intriguing hybrid of Hegel's objective idealism and Henri Bergson's idea of "spontaneous memory." When Stevens writes in "A Collect of Philosophy" that "we do not see the world" except after a "process of seeing,"[41] he is referring to the Bergsonian notion of a prerational, spontaneous processing of sense data that structures perception behind our backs. Bergson calls this process "spontaneous memory" to distinguish it from the conscious, routinized *recognition* of external objects that systematizes perceptions into a stable ensemble of familiar reactions and discards all perceptual data that are not immediately assimilable to present needs. In contrast to this, spontaneous memory consists of a virtual backdrop of memory images upon which we draw continually when we need to adapt ourselves to unfamiliar sensory stimuli, and that in fact "go out to meet" new perceptions continually.[42]

In Stevens's work, this idea of a structuring background to lived experience is often perceptual and social simultaneously. For example, in "The Noble Rider and the Sound of Words," Stevens describes the historical progression from "the comfortable American state of life" in the prewar period to the "much more vital reality" in which "intellectual minorities and social minorities" (26) began to take the place of the Victorians. Stevens likens the false stability of prewar American life to the false stability of an object perceived according to a methodized, habitual sensory mode. Indeed, he offers this sociohistorical portrait as an example of the Bergsonian idea that the world is not a "'collection of solid, static objects extended in space' but the life that is lived in the scene that it composes" (25). In both the perceptual and the social realms, Stevens draws attention to artificially stabilized scenes, beneath which a host of spontaneous impulsions are attempting to make their creative presence felt.

In making this leap from perceptual to social modalities of spontaneous creativity, however, Stevens is not breaking with Bergson but following his lead. In a book titled *The Two Sources of Morality and Religion*, Bergson himself redefines the élan vital as a historical force, operating not just in the realm of biological evolution and perceptual life but also in the realm of large-scale sociopolitical transformations. In this somewhat neglected work of political theory, Bergson describes "great men of action"—saints, founders of religion, social leaders—who grasp the very motive forces of history and gather these forces into a great "forward movement" that "help[s] society further along."[43] To perform this world-historical action, they must "throw[ ] off anything in [their] substance that is not pure enough, not flexible and strong enough" (220) to act as an instrument of human liberation. And their experience in doing so could be likened to what "a machine of wonderfully tempered steel" might experience if it somehow "became conscious of itself as it was being put together" (220).

Stevens refers explicitly to this model of social spontaneity in "The Irrational Element in Poetry," when he describes poets as "biological mechanism[s]" who "purge themselves before reality... in what they intend to be saintly exercises" (226, 231). And in reference to the "mystical *vis* or *noeud vital*"[44] that poets attempt to grasp in their compositional processes, Stevens quotes directly from Bergson's *Two Sources of Morality and Religion*, including a passage in which Bergson describes the "feeling of liberation" experienced by "the founders of religion, the mystic and the saints" (49). So when Stevens describes poets as self-expurgating mechanisms, he is imagining them as undergoing a process of depersonalization similar to that of Bergson's saints and mystics—figures who deliberately suspend their wills in order to render themselves available to a spontaneous life that exists only as a social preexistence.

This, then, is the best way to understand the "unconsidered revelations" and "sequels without thought" of "Owl's Clover" II: as intuitions of social possibility that announce themselves to the poet on prerational levels. Armed with this knowledge, we might expect the poem to progress with images of the poet as a confident exponent of the multitude, an expositor of impulses that the multitude cannot articulate plainly themselves. After all, this is the direction in which Bergson proceeds when he imagines his men of action adapting themselves to a "new social atmosphere" (71) that at the moment is knowable only as a "pre-existence of the possible in the real" (64) but that the saints strive to realize in an "open society" free of compulsory morality and ideological reflex mechanisms.

But this is not the direction in which "Owl's Clover" II heads. Despite the speaker's brassy declarations and Stevens's flirtation with Bergson's grandiose models of spontaneity and social leadership, "Owl's Clover" II immediately deflates the image it has just erected of the poet as an expansive social hero. In a gesture that will recur frequently in "Owl's Clover," Stevens strips himself of any representative claims he has worked himself up to and inquires more deeply into the spontaneous processes to which he seeks to accord large-scale social significance. On this occasion, what he discovers is less the speech of the multitude echoing within him than an embarrassingly conventional set of personal social attunements, which Stevens desperately tries to retrain so that they may be more synchronized with the spontaneous collective processes occurring all around them.

Stubborn Attachments

"Owl's Clover" II thus begins by staging a *failure* of individual spontaneity that we encounter, in different ways, in the work of Williams, Lewis, and Riding as well. As Fredric Jameson argues in *The Modernist Papers*, such modernist failures might be read as semiconscious attempts to avoid the kinds of aesthetic success that "bind[ ] and alienate[ ] us more securely and inextricably into... capitalism itself as a system."[45] I would add to this the suggestion that the general aim of these modernist failures is to show that the artist's *feeling* of spontaneous merger with the multitude often serves to domesticate or otherwise silence the multitude itself, even as it elevates the artist as the redemptive, directive presence the multitude requires.[46] In "Owl's Clover" II, Stevens depicts this failure in a bizarre but highly evocative conceit. He personifies his own imaginative faculties as a group of aristocratic ladies who are timidly attempting to adapt themselves to the multitude's new forms of social organization. In a way that is almost parodic, Stevens portrays these "celestial paramours" as profoundly ambivalent, if not recalcitrant, spiritual entities whom he must instruct and cajole, as if attempting to distract their attention from all the hedonic occupations to which they are accustomed.

This is hardly the picture of artistic spontaneity for which Stevens's heroizing images of "unconsidered revelations" have prepared us. It is true that Stevens conceives the dance of the ladies on a large scale; they represent "all the things in our nature that are celestial.... They are compelled by desire... in the commingling of those two immense reflections."[47] The "two immense reflections" to which Stevens refers here are the past and the future, so the dance of the paramours takes on the significance of a weighty historical transition. But for figures of self-relinquishment and historical transition, the paramours exhibit a strangely stubborn attachment to the past. It seems that on one hand they represent the various emotional complexes that adhere tenaciously to the social epoch that is disappearing, while on the other they represent all the formal capacities frozen, as it were, in this affective landscape—capacities that Stevens attempts to reanimate so they may fulfill the adaptive functions of which he writes.

In other words, the figures whom Stevens addresses are the inhabitants of *his own* affective geography. They represent all of his own faculties, faculties that have taken on the guise of a "sexual other within";[48] aristocratic ladies who must undergo a lengthy process of tutelage instigated by... Stevens himself:

> Come, all celestial paramours,
> Whether in-dwelling haughty clouds, frigid
> And crisply musical, or holy caverns temple-toned,
> Entwine your arms and moving to and fro,
> Now like a ballet infantine in awkward steps,
> Chant sibilant requiems for this effigy. (79)

Note that the statue as it appears here—the epoch of proud, untroubled illusions—is already an "effigy." The indigent woman of "Owl's Clover" I, along with everyone else who was immiserated by the Depression, has transformed its "casual delight... in... nobility"[49] into meaningless "marble skulls"[50]—"a dead thing in a dead time."[51]

But because no new order has emerged from the "tortured wind" (77) of political discontent, the poet imagines that he must take this task on himself: to define, in a completely selfless and unpremeditated way, the social and aesthetic forms that could suffice in the face of such suffering. According to this heroized idea of artistic agency, which Stevens is in the process of deconstructing here, anything less than the most complete kind of spontaneity might produce insufficiently credible results, ideas of order that could be indicted as merely personal fantasies. So Stevens sets in motion a process that is doomed to failure from the outset—to identify all the habituated, static thought forms into which unpremeditated contents must penetrate in order to coax them out of his personality. The dance that results is supposed to permit stark social realities to enter him, in such a way that they could be lent purpose and direction. The general idea here is that if the multitude remains passive, Stevens himself will embrace their negativity and transform his internal faculties into agents of change. At first, these faculties seem well suited to this task insofar as they are themselves ethereal, self-renewing, and bear within themselves the fragile efflorescences of the possible:

> Bring down from nowhere nothing's wax-like blooms,
> Calling them what you will but loosely-named
> In a mortal lullaby, like porcelain.
> Then, while the music makes you, make, yourselves,
> Long autumn sheens and pittering sounds like sounds
> On pattering leaves and suddenly with lights,
> Astral and Shelleyan, diffuse new day (79)

Note, however, how this passage ends. "Diffuse new day"? A jarring shift occurs in the final lines of this passage, as Stevens departs from his relatively modest idea of poetic adaptation, and suddenly endows his timid internal ingenues with the power of social legislation. Shelley appears to guarantee the legitimacy of this act of legislation, derived as it is from Stevens's "unconsidered revelations." And as the paramours are instructed to project this "new day" onto the face of reality—"on this ring of marble horses" to "shed / The rainbow" of social rebirth (79)—it is easy to detect the will to power latent in Shelley's famous dictum that poets are the unacknowledged legislators of the world.

Helen Vendler is on the mark when she compares the "debilitated, fragile, even frigid" paramours of this passage to the simpering Byzantines of "Peter Quince" and concludes that the "squeamishness of concept" embodied in their activity "invalidates [them] as figures of power."[52] Stevens's assertion of a world-historical poetic mandate here is therefore embarrassingly premature. As he notes, the Shelleyan moment arrives "suddenly," indeed, just a few lines after the paramours must be coaxed down from their "holy caverns temple-toned": sacrosanct internal enclaves bathed, it would seem, in the affective timbre of the civilization to which they are accustomed, the "temple" of the old world, as opposed to the "temple ... never quite composed" (82).

This is why the affective personae of this drama—Stevens's own, it is to be remembered—seem to be in need of reassurance that the "new day" they are supposed to have propagated has not reconstituted the material world in a shape that is in any way threatening to them:

> Agree: the apple in the orchard, round
> And red, will not be redder, rounder then
> Than now. No: nor the ploughman in his bed
> Be free to sleep there sounder, for the plough
> And the dew and the ploughman still will best be one.
> But this gawky plaster will not be here (79)

Stevens comments: "The astral and Shelleyan lights are not going to alter the structure of nature. Apples will always be apples, and whoever is a ploughman hereafter will be what the ploughman has always been. For all that, the astral and the Shelleyan will have transformed the world."[53] As a kind of compromise, Stevens evokes the "structure of nature." Though the world may change, nature will not—thankfully, since "nature" designates not merely the "apple in the orchard" but also the hand that picks it and the ploughman who tills the orchard's soil. This abrupt foreclosure of social possibility is startling; indeed, it marks the complete failure of a certain model of poetic spontaneity. Instead of distinguishing his own poetic posture from the "foppish" imagination[54] which resists "the evolution of what ought to be," Stevens simply romanticizes the deadly "need" of the multitude here, incorporating it into a subjectively pleasing but completely static model of poetic spontaneity.

In a 1940 letter to Hi Simons, Stevens implies that he intentionally staged this failure of the interior paramours and the romantic, subjectivist model of spontaneity they represent. He writes of the above passage: "It is impossible to be truly reconciled, if one romanticizes the past (ploughmen, peacocks, doves)" (367). Here, the peacock's "pride" and the dove's "adagio" (80) are not actually natural phenomena, in the sense of being extra-human, asocial things. Instead, they represent social structures of feeling which have become naturalized through habit. This is why Stevens can write, in a 1935 letter to Ronald Lane Latimer, "to the extent that the Marxians are raising Cain with the peacocks and the doves, nature has been ruined by them" (295). In other words, social habit is being unsettled by new mass organizational processes and actors, and Stevens identifies his own project much more closely with these new processes than with the relations they are unsettling. In fact, Stevens even goes so far as to describe the second part of "Owl's Clover" as a "general and rather vaguely poetic justification of leftism" (295). He writes:

> I think we all feel that there is a conflict between the rise of a lower class, with all its realities, and the indulgences of an upper class. This ... is one of the very things which I at least have in mind in MR. BURNSHAW. My conclusion is that, while there is a conflict, it is not an essential conflict ... Marxism may or may not destroy the existing sentiment of the marvellous; if it does, it will create another. (291–92)

In the poetic passage above, then, Stevens stages something of a relapse of the heroic modernist imagination. Initially appointing himself as a representative of the realities of a rising lower class, he concludes with a phony vision of historical rebirth that satisfies the paramours' "natural" attachment to the current social order. This poetic sequence therefore exhibits in an especially vivid way the pitfalls of individual spontaneity, especially insofar as it is meant to guarantee the social universality of the poet's ideas of order. In attempting to be the spontaneous exponent of an emerging set of social relations and actors, Stevens merely ends up voicing the outdated truths that suggest themselves to him most "spontaneously." The content of his poetic creations does arrive unpremeditatedly, but from a source much closer to home than he would wish. Clearly, such a state of affairs is unacceptable, and Stevens interrupts this entire dialectic of deceit with a far different conception of the replacement for the plaster-cast civilization that is disappearing.

"A Drastic Community"

> The stones
> That will replace it shall be carved, *"The Mass*
> *Appoints These Marbles Of Itself To Be*
> *Itself."* No more than that, no subterfuge,
> No memorable muffing, bare and blunt. (80)

This short passage, which follows directly upon the heels of the paramours' dance, emblematizes a model of spontaneity completely different from what we have seen so far and marks a turning point in the poem as a whole. Like the passage that began "Owl's Clover" II, this passage has traditionally been seen as a parody of vulgar Marxism, but some excellent criticism has complicated that reading. Rajeev Patke, for example, notes Stevens's profound investment in the pediment, arguing that "'no memorable muffing' is too Stevensian an exfoliation... to be resisted by the poet or to be ascribed with any kind of plausibility to the Marxist."[55] Similarly, James Longenbach notes that the inscription is "transformed from a naive tenet of socialist realism into the goal of an intricately dialectical process by which art, in all its complexity, engages the world of human speech and makes it 'real.'"[56]

The formal spareness of this passage, as well as the context in which it appears, adds strength to these readings. Its "bareness" and "bluntness" serve as a bracing antidote to what Stevens describes as "subterfuge" and "memorable muffing," in obvious reference to the preceding dance: the "sibilant" chants of the paramours (79) and the embarrassingly baroque climax of "glistening serpentines / Made by the sun ascending seventy seas" (79). *Before* he introduces the blunt reality of the pediment, Stevens is content to let "the poet's politics / ... rule in a poets' world" (80), a static, rusticated "Italy of the mind," pleasing to his aristocratic ladies, who live in "fear before the disorder of the strange" (80). *After* the introduction of the pediment, Stevens chides the paramours for fearing "a drastic community evolved / From the swirling, slowly and by trial" and "Men gathering for a mighty flight of men" into the "possible blue" of the future (82).

The pediment, then, is situated outside the poet's aristocratized sensibility and is necessarily bare insofar as Stevens is not yet in a position to lend it an understandable content. This reflects the fact that, up until now, "Owl's Clover" has been operating according to a fundamentally individual ideal of spontaneity, that of a subjective *adaptation* to changing social realities. The historical imperative of the multitude does arrive, but in the form of a contentless beyond which becomes the catalyst for a subjective process of assimilation. The "men gathering" and "community evolved / From the swirling" of this passage represent an entirely different idea of spontaneity, one that is collective, self-correcting, and irreducible to the subjective fantasies of Stevens's paramours.

It is at this point, then, that Stevens abandons the masquerade of heroic artistic subjectivity and tries to imagine a principle of spontaneous coordination being born *within* the intersubjective terrain of the multitude, as a function of its complex life-activity, rather than as a gift from above. To do this, Stevens imagines a group of workers who are transforming the bare pediment into a synthetic bust of themselves, a "collective self" fashioned from the substance of the pediment and destined to take the old statue's place.[57] This new bust consists of the blended faces of an international assemblage of immigrant workers, "massed for a head they mean to make for themselves, / From which their grizzled voices will speak and be heard" (91). Stevens's phenomenological exteriority to these processes—his inability to "conceive" clearly what they "mean" (91)—is emphasized by the fact that the head being created by the multitude is not that of a recognizable, individual leader, but rather a composite physiognomy: a collective head consisting of their various features (the "English noses and edged, Italian eyes," and so on; 91).

In a second tableau devoted to this image, Stevens makes it clear that this many-featured head has little to do with the central mind or poetic exponent so often present in his poetry. Instead, it is an attempt to imagine how the decentered, differently qualitied multitude could sculpt *themselves* into a dexterous collective body. Stevens tries to evoke the complexified faculties of this new intersubjective body in the following passage:

> This man
> Is all the birds he ever heard and that,
> The admiral of his race and everyman,
> Infected by unreality, rapt round
> By dense unreason, irreproachable force,
> Is cast in pandemonium, flittered, howled
> By harmonies beyond known harmony.
> These bands, these swarms, these motions, what of them?
> They keep to the paths of the skeleton architect
> Of the park. (92)

In this passage, Stevens adopts the voice of the "socialist" or "evolving worker"[58] in order to depict two workers whose quotidian, circumscribed social activity has catalyzed a complexification of sensibility that is organic, in Gramsci's sense of the term. The plurality of birdsongs evokes the heteronomous body of workers, which is able to sustain itself as a unity-in-multiplicity. The intersubjective poise needed to navigate these microcurrents of social activity is also embodied in the second man, whose "race-admiralty" in fact reflects a potentially limiting *particularity* ("Englishness," "Italianness," and so on) that is challenged to find an intelligible common ground within the differential, multiethnic generality of the multitude.

Stevens's suggestion that the bodiless "skeleton architect / Of the park" delimits the range of the multitude's actions and sensibilities (the cheap pleasures of the park available on their "Geranium budgets"; 93) is therefore only partially true. When Stevens ramifies individual consciousness in a miniature "animal kingdom of the spirit," where it is "flittered, howled / By harmonies beyond known harmony," he is staging simultaneously the pandemonium of social crisis *and* the complexification of the multitude's sensibility that results from it, insofar as a seemingly static, unchangeable social reality now appears as a changeable system of relations, of which the multitude constitutes the living body. The fact that the motions and swarms of increasingly numerous workers constitute a possible social harmony beyond a social order that is rapidly being stripped of its life awakens a principle of self-organization in the multitude. "Unreason," or "the transposition of an objective reality to a subjective reality,"[59] now seems to be a transindividual force. In fact, Stevens even poses to this self-organizing multitude the question that he once posed to the heroic, self-abnegating genius:

> But of what are they thinking, of what . . .
> . . . .
> . . . are they being part, feeling the strength . . .
> . . . .
> Is each man thinking his separate thoughts or, for once,
> Are all men thinking together as one, thinking
> Each other's thoughts, thinking a single thought,
> Disclosed in everything, transcended, poised
> For the syllable, poised for the touch? (92–93)

In other words, Stevens asks whether it might be possible for the multitude to achieve the kind of spontaneous ordering capacity that is usually thought to be the sole possession of individual geniuses.

Stevens is not sanguine about such a prospect, in part because he believes that the same kinds of outdated attachments exhibited by the paramours may hold sway in any project of collective self-organization, in part because he believes that the process of social transformation is too easily co-opted by individual dictators, and in part because he believes that such central, dictatorial wills may in fact be necessary to prevent the process of social transformation from devolving into a chaotic war of competing interests. So, despite the guarded optimism of the above passage, Stevens allows his image of spontaneous collective organization to devolve into a crassly individualistic form of pseudoradicalism:

> Then Basilewsky in the band-stand played
> "Concerto for Airplane and Pianoforte,"
> The newest Soviet réclame. Profound
> Abortion, fit for the enchanting of basilisks (93)

This passage represents the worst possible caricature of spontaneous organization: an individual worker setting himself above others and claiming to embody the will of all in his trite improvisations. Crudely juxtaposing the massive noise of the jet engine with his individualistic tinkerings on the pianoforte, he seeks only to wed the multitude to his own egoic sectarianism—to produce small Basilewskys, that is, "basil-isks," or perhaps "basil-ists."

Imagining, then, that collective self-organization will be hopelessly freighted with vulgarity and opportunism, Stevens falls back once more on the Bergsonian model of heroic, selfless genius. According to this model, only great, individual spirits are capable of producing genuine change. The poet must therefore become a neutral "metropolitan of the mind,"[60] must acquire the kind of epistemological centrality that will allow him to oversee social changes that the shortsightedness of the multitude prevents them from detecting.

But this modernist fantasy, however intellectually compelling, becomes slightly more comical each time it is produced in the poem as a solution to the question of credible legislative authority. In fact, the following section, which resurrects the poetic legislator in the somewhat ridiculous forms of "Don Juan turned furious divinity," "oozer and Abraham" (95), and so on, seems to serve as a final, desperately "stubborn" (94) assertion of poetic authority, before Stevens employs his strategy of self-interruption once more. As if calling himself to order, Stevens next allies himself in perfect candor with the we-persona of the workers in the park. It is as if Stevens realizes that even the most rigorous self-renunciations on the part of the modernist amount in the final analysis to a self-interested masquerade. But he finds it impossible to believe that groups of people could constitute anything more than a multiplicity of self-interests. Out of methodological desperation, Stevens steps into the multitude to see what it is composed of. How, he seems to ask, could a collectivity surrender its stubborn attachments to self if individual geniuses are incapable of doing so?

Stevens phrases the question in this way: "When shall lush chorals spiral through our fire / And daunt that old assassin, heart's desire?" (96). He answers: "These people have / A meaning within the meaning they convey, / Walking the paths, watching the gilding sun, / To be swept across them when they are revealed, / For a moment, once each century or two" (95). For a non-Marxist poet, these lines are remarkable. Stevens suggests that for the time being, the multitude sticks to the "paths" of the capitalist circuit. Producing and produced by an individualistic society, they convey the "meanings" proper to it, clutching "crude souvenirs" (94) suffused with the affective forms such a society makes available. But beneath the surface emotions that contain them are undisclosed affective "meanings" that are real and abiding—meanings that have been colonized and redefined in terms more suitable to the limitations of the park.

These potentialities are suddenly revealed when the cyclical pattern of capitalist crisis is repeated "each century or two," and "the tempo... of this complicated shift" (96), the "epical... catastrophe" (95) that discloses the possibility of social transformation, is "a leaden ticking circular in width" (96). In other words, the liquidation of self-feeling the heroic modernist tries to initiate and sustain on an individual basis is here accomplished by a historical "envoi" (96): a moment of crisis that allows for the emergence of suppressed emotional configurations. Infrastructural crisis tends to deprive celebrations of individual agency of their credibility, and, at the same time, it highlights the urgency of evolving new models of collective association. For Stevens, this idea that static attachments to selfhood could be interrupted from without, as a consequence of large-scale social crisis, rather than interrupted exclusively from within, as a consequence of heroic, individual acts of self-renunciation, demands a radical change in perspective.

After all, if the multitude is already having its ideological certitudes and conventional senses of self stripped from them, then the poet's self-renunciations seem just one small part of a larger, intersubjective process of spontaneous destruction and recombination. In this scenario, the poet's acts of self-renunciation guarantee him or her no epistemological centrality. Instead, they are just one performance contending with a host of other performances for some measure of credibility.

A new image of the modernist emerges from this. The finger-paring God awakes to find himself just one element of a vast, intersubjective process of self-organization—one that constitutes itself, at least in part, through its ability to perceive and debunk the pretensions to selflessness advanced by the modernist. A new image of the multitude thus emerges as well. It is no longer identified with the latent negativity of the old woman; instead, it is identified with the active negativity of critique, debate, and mutual transformation.

This idea of the multitude as animated by contradictions that it has internalized and taken up in the mode of critical debate adds something new to Negri's ideas about self-organization. The idea, for example, that economic crisis could in any way motivate a processes of reassessment and critique in the multitude is something Negri repeatedly rejects. In *Marx beyond Marx*, he asks whether the multitude's "social recognition of its own power" should be regarded merely as a "residue of the determination of the critical elements of capitalist development," that is, as a "parasitic and subsequent" response to capitalist crisis.[61] In a pamphlet from 1973, he had already answered this question unambiguously. Capitalist crisis does not predate and stimulate the struggles of the multitude. Instead, "it is the making of the struggle, the incessant internal modification in the relationship between classes... that determines the pace and forms of the crisis."[62] Focusing on "objectivistic" causes of crisis— the tendency of the rate of profit to fall, the problem of overcapacity, the limits to capitalist expansion posed by domestic and international markets—promotes a catastrophist frame of mind and distracts attention from a point Negri repeatedly stresses: that "working-class composition [is] the *only* explanation of the crisis itself."[63]

But does not this idea that class struggle is the *only* motor of capitalist crisis—the idea that the multitude is never forced to reposition itself in relation to extrinsic crises—exhibit precisely the "phobia of the negative" that Rancière detects in Negri's thought?[64] Though Negri's intention in envisioning the multitude as the source of all crisis is to magnify its collective *potenza*, this maneuver actually obscures the critical powers, tactical sensitivities, and rhetorical virtuosities that collective subjects must bring to bear on crisis situations they have not authored. And if, as Ernesto Laclau and Chantal Mouffe remind us, the multitude is not a pregiven unity of interests, worldviews, and subject positions, then it is only by exercising such discursive and practical competences that the multitude can articulate itself as a political body. This kind of articulation requires what Laclau and Mouffe call a "complex strategic movement requiring negotiation among mutually contradictory discursive surfaces."[65] And the success of these negotiations is not pregiven in the collective ontology of the multitude. On the contrary, "the ability and the will to resist are not a gift from heaven but require a set of subjective transformations that are only the product of the struggles themselves *and that can fail to take place.*"[66]

In "Owl's Clover," it is precisely these fallible transformative processes that are on display—the collision of contradictory discursive surfaces, invested with differential ideological investments, worldviews, and strategic intuitions. Stevens has great difficulty representing this larger, collective process of organization, in large part because it is a process that is traditionally conceived as possible only within the mind of the individual genius. This represents a crisis of Stevens's epistemology—one that will lead him to suggest that "the world may . . . be lost to the poet but it is not lost to the imagination."[67] In other words, the time of heroic individual minds may be past. The imagination may have to be conceived as a collective faculty: "We live today in a time dominated by great masses of men and, while the reason of a few men may underlie what they do, they act as their imaginations impel them to act."[68] The spontaneity of the multitude, in other words, may be the new location of the imagination. But where, exactly, do we locate this imagination, if it is not the property of an individual mind?

The Object of Remembrance

Some excellent Stevens criticism has begun to help us conceive the position of collective life in Stevens's work and its relationship to his images of individual poetic agency. Fredric Jameson's *Modernist Papers,* for example, resurrects a remarkable *New Orleans Review* article in which Jameson argues that Stevens's "neutralized landscape[s]" are not so neutral after all, but in fact contain "preconscious grids and associative systems that operate in the same way that Hegel's "objective spirit" does—as a set of "collective, prepersonal capacities."[69] Leon Surette's *The Modern Dilemma: Wallace Stevens, T. S. Eliot, and Humanism* also makes a strong case for the political dimension of Stevens's poetry, as do Jacqueline Vaught Brogan's *The Violence Within/The Violence Without: Wallace Stevens and the Emergence of a Revolutionary Poetics,*[70] Alan Filreis's two lapidary volumes on Stevens, Mark Halliday's *Stevens and the Interpersonal,* and Justin Quinn's

Gathered beneath the Storm, which argues that nature serves as a figural "fund" in Stevens's poetry, allowing him to "test[ ] the reality of all conceptions of the masses of men."[71]

What I hope to contribute to these studies is an analysis of the spontaneous collective imagination in "Owl's Clover," the effort—quite rare in Stevens's work—to depict the multitude as a spontaneously self-regulating complex, operating with the delicate balances and counterweights that are typically imagined as the exclusive property of individual, central minds. Even to begin imagining such a spontaneous complex, however, will mean having to follow Stevens into some unfamiliar territory.

For example, in his exposition of "Owl's Clover" V, which contains the poem's most textured images of collective spontaneity, Stevens appropriates a Jungian terminology that is uncharacteristic of his poetics and rarely seen in his correspondence:

> The sub-conscious is assumed to be our beginning and end.... It follows that it is the beginning and end of the conscious.... In another note I said that the imagination partakes of the conscious. Here it is treated as an activity of the sub-conscious: the imagination is the sub-conscious.[72]

What Steven refers to here is not merely the individual subconscious. It is what Stevens describes in "Owl's Clover" V as a "subman under all / The rest" (96), an "anti-logician, quick / With a logic of transforming certitudes" (96). In the context of this "subman" passage, it becomes clear that this man is not the poet as we have come to recognize him, the self-negating figure who merges with the multitude by way of a phenomenological masquerade. Instead, the subman is Stevens's way of representing spontaneous *collective* forces that are awakened as a consequence of social and political crisis. He is thus a figure of precisely those prerational stirrings that inhabit social landscapes in periods of historical transition—what Steven evokes in "Owl's Clover" as the "fluid ... cat-eyed atmosphere, in which / The man and the man below were reconciled" (98).

The subman thus represents some aspect of the multitude's potentiality, its capacity for social recombination. But how, exactly, is this potentiality to be imagined? What, for example, is feline about it? Why is it cat-eyed?

In a remarkable note on "The Man with the Blue Guitar" in a letter to Hi Simons, Stevens describes the "liquid cats" of that poem to be "sombre cats [that] are merely sombre people going about their jobs" (361). The bodies of these cats are no more than "black blobs on the mind's eye"

(361)—a diffuse, deindividuated atmosphere that shrouds individualist society in darkness. In other words, these cats are meant to represent the movements of the multitude, who merely "go about their accustomed jobs, unconscious of what is occurring" (361). The fluidity embodied in the multitude's movements, therefore, is somehow eroding the basis on which the old order stood. If the multitude itself is unconscious of this, its unconsciousness is, nevertheless, glancingly illuminated with the incipient consciousness of new orders that could emerge from its own ordinary activity. Stevens explains that the term "cat-eyed is a migration of the French word *chatoyant*, changeable, as in the irised glimmering of night" (362). In an extraordinary series of metonyms, then, Stevens evokes a condition of social darkness that is suddenly alight with a multiplicity of interchanging, flickering pupils. In other words, the subconscious impulsions of the multitude suddenly seem to be functioning in the same way as the imagination of the poet.

This attempt to evoke a process of spontaneous collective ordering represents a radical shift in "Owl's Clover" V. It means that Stevens is attempting to locate possibilities for change within actual historical groups, rather than confining them to the actions of selfless, saintly individuals. The Bergsonian saint, whom Stevens finds so compelling, is guided by a mystic élan that descends, as it were, into historical actuality. It is by no means a function of mundane organizational activities. Stevens's subman, by contrast, is described as an "inhabitant" of a "field of lights" (97). That is, he is situated *within* the flickering atmosphere of the multitude's social intuitions. In fact, he could be said to be nothing but the internal logic of these intuitions, a logic in which the social relations that govern the multitude's "accustomed jobs" suddenly appear to be as changeable as the play of associations that traverse their collective subconscious.

Here is the passage where Stevens most fully explicates the spontaneous movements of this collective subconscious:

> He dwells below, the man below, in less
> Than body and in less than mind, ogre,
> Inhabitant, in less than shape, of shapes
> That are dissembled in vague memory
> Yet still retain resemblances, remain
> Remembrances, a place of a field of lights,
> As a church is a bell and people are an eye,

> A cry, the pallor of a dress, a touch.
> He turn us into scholars, studying
> The masks of music. We perceive each mask
> To be the musician's own and, thence, become
> An audience to mimics glistening
> With meanings, doubled by the closest sound,
> Mimics that play on instruments discerned
> In the beat of the blood (97)

In this astonishingly rich passage, the subman is clearly neither an individual agent nor a mystic élan. Instead, he represents the possibility that Stevens's we-subject might collectively "remember" the unrealized social possibilities that are latent in its everyday activity.[73]

In this passage, then, remembrance does not designate an individual act. It is not accomplished through the psychological operations of the poet. Instead, it designates the ways that a collectivity might recall itself as a vast network of untapped faculties. Stevens's "remembrance" is thus most similar to the Hegelian process of re-collection *(Erinnerung)*. In this process, the faculties summoned through collective memory exist "in themselves" only once they are "gathered in" as part of an intersubjective process of debate.[74]

In this context, the problem of whether the poet can become selfless enough to perceive reality "as it is" loses much of its urgency. Stevens shows that this problem relies on a specific model of political advocacy—one in which the individual must speak on behalf of "external realities" that are separate from his or her existence. This means that the entire project of knowledge and representation is structured around a strange act of epistemic benevolence. Only individual will and candor can guarantee that the self-interest of the knower will not corrupt him or her as an advocate of the outside world.

By contrast, notice how the passage above does not hinge on individual candor or self-renunciation. In it, the dissemblances of the knower are not fatal to the project of knowledge. In fact, all of the recollections of the agents in the passage are "dissembled in vague memory," and it is precisely these dissemblances that make "us . . . scholars, studying / The masks of music" (97). In other words, Stevens does not represent "external reality" as a passive object of knowledge, to which one must benevolently extend one's perceptions. Instead, external reality is represented as a network of social relations, constituted by a multitude that is taking the work of ordering reality upon itself. In the process of composing the harmonious music that will unite them, they act deceitfully, they dissemble and wear masks. But in the process, they also learn to detect others' dissemblances and masks, which allows them to define what is worth mimicking in others' performances and what is not. Through this reciprocal play of deception, and not through the benevolence of external representatives, collective requirements are transformed into mutually verified representations—representations in which the epistemological and the political constitute a dialectical continuum.

In such a process, masquerades such as Basilewsky's musical performance are subjected to the spontaneous scrutiny of "scholars": the multitude conceived as a mutually corrective interplay of individualities. Taking the bandstand and trying to pass off his technical contortions as adequate ideas of social order, Basilewsky would meet not with a passive audience but with a dynamic collectivity capable of detecting the mask of egotism in every individual attempt to lend shape to social requirements.

All of this means that the play of dissemblance and critique Stevens models does not resolve itself into some collective moral imperative or abstract "humaneness."[75] Instead, Stevens stages a dialectic of deceit, in which many individuals bring forth individual works, each one staking a claim to intersubjective significance. It is in this very "interplay of . . . mutual deceits"[76] that a field of intersubjective contention and activity is opened, with each partial, subjective representation of the social body calling out in such a way as to elicit collective involvement.

Thinking, in these terms, about a form of spontaneity that is at the same time a forum of critique, debate, and political self-constitution invites us to reconsider the entire category of spontaneity, especially insofar as the term is associated with inviolable forms of inwardness, privacy, and personal authenticity. In Stevens's imagined scenario, spontaneity is possible only as a function of reciprocal critique and correction. The image of Bergson's benevolent, depersonalized mystics at first furnished "Owl's Clover" with its model of spontaneous agency and social change. But the poem reveals the limitations of this model of spontaneity by testing it against the increasingly complex conceptions of the multitude it evolves. Initially, the multitude was imagined as an undifferentiated flux whose only content was the anguished cry it directed toward the central mind of the artist. But by the end of the poem the multitude has become so dynamized and self-organizing that the artist's ordering processes are stripped of any centrality they once appeared to possess.

Now, Bergsonian mystics, social leaders, and Stevensian artists are all deposited in a social milieu in which they possess no centrality whatsoever. In fact, this social milieu could be said to have turned the tables on the artist. Its members "remember" themselves in the artistic work and validate the work's claim to social significance only once the artist's mask of subjectivism becomes publicly, embarrassingly, visible. In such a scenario, poetic exponency is no longer guaranteed by a romantic self-purification seeking to "appropriate the world under some single synthetic, compositional force."[77] Instead, it is framed as something collectively recognizable, after the creative act, if and when the poem's "invitation to participate in the processes of fit that it composes"[78] successfully mobilizes "publicly significant emotional intensities."[79]

This represents a dramatic break with the Bergsonian model of the imagination, which relies on the idea that poets can purge their imaginative faculties of subjective content and thus become, in a sense, nothing but the active aspect of potentialities implicit in the life-activity of the multitude. By contrast, the form of remembrance Stevens evokes in "Owl's Clover" functions much more like Marcuse's imagination, which both "envisions the reconciliation of the individual with the whole" and "preserves the 'memory' of the subhistorical past when the life of the individual was the life of the genus, the image of the immediate unity between the universal and the particular."[80] In this modality of the imagination, the recombinative possibilities dormant in the multitude appear as an unarticulated excess with respect to each concrete social constellation that is articulated within its collective body—an excess that announces itself as if from some psychic representative of the archaic past. In this context, the imagination denotes a form of social reflection that is somehow indistinguishable from primary affective states. It is a form of collective, sensuous autocriticism in which "Ananke [*Lebensnot*, "necessity"] itself becomes the primary field of libidinal development."[81]

Stevens's subman passage thus constitutes a speculative vista, an imagination of the inner workings of the multitude's organizational processes. But, like the speculative vistas opened by each of the other modernists in this book, Stevens's is exceedingly abstract. It is not clear where Stevens's multitude is gathering, what concrete political problems it is turning over, or how its constituent members are discovering and engaging each other. Like the imagined social metabolisms of *Paterson, Enemy of the Stars*, and "Disclaimer of the Person," those of "Owl's Clover" seem to exist as a nonsite, a potential space in which the multitude's suppressed capacities for creative agency and critical judgment could be awakened. But just as with the other works I examine here, it is possible to triangulate some concrete political hopes and anxieties that the utopian cityscape of "Owl's Clover" expresses, however obliquely.

To begin with, the poem's utopian impulses are situated within the complex, collective body of "workers" who "do not rise, as Venus rose, / Out of a violet sea"—who rise, instead, "inch / By inch" (91). Thus, however counterintuitive it may seem, "Owl's Clover" operates somewhere within a broad spectrum of Marxist debates about political spontaneity and organization. Indeed, as Stevens indicates to one of his many Marxist correspondents, "Owl's Clover" was an attempt to "apply the point of view of a poet to Communism."[82] And as Harvey Teres notes, Stevens's political poetry of the 1930s represents his attempt to "revise leftist political discourse through [a] trenchant but patient and relatively sympathetic critique of orthodox Marxism."[83] It makes sense, therefore, that by the last section of "Owl's Clover," the central mind of the poet is explicitly aligned with the aporias and impostures of the Marxist central committee—a transcendent ordering structure that is, in Gramsci's terms, "complete and fully-formed only when [it] no longer exists[s]."[84] This Gramscian self-abolition of the party is rescripted at the level of the Stevensian imagination, which offers itself as a depersonalized set of ordering faculties that is functionally identical with the general intellect of the multitude—with its creative know-how and associative potential. The failure of this self-abolition at the level of the imagination thus simultaneously stages the failure of the self-abolishing vanguard party. The Gramscian ambition that a theoretico-practical elite should "give a personality to the amorphous mass element"[85] does not result in an identity of the directive will and the multitude in Stevens. Instead, it arouses the negativity and critical awareness of this "mass element," which does not wait for the promised self-abolition of the vanguard but instead brings it about actively through a collective process of unmasking and strategic realignment.

At the same time, what Stevens opposes to the "Soviet réclames" of "Owl's Clover" is not the idyll of liberal democracy or the public sphere of "civil society." "The civil fiction," Stevens writes, "the calico idea, / The Johnsonian composition, abstract man, / All are evasions" (95). Instead, Stevens's corrective to the central minds proposed by Marxism and representative democracy alike is to be found in an idea of the multitude as a self-organizing force, a collective body "flashed through / With senses chiseled on bright stone" (94). In other words, "Owl's Clover" absorbs an essentially Marxist conception of the multitude as an evolving, socially constitutive force, and then challenges doctrinaire Marxism with this social body—one whose sensuous and intellectual development occurs outside the leadership structures of parties and sects and does not depend on them for its coherence.

Stevens's emphasis on the "chiseled senses" of the multitude also speaks to his sense of the multitude as something more than it appears to be within the logics of either liberal democracy or doctrinaire Marxism. The site of the multitude's self-constitution is definitely not that of liberal democracy's communicative reason. Reason makes out very poorly in "Owl's Clover," appearing primarily as a "fatuous fire / ... only another egoist wearing a mask" (93). But doctrinaire Marxism's "scientific" education of the multitude also falls flat in Stevens's poem—or rather is resorbed as one element within the spontaneous self-educative process of the multitude itself. This spontaneous process, conducted at the level of the multitude's evolving senses, is the site of the utopian speculations of "Owl's Clover." Unlike the self-suspending, spontaneous *individuals* of much of Stevens's poetry, this spontaneous process is not the product of social benevolence, deliberate depersonalization, or even conscious intention. Indeed, it occurs involuntarily, when the leaden ticking of the industrial production process has completed one of its cycles, descended into crisis, and severed the bond between the multitude and its conventional ideas of selfhood and order.

It makes sense, then, that the critical discernment that is awakened in Stevens's collective audience is not disembodied, scientific, or disinterested. It is felt as a primordial "beat of the blood" (97) and is therefore indissociable from collective forms of affect memory. This accords nicely with the fact that what impels the multitude in Stevens's vision is not consciously held commitments but economic crisis—specifically the crisis of the Great Depression—which primordially dislocates the social body, threatening its very capacity to reproduce itself. This primordial threat sets in motion an equally primal reassessment of the multitude's life processes. What results is the kind of "universal intercourse" that Stevens describes in a letter to Hi Simons: "Cross-reflections, modifications, counter-balances, complements, giving and taking are illimitable. They make things interdependent, and their inter-dependence sustains them and gives them pleasure" (368). This idea of dynamic counterbalances perfectly expresses Stevens's vision of a social body that is mutually dependent and whose critical processes cannot be disentangled from its actual, necessitous, conditions of existence. What it makes visible is a model of spontaneity that exists only as an embedded, reciprocal social process, not as the possession of the central minds of doctrinaire Marxism, liberal democracy or even Stevens's more familiar forms of artistic exponency.

Imagined Futures

In sum, then, the spontaneous collective processes we see in "Owl's Clover" may occur in parks, around statues, and in cafés, but their *site*, their sphere of activity, is an imagined future in which the multitude's critical and creative faculties possess a socially constitutive function that is now exercised only virtually, at the level of intuition or recollection. So, even if it is possible to map out the political hopes from which "Owl's Clover" springs, the scene of their fulfillment remains highly abstract in Stevens's poem, just as it does in the other modernist works I examine in this book. This is because each of these works approaches society as a network of immensely productive minds and bodies whose capacity to direct and recombine its own energies remains, for the most part, untapped. The various concrete political remedies that these authors explore—from Williams's Social Credit and Lewis's fascism to Riding's and Stevens's models of exponency—all fail miserably in their promises to actualize these dormant energies. So, rather than stubbornly advocate for these crumbling social ideas, each of these modernists uses failures of political imagination as catalysts for unique kinds of speculative research.

The object of this research is the collective capacities of "the multitude"—a term I have used in this book to describe the immense ensemble of producers who continually re-create the material and immaterial fabric of society. This term, with all of its elisions and lacunae, efficiently expresses a modernist fantasy that all of the authors I examine share: that of a social body whose powers of creative association are suppressed—leading a merely subterranean existence—and that therefore cry out for aesthetic and political expression. Once their various political cures prove unable to recuperate and represent this collective body, the modernists I consider turn to highly abstract figurative modes, attempting to create emblems or analogies of what the multitude's creative mechanisms might look like in differently imagined social worlds.

In *Paterson*, these creative mechanisms take on the guise of an androgynetic social body, able to resorb and redistribute wealth without the time lag that Williams believes to be the source of private profit. In *Enemy of the Stars* and *The Lion and the Fox*, there is the image of a multitude that educates itself in the deceptions being practiced upon it and that therefore appropriates its own powers of social direction in a complex, regicidal ritual. In *The World and Ourselves* and "Disclaimer of the Person," we encounter social worlds in which the impersonality of commodity exchange has been replaced by mutually embedded and "civically locatable" councils. And in "Owl's Clover" we are invited to imagine a process of collective critique and sensuous development so intricate that it takes on a creative potency often imagined to be the exclusive province of individual, central minds.

What all these visions and emblems have in common is that they locate the ability to reimagine and re-create society within the horizontal networks of the multitude itself. No doubt, the starting point for all of these modernists is the heroized, individual mind merging with the multitude and expressing the fleeting intuitions of order discovered in its midst. But in each of the works I have examined, this model of individual spontaneity is exposed and debunked. What emerges in its place are a number of highly variegated models of collective spontaneity, some of which are visible only between the lines or in the conceptual fissures of these authors' texts.

In this book, I have tried to borrow, steal, or forge the tools that might make some of these collective processes visible. Doing so, I hope, will allow us to approach modernism not as a cult of individual egos but as an imagination of collective powers and associative forms that, even today, can be difficult to dare to believe in.

CONCLUSION
Beginning Again

COMING TO TERMS WITH MODERNISM'S FIGURATIONS of collective life from a contemporary standpoint can be a delicate, even an unsettling, proposition. Grandiose images of a universally self-mediating body such as Riding entertains and Stevens's image of a global, collective subconscious seem awkwardly out of step with the image of the world as a "generation by models of a real without origin or reality."[1] Much more familiar from a postmodern standpoint is a social vision such as Lyotard's, with its contention that there is no "referent"—such as production, surplus value, or, indeed, the multitude—outside the contingent play of exchange. In a work such as *Des dispositifs pulsionnels*, this gives rise to the image of capitalism as a sign system that, like other sign systems, refers only to itself, and whose tendency to exceed its own limits is, like the constant slippage of the signifier, continually mapped back onto the sign system itself:

> The *socius* ... has no limit; it folds everything into itself, returns upon itself, captures and directs the innumerable fluxes that the "economic" libidinal-political *dispositifs* branch into each other in a metamorphosis without end.[2]

A familiar postmodern narrative of agentless recalibration, to be sure. But looked at a bit more closely, is there not something uncannily *modernist* about this image of a self-mediating socius? As it turns out, Lyotard's is a social vision that relies on the same, fairly straightforward, economic propositions that guided Pound's and Williams's own amateur economics, namely, that *credit* and state-sponsored *redistribution* can perpetuate capitalist exchange by permanently deferring economic crisis.

As part of his postmodern economic system, Lyotard even revives the early twentieth-century fantasy of a "looting" faction of capitalists who, unlike good capitalists, insist on "hoarding" wealth, "tak[ing it] out of the cycles and the measures of exchanges" and "block[ing] what assures reproduction in principle."[3] Here, usury is singled out as a threat to capitalism's self-reproduction in ways that are almost identical to what we find in the Social Credit theories of Pound and Williams. Finally, in *Libidinal Economy* Lyotard develops a sexual metaphorics of credit strangely similar to what we find in Williams's *Paterson*. For Lyotard, credit represents a form of "coitus reservatus" completely different from that of economic hoarding. Credit "put[s] wealth into reserve as semen . . . while on the other hand it excites those regions (the woman) capable of providing it with energy" (217). In advancing itself and yet "postponing its fulfillment . . . it . . . create[s] a reserve or a reservoir of energy" and becomes "swollen with the inhibited energy in a cumulative process of retention" (219). As in a poem such as *Paterson*, this sexual metaphorics is meant to evoke a system of exchange whose need for cumulative expansion presents no threat to it long-term stability. Credit, as a permanent economic excitation, becomes an almost mystical force, allowing the capitalist economy to stave off crisis indefinitely.

Within the writerly culture of postmodernism, then, Lyotard resuscitates some of modernism's most crude and inaccurate fantasies, almost as if modernism testified to some historical limit or lacuna that the refinements of postmodernism continually revisit and encode. Returning to modernist texts can therefore feel strangely like revisiting spheres of historical memory that reappear in postmodern theoretical discourse only as traumatic residues or as the *Verneinungen* of the analysand. Unrefined and untimely, a poem such as *Paterson* bluntly interrogates propositions that are strangely naturalized within Lyotard's theoretical tropology. Can state redistribution really restore to the social body the kind of endless self-creative power that commodity society seems to promise? Are the divisions between employer and employee, corporate executive and textile worker, really nothing more than optical illusions, to be erased within a utopia of unrestrained consumption? Despite its very "postmodern" dreams of economic harmonization, *Paterson* rejects these propositions again and again. The primary images in the poem remain those of a social body being drained of creative powers that cannot be recuperated through consumption, an alien productive apparatus impermeable to the self-directing capacities of Paterson's inhabitants, and a collective subject with the potential to organize its own production and consumption in the absence of employers, parties, and centralized bureaucracies of all kinds. In other words, the traumatic absence, the foreclosed memory around which postmodern discourse revolves with such obsessive discretion, is precisely what texts such as *Paterson* resurrect so persistently: the image of a self-organizing network of producers, of a *multitude* capable of comprehensive self-direction and self-valorization.

In recent years, more and more theorists seem willing to stage rapprochements with such specters of the early twentieth century—the very specters that the figures of high postmodernism sought so hard to exorcise. In chapter 2, I mentioned Badiou's and Agamben's recuperation of the mass movement and the workers' councils of 1917 and 1919 as images of constituent power. More recently, in Douzinas and Žižek's edited collection *The Idea of Communism,* we find Jean-Luc Nancy writing that communism is "something which is still in front of us, which is still to be discovered, or which is still to *come*" and Gianni Vattimo advocating "weak communism," which is distinct from authoritarian communism and capitalism in that it is "an undisciplined social practice which shares with anarchism the refusal to formulate a system, a constitution, a positive 'realistic' model according to traditional political methods."[4]

Most instructive is probably the contribution of volume coeditor Slavoj Žižek, who refers to the historical present in explicitly modernist terms. After the historical defeat suffered by the idea of communism in 1989, we must do as Beckett suggests in *Worstward Ho:* "Try again. Fail again. Fail better" (210). Moreover, the subject who must begin again the project of universal emancipation is none other than the contemporary proletariat, described in Hardt and Negri's terms as all those separated from "the shared substance of our social being" (212)—in other words, those separated from the "commons," defined as "the immediately socialized forms of 'cognitive' capital, primarily language, our means of communication and education, but also the shared infrastructure of public transport, electricity, post, etc." (212). In other words, the idea of the multitude—as a "proletarianized majority" (214) divorced from its own commons—emerges in Žižek's essay as the revolutionary subject that, like the communist idea itself, "survives the failures of its realization as a spectre which returns again and again" (217).

And yet it is not merely modernism's revolutionary optimism that Žižek resurrects in his recent work, but its political anxieties and intransigencies as well. In his *In Defense of Lost Causes,* Žižek correctly identifies the workers' councils of the early twentieth century as the most robust embodiment of Negri's ideal of the "direct democracy of the 'expressive' multitude."[5] But he goes on to claim that self-government by means of workers' councils is "unable to serve as the permanent basic organizing principle of society" (376). For Žižek, such a model of transparent self-organization is far too similar to the kind of feigned "transparency" of totalitarian states, in which "the Leader is supposed to directly present the will of the people" (378) and "the Party... perceives/posits itself" as their "*Selbst-Aufhebung* (self-sublation)" (377). It is therefore wiser, Žižek claims, to abandon the entire idea of direct democracy in favor of "the resigned 'postmodern' acceptance of the fact that society is a complex network of 'subsystems,'" and that "a certain level of 'alienation' is constitutive of social life" (376–77). From this perspective, representative democracy, with its "abstract-universal formal character (one person one vote and so on)," is the wisest option, since it institutionalizes the tension between the state and the political movements of the multitude, thereby providing a "neutral ground" for the multitude's "exercise of expressive freedom" (377).

What is fascinating about this series of arguments is that it recapitulates some of the key political antinomies to which modernist authors such as Williams, Lewis, Riding, and Stevens obsessively return. The most interesting for our purposes is the relationship here between the self-organizing multitude and the figure of the party and its leadership apparatus. Historically, syndicalist councils and "left communist" groups evolved government by workers' councils as a direct *refusal* of the kinds of totalitarian bureaucracies that developed in the early twentieth century under the auspices of centralist parties and leaders. This is why so many modernists were attracted to the informal networks of communication and self-organization possessed by the multitude; they represented an elastic and self-transforming alternative to the dogmatic party-states of the early twentieth century. And yet when these same modernists try to imagine the multitude's organs of self-government as "the permanent basic organizing principle of society" it is to the image of the party, the dictator, that they tend to revert. At such moments, it is as if the multitude, as a self-organizing, self-governing complex, represents a figural limit to which modernism returns again and again: a collective body whose metabolic rhythms are almost impossible to imagine in the absence of a coordinating "center" or personality.

This figural limit—the specter of the multitude—continues to haunt contemporary social theory. It is visible in Žižek's invocation of representative democracy as a "neutral ground": a quintessentially modernist political fantasy of "impersonal" political space that Williams, Lewis, Riding, and Stevens all resurrect at various times, despite knowing that one of the characteristic features of representative democracy is, as Žižek himself points out, "the unconditional exercise of Power."[6] It is a figural limit that Alberto Toscano approaches in his description of the "legacies of commune, council and soviet," whose promise to "overcome the antinomy between organization and association" has been obscured by centralized accumulations of power.[7] It is visible in what Jacques Rancière calls the "capacity of anybody," which is documented in "moments, famous or obscure, when simple workers and ordinary men and women proved their capacity to . . . run factories, companies, administrations, armies, schools, etc. by collectivizing the power of the equality of anyone with everyone."[8]

The combination of tentativeness and speculative passion in such authors exactly mirrors the disposition of modernist authors who were, in their own moment, also grappling with the betrayals of institutional communism and the networks of human capacities that party-states failed to include and represent. How to name and describe these capacities, how to figure the human networks that bring them to life, how to imagine their development into organs of self-rule—these are questions that span the divide between the contemporary world and that of modernist literature. At their heart is the image of a self-organizing collective that is hijacked and arrested in the image of the party, the state, the leader: an ur-narrative that we have inherited from the early twentieth century and whose trauma is still, at its core, our trauma, renewing itself globally in tragically similar forms up to the present day. The imperative to leave behind mystified ideas of spontaneity—what Rancière calls the "worn-out sermons" that link the idea of spontaneity to social chaos and directionlessness—is therefore as crucial as ever. As Rancière's early work reminds us, what is often referred to as "spontaneity" actually consists of complex organizational processes that have been lost to official history: "*l'initiative créatrice des masses*," which Rancière locates in the everyday affective bonds and political seductions that occur between coworkers, neighbors, friends, family members, and strangers.[9] On this micropolitical level, the abstraction "spontaneity" reveals itself to consist of exactly the highly mediated, mutually embedded, and reciprocally correcting relational processes that a modernist such as Laura Riding documents.

Seen in this context, modernism could be viewed as an archive of political tropes and figural resources that are continually resurrected wherever questions of collective life and political representation are broached. At the same time, however, it is important to register the profound otherness of the modernists I consider. Stevens's ideas about the creative potentiality of collective life are simply irreducible to any constellation of contemporary theories about the multitude or revolutionary temporality. Though Negri's ideas about self-organization can help us understand certain aspects of "Owl's Clover," Stevens's text exceeds these formulations, teaching us how forms of negativity—skepticism, deceit, and argument—could be imagined not as fatal to the multitude but rather as essential to its immanent creative dynamism. Similarly, Williams's ideas about counterbalancing measures in the social metabolism, Lewis's investment in the "Not-Self" as a figure of political agency, and Laura Riding's ideas about the roles that subjective risk and mutual correction play in social constitution all cut against multitude theory in fundamental ways.

Throughout this book, therefore, I have tried to show how modernist texts are already a part of our most urgent political debates and, at the same time, how they supplement our historical memory with figures and relational processes too often foreclosed in contemporary theory. In doing so, I have hoped to exhibit them not as seamless works of prophetic genius—none of the works I examine is aesthetically "whole," even by modernist standards—but precisely as works that continually risk crassness, disharmony, idiosyncrasy, and embarrassment in the service of a figural ambition that is still, in some sense, our own. When Williams and Lewis imagine the multitude, respectively, as a hermaphroditic flower and as a creatively evolving insect, they commit themselves to partial and highly abstract representations of the multitude's recombinative powers. In doing so, they constantly risk indelicacy, bluntness, and aesthetic failure. But is this not precisely the kind of risk that we must allow ourselves to take in our own acts of theoretical speculation? Is it not possible that we are struggling to emerge from our own fin de siècle, with its own discursive seductions and hermetic refinements?

In such a context, the figural ambition of modernism, its faith in the ability of even the "unrefined" to borrow, invent, or reengineer the tools of social diagnosis and speculation, may be more relevant than ever. The problems of spontaneous political activity and the roles of the revolutionary group, the party, and the state have clearly not disappeared—on the contrary, they have played a central role in recent conflicts in Libya, Egypt, Tunisia, Kyrgyzstan, Greece, France, Mexico, Ecuador, Bolivia, Iraq, South Korea, Argentina, Brazil, Venezuela, and Indonesia. But to what extent are our sensory and cognitive apparatuses, not to mention our theoretical systems, equipped to register the inner dynamism, potentialities, and limits of such collective upheavals? Modernist texts could be read as attempts to train the sensorium into a sensitivity to precisely these kinds of potentialities and limits—to cultivate a sense that the individual's own potentialities and limits are impossible to gauge and recognize except in relation to such collective objectifications. If today we have ceased to have this sense, perhaps allowing ourselves to learn from modernism is just the way to begin again.

NOTES

Introduction

1. "Spontaneous," *Webster's New Universal Unabridged Dictionary*, 2nd ed., 1979.
2. "Spontaneous," *Oxford English Dictionary*, 2nd ed., 1989.
3. William Carlos Williams, *Selected Essays* (New York: Random House, 1954), 270.
4. Laura (Riding) Jackson, *The Telling* (New York: Harper & Row, 1972), 112.
5. Wyndham Lewis, *The Art of Being Ruled*, ed. Reed Way Dasenbrock (Santa Rosa, Calif.: Black Sparrow Press, 1989), 148.
6. Ibid., 131.
7. (Riding) Jackson, *The Telling*, 65.
8. Wyndham Lewis, *Creatures of Habit and Creatures of Change: Essays on Art, Literature, and Society, 1914–1956*, ed. Paul Edwards (Santa Rosa, Calif.: Black Sparrow Press, 1989), 124.
9. Williams, *Selected Essays*, 186.
10. Wallace Stevens, *The Collected Poems* (New York: Vintage Books, 1982), 310–11.
11. Daniel Belgrad, "The Ideal of Spontaneity," in *The Encyclopedia of American Cultural and Intellectual History*, ed. May Kupiec Cayton and Peter W. Williams (New York: Charles Scribner's Sons, 2001). See also Belgrad's important *The Culture of Spontaneity: Improvisation and the Arts in Postwar America* (Chicago: University of Chicago Press, 1999).
12. Though Michael Warner, in *Publics and Counterpublics* (New York: Zone Books, 2005), offers a highly compelling idea of a public as a "self-creating and self-organized" virtuality, taking shape "independently of state institutions, laws, formal frameworks of citizenship, or preexisting institutions" (68–69), his model of publicness as a way to imagine "membership by mere attention" (89) is ultimately distinct from the image of collective transformative power I trace here. Much closer is Justus Nieland's idea of an Arendtian "publicness-as-potentiality," in *Feeling Modern: The Eccentricities of Public Life* (Urbana: University of Illinois Press, 2008), 16, which "precedes all formal constitution of the public realm"; see Hannah Arendt, *The Human Condition* (Chicago: University of Chicago Press, 1958), 199, cited in Nieland, *Feeling Modern*, 15. This idea of a virtual public helps

Nieland to imagine a "feeling multitude" (248), in which we see "the potential for modernism's public world to unsettle and rearticulate itself" (5). The idea of virtuality that most informs this study is that of Michael Hardt and Antonio Negri, who in *Empire* (Cambridge, Mass.: Harvard University Press, 2000) describe virtuality as "the set of powers to act . . . that reside in the multitude" (357). Hardt and Negri differentiate their idea of virtuality from the Deleuzian–Bergsonian model in its emphasis on "the reality of the being created, its ontological weight, and the institutions that structure the world, creating necessity out of contingency" (468). Virtuality is thus conceived as a constructive capacity continually realizing itself in social life: "a power of self-valorization that exceeds itself, flows over onto the other, and, through this investment, constitutes an expansive commonality" (358).

13 Vincent Sherry and Hal Foster provide essential insight into this aspect of Lewis's work. Sherry argues that Lewis's hostility to "demotic giganticism" is part and parcel of his critique of mass political movements. Vincent Sherry, *Ezra Pound, Wyndham Lewis, and Radical Modernism* (New York: Oxford University Press, 1993), 93. Foster also correctly observes that Lewis often demonstrates a paranoiac fear of the "commutability . . . of 'the outside' and 'the inside'" and attempts to erect "'the protective shell'" of the ego as a boundary between them. Hal Foster, "Prosthetic Gods," *Modernism/Modernity* 4, no. 2 (1997): 19.

14 Lewis, *Creatures of Habit*, 120.

15 Wyndham Lewis, *Collected Poems and Plays*, ed. Alan Munton (New York: Persea Books, 1979), 197.

16 Lewis, *The Art of Being Ruled*, 149.

17 Ibid., 149, 147–48.

18 Michael Levenson and Paul Peppis contribute to this perspective on Lewis by attending to Lewis's ambivalences about the idea of the ego as a defensive shield. In *Modernism and the Fate of Individuality: Character and Novelistic Form from Conrad to Woolf* (New York: Cambridge University Press, 2005), Levenson argues that Lewis undermines the fiction of autonomous personal identity by exhibiting the ego as immured in the vagaries of bodily experience. Peppis provides another valuable contribution to this antiegoistic conception of Lewis, claiming that in *Tarr* "identity . . . is a transitory concatenation of contradictory desires and compulsions." Paul Peppis, *Literature, Politics, and the English Avant-Garde: Nation and Empire, 1901–1918* (New York: Cambridge University Press, 2000), 147.

19 Williams, *Selected Essays*, 189, 185.

20 Ibid., 56.

21 Laura Riding, *The World and Ourselves* (London: Chatto & Windus, 1938), 455, 454.

22 Ibid., 455.

23 (Riding) Jackson, *The Telling*, 132.

24 Ibid., 105.

25 Wallace Stevens, "Owl's Clover," in *Opus Posthumous*, ed. Milton J. Bates (New York: Vintage Books, 1990), 97, 98.

26 Stevens, *The Collected Poems*, 396–97.

27 Wyndham Lewis, *The Caliph's Design: Architects! Where Is Your Vortex?*, ed. Paul Edwards (Santa Barbara, Calif.: Black Sparrow Press, 1986), 119. In *Solid Objects: Modernism and the Test of Production* (Princeton, N.J.: Princeton University Press, 1998), Douglas Mao begins his chapter on Lewis by examining his concept of "the common life" in the 1910s, when Lewis stressed "the artist's ability to reform the common life" (95). But in the late 1920s and 1930s, according to Mao's incisive account, Lewis shifted his attention to the need of the common life, and in particular the world of objects, to be protected from the manipulative incursions of the subject. My account of Lewis's anxieties about political vanguards and their attempts to reengineer the multitude is thus in close dialogue with Mao's account of Lewis's epistemology and politics in the late 1920s and 1930s.
28 Williams, *Selected Essays*, 103.
29 (Riding) Jackson, *The Telling*, 148.
30 In his remarkable *Anonymous Life: Romanticism and Dispossession* (Stanford, Calif.: Stanford University Press, 2009), Jacques Khalip engages with a similar model of authorship, in which artistic subjectivity is "suspended in the gap between subject and object," its relation to others defined by "an obligation it is compelled to honor in spite of its impoverishment" (2). He relates this conception to Sharon Cameron's idea of "impersonality" as a "penetration through or a falling outside of the boundary of the particular" and Alan Liu's idea of a nonintentional creative agent, existing in a social universe where instead of a "central controller" there is an "ensemble self-organizing into the fluctuating networks of distributed dependency and feedback that we call identity." See Sharon Cameron, *Impersonality: Seven Essays* (Chicago: University of Chicago Press, 2007); and Alan Liu, "'A Forming Hand': Creativity and Destruction from Romanticism to Emergence Theory," in "Development, Creativity, and Agency: New Approaches," workshop held at the meeting of the North American Society for the Study of Romanticism, Montreal, August 16, 2005, cited in Khalip, *Anonymous Life*, 4, 16. What my study adds to these impressive accounts is a model of self-extinguishing that is active and migratory, not preaccomplished and ontologically given, "since no identity ever existed in the first place"; Cameron, *Impersonality*, xi. Moreover, I treat modernist aspirations toward depersonalization as allegories of political engagement, whose existential categories are at the same time political diagnostics, fraught with anxieties about collective spontaneity and authoritarian leadership. All the same, the forms of dispossession and impersonality that Khalip, Cameron, and Liu track all appear at some point in the works I examine, which suggests that some fascinating continuities exist between romantic and modernist models of egoic despoilment.
31 Fredric Jameson, *A Singular Modernity: Essay on the Ontology of the Present* (New York: Verso, 2002), 135.
32 Indeed, Jameson himself is one of the greatest theorists of modernism as an "inward turn," which makes his shift to the theory of depersonalization all the more noteworthy. In his *Fables of Aggression: Wyndham Lewis, the Modernist as Fascist* (Berkeley: University of California Press, 1979), he claimed that "the most influential

formal impulses of canonical modernism have been strategies of inwardness" (2). And in *The Political Unconscious: Narrative as a Socially Symbolic Act* (Ithaca, N.Y.: Cornell University Press, 1981), Jameson reads Conrad's "impressionism" as emblematic of the modernist ambition to "recode or rewrite the world and its own data in terms of perception as a semi-autonomous activity" (230). In both of these texts, modernism's private languages function as a "Utopian compensation" for capitalism's alienations and thus have a collective dimension that is important not to overlook (*The Political Unconscious*, 236). But Jameson's emphasis on depersonalization in *A Singular Modernity* does mark a shift in his theory of modernism, the implications of which are richly borne out by the authors I analyze.

33 Michael Hardt and Antonio Negri, *Multitude: War and Democracy in the Age of Empire* (New York: Penguin Press, 2004), 106, 192.

34 Ibid., 339.

35 In Antonio Negri's *Insurgencies: Constituent Power and the Modern State*, trans. Maurizia Boscagli (Minneapolis: University of Minnesota Press, 1999), it is clear that the history of the multitude is intertwined with the birth and efflorescence of capitalism. In that book, he describes "constituent power" as "the passion of the multitude" (305). In other words, the power of reciprocal counsel and collective association that gave rise to the American, French, and Russian Revolutions is "the *virtus* of the multitude" (304). In later works, he sometimes defines the multitude as a specifically post-Fordist phenomenon, defined by the transition from "industrial exploitation" to a more comprehensive "social exploitation," which implicates all forms of labor, manual and intellectual; see Antonio Negri, *Empire and Beyond*, trans. Ed Emery (Cambridge: Polity Press, 2008), 42. Because of my focus on the organizational dynamics of the multitude in the early twentieth century, I stick to Negri's early conception of the multitude, as the force of "associated living labor," which "as capital develops ... becomes a political subject" (*Insurgencies*, 306, 260–61).

36 Paolo Virno, *A Grammar of the Multitude*, trans. Isabella Bertoletti et al. (Los Angeles: Semiotext[e], 2004), 81.

37 Ibid., 64, 78.

38 Ibid., 37.

39 Alex Callinicos, "Toni Negri in Perspective," in *Debating "Empire,"* ed. Gopal Balakrishnan (London: Verso, 2003), 134.

40 Ernesto Laclau, "Can Immanence Explain Social Struggles?" *Diacritics* 31, no. 4 (2001): 7.

41 Timothy Brennan, "The Empire's New Clothes," *Critical Inquiry* 29, no. 2 (Winter 2003): 344.

42 Hardt and Negri, *Empire*, 285.

43 For an excellent analysis of the practical struggles that lay behind Negri's intellectual development, see Steve Wright, *Storming Heaven: Class Composition and Struggle in Italian Autonomist Marxism* (London: Pluto Press, 2002).

44 Antonio Negri, *Reflections on "Empire,"* trans. Ed Emery (Cambridge: Polity Press, 2008), 99.

45 Negri, *Insurgencies*, 331, 251.

46 Ibid., 260.
47 Antonio Negri, *Books for Burning: Between Civil War and Democracy in 1970s Italy*, trans. Arianna Bove et al. (London: Verso, 2005), 160, 159, 160.
48 Karl Marx, *Grundrisse*, trans. Martin Nicolaus (London: Penguin Books, 1973), 295–96, cited in Antonio Negri, *Marx beyond Marx: Lessons on the "Grundrisse,"* trans. Harry Cleaver et al. (Brooklyn: Autonomedia, 1991), 69.
49 Marx, *Grundrisse*, 325, cited in Negri, *Marx beyond Marx*, 160.
50 See Ellen Minkins Wood, "A Manifesto for Global Capitalism?" and Michael Rustin, "*Empire:* A Postmodern Theory of Revolution," both in Balakrishnan, *Debating "Empire."*
51 Georg Lukács, "The Spontaneity of the Masses and the Activity of the Party," in *Tactics and Ethics: Political Essays, 1919–1929*, trans. Michael McColgan (New York: Harper & Row, 1972), 99, 98.
52 Ibid., 99, 101.
53 Rosa Luxemburg, "Was Weiter?" in *Gesammelte Werke* (Berlin: Dietz Verlag, 1972), 2:295. Translation available in Rosa Luxemburg, "Theory and Practice," trans. David Wolff (1980), at http://marxists.org/archive/luxemburg/1910/theory-practice.
54 Rosa Luxemburg, *"The Russian Revolution" and "Leninism or Marxism?,"* trans. Bertram D. Wolf (Ann Arbor: University of Michigan Press, 1970), 91, 90.
55 Negri, *Books for Burning*, 75.
56 Ibid., 34.
57 Ibid.
58 Antonio Negri, *The Politics of Subversion*, trans. James Newell (Cambridge: Polity Press, 1989), 118.
59 Leon Trotsky, *1905*, trans. Anya Bostock (New York: Random House, 1971), 104, cited in Negri, *Insurgencies*, 273.
60 Laura Riding, *Anarchism Is Not Enough*, ed. Lisa Samuels (Berkeley: University of California Press, 2001), 92–93.
61 Harold Callender, "The Truth about the I.W.W.," *The Masses* 10, nos. 1–2 (November–December 1917): 9.
62 Jack Conroy, "A Factory Lives," *Partisan Review* 1, no. 3 (June–July 1934): 53.
63 Antonio Gramsci, *The Prison Notebooks*, trans. Quintin Hoare and Geoffrey Nowell Smith (New York: International Publishers, 1999), 198.
64 See Daniel Aaron, *Writers on the Left: Episodes in American Literary Communism* (New York: Columbia University Press, 1992); Charlotte Nekola and Paula Rabinowitz, *Writing Red: An Anthology of American Women Writers, 1930–1940* (New York: Feminist Press at the City of New York, 1987); Barbara Foley, *Radical Representations: Politics and Form in U.S. Proletarian Fiction, 1929–1941* (Durham, N.C.: Duke University Press, 1993); Carey Nelson, *Repression and Recovery: Modern American Poetry and the Politics of Cultural Memory, 1910–1945* (Madison: University of Wisconsin Press, 1989); and Carey Nelson, *Revolutionary Memory: Recovering the Poetry of the American Left* (New York: Routledge, 2001).
65 William Carlos Williams, *Paterson*, ed. Christopher MacGowan (New York: New Directions, 1992), 180.

66 Stevens, "Owl's Clover," 91.
67 See Alan Wald, *The Revolutionary Imagination: The Poetry and Politics of John Wheelwright and Sherry Mangan* (Chapel Hill: University of North Carolina Press, 1983).
68 Wyndham Lewis, *Blasting and Bombardiering* (London: Eyre & Spottiswoode, 1937), 85.
69 Ezra Pound, *The Cantos* (New York: New Directions, 1979), 61.
70 I make these distinctions not to police a boundary between a supposedly apolitical modernism and the politically revolutionary literatures of the early twentieth century. This boundary simply does not exist, as Wald's analyses of revolutionary modernists John Wheelwright and Sherry Mangan, and Michael Thurston's analyses of Edwin Rolfe, Langston Hughes, Ezra Pound, and Muriel Rukeyser so eloquently attest. Instead, I am attempting to account for a tendency within this larger tradition of politically dynamic twentieth-century literature—one whose authors, unlike Wheelwright, Mangan, Rolfe, Hughes, and Rukeyser, never espoused Marxist ideas, and yet that continually revisits the mass revolutionary phenomena toward which Marxist theory is oriented. There is something strange and unique about such a wavering imaginative relationship to the multitude, and to my mind it has much to teach us about what Robert Shulman calls "the panorama of left creative work." Robert Shulman, *The Power of Political Art: The 1930s Literary Left Reconsidered* (Chapel Hill: University of North Carolina Press, 2000), 15. See Wald, *The Revolutionary Imagination;* and Michael Thurston, *Making Something Happen: American Political Poetry between the World Wars* (Chapel Hill: University of North Carolina Press, 2001).
71 (Riding) Jackson, *The Telling*, 155.
72 Jules Romains, "To the Multitude Which Is Here," *Contemporary French Poetry*, ed. and trans. Jethro Bithell (London: Walter Scott, 1912), 164.
73 D. Burliuk et al., "A Slap in the Face of Public Taste," *Russian Futurism through Its Manifestoes, 1912–1928*, ed. and trans. Anna Lawton and Herbert Eagle (Ithaca, N.Y.: Cornell University Press, 1988), 51.
74 William Carlos Williams, *Selected Letters*, ed. John C. Thirwall (New York: New Directions, 1957), 158.
75 Theodor W. Adorno, *Aesthetic Theory*, trans. Robert Hullot-Kentor (Minneapolis: University of Minnesota Press, 1997), 115.
76 As Adorno's extremely sensitive writings on surrealism make clear, his remarks here about automatic writing refer to a heuristic schema of automaticity, rather than to surrealist practice as a whole. In fact, in "Looking Back on Surrealism" Adorno combats the received idea that surrealist works should be approached as purely automatic documents. Unlike the automaticity of the dream, in which the agency of the subject is completely effaced, the surrealist work "directs its energy toward its own self-annihilation" and thus exhibits a form of "spontaneity... [that] is by no means spontaneous," since immense effort is required "to master the involuntary expression that occurs through these efforts." Theodor W. Adorno, *Notes to Literature* (New York: Columbia University Press, 1992), 1:87. Through this pro-

cess, which discovers libidinal investments in historical objects, the "subject's innermost core becomes aware that it is something external, an imitation of something social and historical" (1:87, 89).

77 Herbert Marcuse, *The Aesthetic Dimension: Toward a Critique of Marxist Aesthetics* (Boston: Beacon Press, 1978), 51–52.
78 Ibid., 51.
79 Herbert Marcuse, *The New Left and the 1960s*, ed. Douglas Kellner (New York: Routledge, 2005), 126.
80 Herbert Marcuse, *Counterrevolution and Revolt* (Boston: Beacon Press, 1972), 42, 45.
81 Marcuse, *The Aesthetic Dimension*, 52.
82 Ibid., 50.
83 Adorno, *Aesthetic Theory*, 108.
84 Michael Hardt and Antonio Negri, *Commonwealth* (Cambridge, Mass.: Harvard University Press, 2009), 97.
85 Ibid., 99.
86 Antonio Negri, *The Savage Anomaly*, trans. Michael Hardt (Minneapolis: University of Minnesota Press, 2008), 21.
87 See Wright, *Storming Heaven*, esp. 168–71 and 216–23.
88 Antonio Negri, *Subversive Spinoza: (Un)contemporary Variation*, trans. Timothy S. Murphy et al. (Manchester: Manchester University Press, 2004), 83–84.
89 Michael Hardt and Antonio Negri, *Labor of Dionysus: A Critique of the State-Form* (Minneapolis: University of Minnesota Press, 1994), 61–62.
90 Negri, *Subversive Spinoza*, 47.
91 Negri, *The Savage Anomaly*, 75, 55.
92 Baruch Spinoza, *Complete Works*, trans. Samuel Shirley (Indianapolis: Hackett, 2002), 533.
93 Étienne Balibar, *Masses, Classes, Ideas: Studies on Politics and Philosophy before and after Marx*, trans. James Swenson (New York: Routledge, 1994), 23.
94 Negri's analysis of Machiavelli in *Insurgencies* stresses the multitude's role as a force of constituent power; Negri dwells on Machiavelli's articulation in the *Discourses* of a "very radical image of a people capable of truth, equality, organized in its rallies, ethically sustained by civil religion, capable of arms and victory" (69). But the status of the multitude as a perpetual, functional limit to tyranny is never far away from such formulations. The multitude is involved in "the relations between magistratures and . . . counterpowers" and "oppose[s] tyrannical dominion and corruption, the church and fortune" (80) in a host of ways, many of which evoke Balibar's image of institutional mediation. No doubt this is why, in developing his own concept of the multitude, Negri draws on Spinoza's cosmic and autochthonous models of collective organization more than on those of Machiavelli.
95 Ibid., 293.
96 Antonio Negri, *Time for Revolution*, trans. Matteo Mandarini (New York: Continuum, 2003), 103.
97 Williams, *Selected Essays*, 178, 192.

98 Ibid., 186.
99 Ibid., 184.
100 See Reed Way Dasenbrock, "Wyndham Lewis's Fascist Imagination and the Fiction of Paranoia," in *Fascism, Aesthetics, and Culture*, ed. Richard J. Golsan (Hanover, N.H.: University Press of New England, 1992).
101 Lewis, *Collected Poems and Plays*, 164.
102 Wyndham Lewis, "Physics of the Not-Self," in *Collected Poems and Plays*, 203.
103 Lewis, *The Art of Being Ruled*, 316.
104 Wyndham Lewis, *The Lion and the Fox: The Rôle of the Hero in the Plays of Shakespeare* (London: Methuen, 1966), 132.
105 Riding, *The World and Ourselves*, 455.
106 (Riding) Jackson, *The Telling*, 107.
107 Wallace Stevens, *Letters*, ed. Holly Stevens (Berkeley: University of California Press, 1981), 295.
108 Stevens, "Owl's Clover," 96.
109 Hardt and Negri, *Empire*, 357.
110 Sean McCann, *A Pinnacle of Feeling: American Literature and Presidential Government* (Princeton, N.J.: Princeton University Press, 2008), 24.
111 Pericles Lewis, *Modernism, Nationalism, and the Novel* (New York: Cambridge University Press, 2000), 11.
112 Jessica Berman, *Modernist Fiction, Cosmopolitanism, and the Politics of Community* (New York: Cambridge University Press, 2001), 15.
113 Rebecca Walkowitz, *Cosmopolitan Style: Modernism beyond the Nation* (New York: Columbia University Press, 2006), 27.
114 Berman, *Modernist Fiction*, 18.
115 Michael Tratner, *Modernism and Mass Politics: Joyce, Woolf, Eliot, Yeats* (Stanford, Calif.: Stanford University Press, 1995), 9.
116 Nicholas Brown, *Utopian Generations: The Political Horizon of Twentieth-Century Literature* (Princeton, N.J.: Princeton University Press, 2005), 127.
117 Nieland, *Feeling Modern*, 19.
118 See Douglas Mao and Rebecca Walkowitz, "The New Modernist Studies," *PMLA* 123, no. 3 (2008): 737–48.
119 Michael Szalay, *New Deal Modernism: American Literature and the Invention of the Welfare State* (Durham, N.C.: Duke University Press, 2001), 126.
120 Another important tradition of thought addressing modernism's relationship to mass culture is defined by works such as the following: Alissa G. Karl, *Modernism and Marketplace: Literary Culture and Consumer Capitalism in Rhys, Woolf, Stein, and Nella Larsen* (New York: Routledge, 2008); John Xiros Cooper, *Modernism and the Culture of Market Society* (New York: Cambridge University Press, 2004); Mark S. Morrisson, *The Public Face of Modernism: Little Magazines, Audiences, and Reception, 1905–1920* (Madison: University of Wisconsin Press, 2001); Lawrence Rainey, *Institutions of Modernism: Literary Elites and Public Culture* (New Haven, Conn.: Yale University Press, 1998); and Stephen Watt and Kevin J. H. Dettmar, *Marketing Modernisms: Self-Promotion, Canonization, Rereading* (Ann Arbor: University

of Michigan Press, 1996). I do not engage closely with this scholarly tradition, but the continuities between these examinations of modernism's crowds, publics, and masses and my analysis of modernism's multitudes are greater than the differences, as Rod Rosenquist's emphasis on late modernism's "desire to see art more firmly integrated into the praxis of life" richly suggests. Rod Rosenquist, *Modernism, the Market, and the Institution of the New* (New York: Cambridge University Press, 2009), 28.

121 Jeffrey T. Schnapp, "Mob Porn," in *Crowds*, ed. Jeffrey T. Schnapp and Matthew Tiews (Stanford, Calif.: Stanford University Press, 2006), 16.

122 Jobst Welge, "Far from the Crowd: Individuation, Solitude, and 'Society' in the Western Imagination," in Schnapp and Tiews, *Crowds*, 348, 336.

123 Negri, *Reflections on "Empire,"* 117.

124 Michael Hardt, "Bathing in the Multitude," in Schnapp and Tiews, *Crowds*, 40, 39.

125 See Ann L. Ardis, *Modernism and Cultural Conflict, 1880–1922* (New York: Cambridge University Press, 2002); Tyrus Miller, *Late Modernism: Politics, Fiction, and the Arts between the World Wars* (Berkeley: University of California Press, 1999); and Andreas Huyssen, *After the Great Divide: Modernism, Mass Culture, Postmodernism* (Bloomington: Indiana University Press, 1986).

126 Mary Esteve, *The Aesthetics and Politics of the Crowd in American Literature* (New York: Cambridge University Press, 2003), 26, 20.

127 One excellent example of the dynamic debates surrounding centralization and decentralization today is the essay collection *Lenin Reloaded: Toward a Politics of Truth*, edited by Sebastian Budgen, Stathis Kouvelakis, and Slavoj Žižek (Durham, N.C.: Duke University Press, 2007), in which thinkers suspicious of political centralization, such as Jameson and Negri, appear alongside democratic centralist thinkers such as Alan Shandro and Alex Callinicos. In this discursive context, questions of spontaneity and vanguardism are addressed according to the same problematic I use to analyze literary modernism. Indeed, in his contribution to the collection, Jameson describes the party and the leader as "allegories of the collective," which would ideally subsist as "merely formal point[s] without content"— exactly the formula of the modernist imagination whose ambivalences I recover in this book. Fredric Jameson, "Lenin and Revisionism," in Budgen et al., *Lenin Reloaded*, 67, 72. Similarly, the critique of Ernesto Laclau's populism that Slavoj Žižek levels in the volume, and that he expands upon in *In Defense of Lost Causes*, has a very modernist question at its root, namely, how can an inclusive and ecumenical collective—such as the term "populism" denotes—resist what appears to be its ineluctable tendency: to recentralize its political commitments around strong leadership figures who promise to combat an imaginary enemy that "is externalized or reified into a positive ontological entity... whose annihilation would restore balance and justice"? Slavoj Žižek, "A Leninist Gesture Today: Against the Populist Temptation," in Budgen et al., *Lenin Reloaded*, 81. What I demonstrate in this book is that such anxieties about leadership and collective action as are evinced by today's most intellectually ambitious political theory rescript a problematic that modernist authors approached with at least as much urgency in their

own historical moment. See Ernesto Laclau, *On Populist Reason* (London: Verso, 2005); and Slavoj Žižek, *In Defense of Lost Causes* (London: Verso, 2008).

1. Rising from Nowhere

1. William Carlos Williams, *Kora in Hell: Improvisations*, in *Imaginations*, ed. Webster Scott (New York: New Directions, 1971), 14.
2. William Carlos Williams, *I Wanted to Write a Poem: The Autobiography of the Works of a Poet* (New York: New Directions, 1977), 27.
3. William Carlos Williams, *Autobiography* (New York: New Directions, 1951), 158.
4. Ibid.
5. Williams, *I Wanted to Write a Poem*, 27.
6. Peter Kropotkin, *The Conquest of Bread, and Other Writings*, ed. Marshall Shatz (New York: Cambridge University Press, 1995), 178.
7. Ibid., 233.
8. Williams was attracted to the IWW because it represented a large-scale system of political organization whose power structure was located strictly in self-governing local councils of producers. In "Against the Weather," Williams makes it clear that it is such a balance of "joint action" and political autonomy that constitutes his political ideal; in William Carlos Williams, *Selected Essays* (New York: Random House, 1954), 209. In this essay, Williams condemns party politicians who "seek to impose a fixed order from without" (211) but does not celebrate pure individualism as an alternative. Instead, he celebrates models of council governance, such as that of medieval Norway, and insists that "the real character of the people is not toward dispersion except as a temporary phase for the gathering of power, but to unite. To form a union" (209). Williams repeats the IWW's motto, "One Big Union" in *The Great American Novel*, using it as an image of aesthetic wholeness. And in a 1939 interview with the *Partisan Review*, he eulogizes the founder of the IWW: "Long live in America the memory of Eugene Debs!"; "The Situation in American Writing," *Partisan Review* 4, no. 4 (Summer 1939): 44.
9. In *The Great American Novel*, Williams mentions Kropotkin in an imaginary dialogue about the relationship of art and politics. Williams responds to the questions of an incredulous interlocutor: "Do you mean to say that art does any WORK?—Yes. Do you mean—? Revolution. Russia. Kropotkin. Farm, Factory and Field.—CRRRRRRASH.—Down comes the world. There you are gentlemen, I am an artist" (*Imaginations*, 170). Williams's point here is not that art is literally capable of overturning society but that the *work* of verbal destruction and recombination effected by vital literary creations is governed by the same logic as forms of destruction and recombination that occur within the political sphere. Williams names Kropotkin in this connection—rather than, say, Lenin or Rosa Luxemburg—because Kropotkin's *The Conquest of Bread* explains, industry by industry, exactly how the world of work could be reorganized by spontaneously self-organizing associations of producers. For Williams, the spontaneous association of words that occurs in his literary works has the same structure as this kind of political spontaneity. Organization does not come from without to impress itself upon the raw material of language.

Instead, the work of organization is immanent to the work of production: organization and production form a creative continuum. This is why in the political realm only a vision such as Kropotkin's, in which workers are simultaneously the organizers of the conditions of work, satisfies Williams's model of spontaneous association.

10 William Carlos Williams, *A Recognizable Image: William Carlos Williams on Art and Artists*, ed. Bram Dijkstra (New York: New Directions, 1978), 112.
11 Michael Hardt and Antonio Negri, *Empire* (Cambridge, Mass.: Harvard University Press, 2000), 358.
12 Antonio Negri, *Books for Burning: Between Civil War and Democracy in 1970s Italy*, trans. Arianna Bove et al. (London: Verso, 2005), 254.
13 Theodor Adorno, *Minima Moralia: Reflections from Damaged Life*, trans. E. F. N. Jephcott (London: Verso, 2000), 231.
14 Ron Loewinsohn provides an extremely helpful analysis of this phenomenological dimension of Williams's poem. He describes Williams's fixed perceptual array as "the patterns of relation and value established by science, religion, and philosophy—even art—[which] cast a spell over us... sanctified by time, they appear to us as part of the nature of things, accepted without question." Williams's poetic method therefore involves deliberately "clearing the world not only of the values he inherits from preceding artists, scientists, and philosophers, but also of *his own* preceding perceptions. Ron Loewinsohn, "'Fools Have Big Wombs': William Carlos Williams' *Kora in Hell*," *Essays in Literature* 4, no. 2 (Fall 1977): 225–26.
15 "Kora" is a variant of "Kore," another name for the Greek goddess Persephone. As Audrey T. Rodgers notes, "Kora," which literally means "maiden," represents a condition of "elemental virginity," which Williams sometimes associates with a "nourishing, inspirational life force within the poet" and sometimes with "the real world," whose innocence and creative possibilities have been destroyed by World War I. Audrey T. Rodgers, "'Spring and All': The Myth of Kore in the Poetry of William Carlos Williams," *Mosaic: A Journal for the Interdisciplinary Study of Literature* 14, no. 1 (Winter 1981): 96, 100, 91.
16 Ron Loewinsohn describes this paradox in terms of "planned spontaneity"—something he associates with Marcel Duchamp, who, as Williams notes in *Kora in Hell*, "decides" to set out on spontaneous searches for his famous found objects. Loewinsohn, "'Fools Have Big Wombs,'" 224.
17 Jesse D. Green's deft analysis of *Kora in Hell* also points in this direction. He describes the passage in question as "a kind of dramatic monologue spoken... to the poet himself by his own imagination." The protagonists of the drama are like two poles of the artist's own subjectivity. On one hand, there is "egocentric principle," or the "self as the arbiter of the information it receives of the world," and on the other, "the radically autonomous powers of the imagination," instinct with Williams's "direct sense of things." Jesse D. Green, "Williams' *Kora in Hell:* The Opening of the Poem as 'Field of Action,'" *Contemporary Literature* 13, no. 3 (Summer, 1972): 311, 313.
18 Some noteworthy criticism has addressed this phenomenological schism in *Kora in Hell*. Mitchum Huehls, for example, notes that "by the time Williams' apprehension

of the thing has been articulated and has reached the reader, the empirically determined, ontological reality of the thing has been left far behind." Mitchum Huehls, "Reconceiving Perceiving: William Carlos Williams' World-Making Words of 'Kora in Hell: Improvisations,'" *Paideuma: Studies in American and British Modernist Poetry* 32, nos. 1–3 (Spring–Winter 2003), 58. Similarly, Thomas P. Joswick writes that the poet of *Kora in Hell* "must... come to see the abstract forms of the mind and the sensual immediacy of experience as necessary antagonists that draw nearer by each reciprocally limiting and displacing the other." This means that "the Dionysian plenitude" Williams evokes through the underground poet "cannot achieve real completeness by itself nor by the direct sensual immersion into it by a subject. It lacks, as Lukács might say, 'the form of totality for itself as a whole.'... In short, the presence of the immediate lacks the power of re-presentation, and only in re-presentation will the dissonance of a flowering and decaying world take on life *and* meaning." Thomas P. Joswick, "Beginning with Loss: The Poetics of William Carlos Williams's *Kora in Hell: Improvisations*," *Texas Studies in Literature and Language* 19 (1977): 109, 107. Joswick's provocative invocation of Lukács suggests that the problems of perceptual representation he analyzes might simultaneously be problems of political representation, that the perceptual dichotomy between sensual immersion and cognitive representation in *Kora in Hell* might encode another dichotomy involving political totalities and the subjects debarred from active, conscious participation in them. Joswick does not pursue such a line of argument, but, according to my analysis, it is precisely such a simultaneous existence of political and phenomenological divisions that is at stake in *Kora in Hell*'s representation of the crude, promiscuous, underground poetic faculty and the haughty, isolated poetic faculty.

19 Christine Holbo is one critic who focuses rewardingly on the social divisions that this phenomenological split encodes. She argues that in contrast to *Kora in Hell*'s "opening invocation of poetic fastidiousness," its "final notion of aesthetics is a poetics of 'the ruck,' of dirt and sexuality, brokenness and abortion; one which redeems by renouncing, not the world, but the ideal of a pure and separate sphere of avant-garde poetics." Christine Holbo, "Contraception as Revelation: Objectivity, Authority, and the Politics of Fertility in *Kora in Hell*," *William Carlos Williams Review* 24, no. 1 (Spring 1998): 32, 23.

20 Theodor W. Adorno, *Aesthetic Theory*, trans. Robert Hullot-Kentor (Minneapolis: University of Minnesota Press, 1997), 110.

21 In ironizing "the countless composers of music that can only be understood with the aid of diagrams," Adorno writes: "The more urgently the structural arrangements insist through their own shape on their own necessity," the more the composer "sinks to the level of the ephemeral and the arbitrary, even though the rules he is confronted with are administrative prescriptions." Theodor W. Adorno, *Quasi una fantasia*, trans. Rodney Livingstone (London: Verso, 1992), 277.

22 Ibid., 319.

23 Theodor W. Adorno, *Essays on Music*, ed. Richard Leppert, trans. Susan H. Gillespie (Berkeley: University of California Press, 2002), 639.

24 Ibid.
25 Adorno, *Aesthetic Theory*, 115, 184.
26 Williams, *Autobiography*, 158.
27 Fredric Jameson, *The Modernist Papers* (London: Verso, 2007), 14, 27.
28 Ibid., 42.
29 Michael Tratner, *Deficits and Desires: Economics and Sexuality in Twentieth-Century Literature* (Stanford, Calif.: Stanford University Press, 2001), 128.
30 Ibid., 171, 172.
31 Ibid., 132.
32 Paolo Virno, *A Grammar of the Multitude*, trans. Isabella Bertoletti et al. (Los Angeles: Semiotext[e], 2004), 65.
33 William Carlos Williams, *Paterson*, ed. Christopher MacGowan (New York: New Directions, 1992), 47.
34 William Carlos Williams, "A Social Diagnosis for Surgery," *New Democracy* 6 (April 1936): 27.
35 Ibid., 26.
36 Ibid.
37 Williams, *A Recognizable Image*, 114.
38 Critics who focus on Williams's relationship to Social Credit tend to emphasize that the economic doctrine promises a social cure without revolutionary upheaval or mass mobilization of any kind. Thus Bob Johnson indicates that Williams was attracted to Social Credit as "a radical reformist solution premised on the democratization of credit rather than the overthrow of capitalism itself." Bob Johnson, "'A Whole Synthesis of His Time': Political Ideology and Cultural Politics in the Writing of Williams Carlos Williams," *American Quarterly* 54, no. 2 (June 2002): 194. Similarly, Richard Sieburth notes Social Credit's difference from Marxist economics. Sieburth correctly argues that Social Credit's "gap or threatening lack with capitalism" is "akin, but not identical to Marx's notion of surplus value." Richard Sieburth, "In Pound We Trust: The Economy of Poetry/The Poetry of Economics," *Critical Inquiry* 14, no. 1 (Autumn 1987): 159. This is because, as Hugh Kenner argues in *The Pound Era* (Berkeley: University of California Press, 1973), followers of Social Credit did not "suppose[ ] that the discrepancy between costs and wages was explained by profits" (34). Kenner notes that for the founder of Social Credit theory, C. H. Douglas, profit represents fair payment apportioned to the "man who founds or organizes or supervises" (311). But Silvio Gesell, whom Williams was reading in the 1940s, and whose economic system is incomparably more sophisticated than Douglas's, literally begins his book *The Natural Economic Order*, trans. Philip Pye (London: Peter Owen, 1958) by considering the relation of "surplus value"—which he defines as the "unearned income" of "the capitalist"—to the problem of interest, which conventional Social Credit theorists isolate from the problem of profit (27, 36). Gesell is far more radical in discerning that "the common or collective right to the whole proceeds of labour... implies the total abolition of all unearned income, i.e. interest and rent" (38–39). *Paterson*'s images of spontaneous reinvestment therefore exist in an uneasy tension between reform-oriented and anticapitalist economic ideologies.

39 Edward Bell stresses this idea of a "spontaneous integration of local, regional, national, and international economic activity" as well as C. H. Douglas's more general philosophy of "free and spontaneous association" in *Social Classes and Social Credit in Alberta* (Quebec City: McGill-Queens University Press, 1993), 48.

40 Brian A. Bremen helps make clear the comprehensive importance of Social Credit to Williams in *William Carlos Williams and the Diagnostics of Culture* (New York: Oxford University Press, 1993). He shows that Social Credit was more than a recondite economic ideology for Williams; it "became the 'gist' of Williams's notion of culture: 'a whole way of life'" analogous to what Bremen, following Bourdieu, calls "the habitus" (187).

41 This accords well with Michael André Bernstein's observation that "the proper direction for a modern epic, in Williams's eyes, is a total relativization of the poem's assertive authority; emotionally and structurally the text must present itself as a 'testing,' as an exploration which is always willing to recognize false directions and to adjust its expectations accordingly." Michael André Bernstein, *The Tale of the Tribe: Ezra Pound and the Modern Verse Epic* (Princeton, N.J.: Princeton University Press, 1980), 222. This idea of *Paterson* as a dynamic series of failures and testing operations has been given a great deal of nuance in Williams criticism. Bernard Duffey, for example, argues in *A Poetry of Presence: The Writing of William Carlos Williams* (Madison: University of Wisconsin Press, 1986) that "the poet debarred from resolving his work in a single focus enacts his structure instead by finding, leaving, and refinding its shaping principle" (74). Similarly, Fredric Jameson begins his essay on *Paterson* by referring to its modernist "aesthetics of failure"; see Jameson, *The Modernist Papers*, 3.

42 Gesell, for example, likens the current state of credit to an "unreliable canal, sometimes silted up and sometimes frozen over" in *The Natural Economic Order*, 215; Douglas compares it to a thin stream of water, insufficient to power the mill of consumption, in *The Monopoly of Credit* (London: Eyre & Spottiswoode, 1937), 43; and Ezra Pound, in *ABC of Economics* (London: Faber & Faber, 1933), sees it as a form of "constipation" unable to respond to the massive "raw supply" of industrial labor, which he evokes in the image of a waterfall: "the simple device of letting water run down hill through a pipe onto a turbine" (83, 101).

43 George Zabriskie, "The Geography of 'Paterson,'" *Perspective* 6 (Autumn 1953): 208, cited in Benjamin Sankey, *A Companion to William Carlos Williams's "Paterson"* (Berkeley: University of California Press, 1971), 35.

44 John Beck provides an excellent critique of Social Credit in *Writing the Radical Center: William Carlos Williams, John Dewey, and American Cultural Politics* (Albany: State University of New York Press, 2001). He points out that it assumes "the social and economic framework need not be dismantled, simply repaired. Initiative is thus removed from the political to the administrative sphere, with the emphasis placed on making changes without presenting a thoroughgoing analysis of class and power structures. Financial credit, as the dysfunctional element, becomes the enemy, rather than the capitalist system that creates the institution in the first place" (147).

45 Sieburth makes the excellent point that Pound focuses "almost exclusively on issues of monetary representation, inscription, and circulation... while virtually bracketing the question of economic *production*." Sieburth, "In Pound We Trust," 166. This allows Pound to conflate employer and employee into an imagined continuity of interest, represented, in the abstract, by what he calls "producers" or "makers." This maneuver is most immediately traceable to Gesell's idea that there exists a "natural affinity" between employer and employee—that "money... intervene[s] between consumer and producer, between workman and workgiver, separating those who were naturally destined to unite and exploiting the embarrassments so arising"; *The Natural Economic Order*, 334. But Pound fails to articulate even the very basic relationship—which Gesell himself establishes with remarkable lucidity—between the owner's interest-bearing capital and the surplus value he or she must extract from workers in order to reconstitute this capital. Pound is thus reduced to vague generalizations about "a certain part of the credit-slips received by the *entrepreneur*" being "wormed down a sort of tube" and "flow[ing] continually down into the ground, down into somebody's pocket"; *ABC of Economics*, 83–84. For Williams, by contrast, usury does not insinuate itself into an idyllic fraternity of employer and employee. His central poetic fantasies, then, do not revolve around the image of strongmen capable of eradicating usurers.

46 Antonio Negri, *Time for Revolution*, trans. Matteo Mandarini (New York: Continuum, 2003), 95.

47 Antonio Negri, *Books for Burning: Between Civil War and Democracy in 1970s Italy*, trans. Arianna Bove et al. (London: Verso, 2005), 219.

48 Ibid., 47.

49 Karl Marx, *Grundrisse*, trans. Martin Nicolaus (London: Penguin Books, 1973), 153.

50 Williams, *Autobiography*, 385.

51 William Carlos Williams, *In the American Grain* (New York: New Directions, 1933), 195.

52 Buffalo manuscript, cited in Sankey, *A Companion to William Carlos Williams's "Paterson,"* 43.

53 To understand Williams's constant evocation of "primitive" social violence as a permanent principle of *psychic life*, it helps to keep in mind Jason Read's excellent exposition, in *The Micro-Politics of Capital: Marx and the Prehistory of the Present* (Albany: State University of New York Press, 2003), of primitive accumulation as a continuous process. The "normalization" of primitive accumulation, which is "constitutive of the regularity and functioning of the capitalist mode of production is actualized not only at the levels of laws or institutions but also at the level of subjectivity," that is, at the level of "knowledges, affects, and desires" (64, 65). Read does not develop this observation in a psychoanalytic direction, but it is easy to see how for Williams this occult, yet omnipresent and socially regenerative, element of primal violence is inscribed at the psychic level as a violent divorce—one that is similarly normalized at the level of desire and affect.

54 Marx, *Grundrisse*, 504.

55 Werner Bonefeld, "The Permanence of Primitive Accumulation: Commodity Fetishism and Social Constitution," *The Commoner* 2 (September 2001): 1, 7, 5.
56 Read, *The Micro-Politics of Capital*, 28.
57 Marx, *Grundrisse*, 504.
58 Read, *The Micro-Politics of Capital*, 25.
59 Michael Hardt and Antonio Negri, *Commonwealth* (Cambridge, Mass.: Harvard University Press, 2009), 138.
60 Antonio Negri, *Marx beyond Marx: Lessons on the "Grundrisse,"* trans. Harry Cleaver et al. (Brooklyn: Autonomedia, 1991), 70.
61 Michael Hardt and Antonio Negri, *Labor of Dionysus: A Critique of the State-Form* (Minneapolis: University of Minnesota Press, 1994), 47.
62 Negri, *Marx beyond Marx*, 184, 183.
63 Antonio Negri, *The Politics of Subversion*, trans. James Newell (Cambridge: Polity Press, 1989), 207, 87.
64 Negri, *Marx beyond Marx*, 162.
65 At such moments, Williams really does seem eager to "eradicate and denounce the inauthenticity of mass culture," as Carla Billitteri argues. In one of the best analyses of the status of the crowd in *Paterson*, Billitteri claims that "*Paterson* is a poetic structure meant to contain the mob crowding the 'debased city' of Paterson" and that Williams symbolically "ravages" Paterson "in what can be read as an apocalyptic gesture of containment through destruction." In my analysis, I focus on Williams's only partially legible desire for a self-containing multitude, one capable of destroying and remaking itself processually, but Billitteri's "distracted *and* destructive" crowd certainly appears more regularly and more noisily in *Paterson* than the multitude I detect between the lines of Williams's epic. See Carla Billitteri, "William Carlos Williams and the Politics of Form," *Journal of Modern Literature* 30, no. 2 (Winter 2007): 59, 58, 59.
66 William Carlos Williams and Kenneth Burke, *The Humane Particulars: The Collected Letters of William Carlos Williams and Kenneth Burke*, ed. James H. East (Columbia: University of South Carolina Press, 2003), 115.
67 Wilhelm Reich, *The Discovery of the Orgone*, vol. 1, *The Function of the Orgasm: Sex-Economic Problems of Biological Energy*, trans. Theodore P. Wolfe (New York: Orgone Institute Press, 1942), xxv. Confusingly enough, the book Williams was reading while he wrote *Paterson* was neither Reich's 1927 *Die Funktion des Orgasmus* nor an English translation of it. In fact, Reich's 1927 *Die Funktion des Orgasmus* was not the source for the English book *The Function of the Orgasm* that appeared in 1942; the two texts, while exploring some similar themes, are actually unrelated. The source from which Theodore P. Wolfe did translate was a manuscript originally titled "Das Lebendige," which was previously unpublished and would not appear in the German until well after the English translation appeared. Although Williams did have some proficiency in the German language, he was not reading the 1927 *Die Funktion des Orgasmus* (which was not published in an English translation until 1980 under the title *Genitality in the Theory and*

Therapy of Neuroses); he was reading the book cited above, which at the time had no published German-language source text.
68 Williams and Burke, *The Humane Particulars*, 114.
69 Ibid., 117.
70 Brian A. Bremen notes that "Williams' 'psychology' takes its view from the pre-oedipal stages of nurturing and separation" and holds as an ideal the "mutual recognition between equal subjects... that sustains the tension between contradictory forces" of "identity and difference." Williams's model of pre-oedipal unrelief, then, possesses a political significance according to which the "relieving of tensions" corresponds to a "structure of domination" based on the repudiation of the feminine as the embodiment of lack. Bremen, *William Carlos Williams*, 53, 58, 54, 56, 197. On the other hand, "maintaining those tensions" (ibid.) corresponds to a form of intersubjectivity that, in my analysis, is coextensive with Williams's desideratum: a spontaneously self-mediating socioeconomic body. The centrality of the component drives, and specifically of a "constantly unsatiated state of arousal"—see Shane Rhodes, "Matrimony of the Sign: The Idea and the Thing in William Carlos Williams's *Paterson*," *Sagetrieb* 18, nos. 2–3 (2002): 244—to this political model is difficult to overestimate.
71 Williams, *Autobiography*, 221.
72 Ibid., 224.
73 Gilles Deleuze and Félix Guattari, *Anti-Oedipus: Capitalism and Schizophrenia*, trans. Robert Hurley et al. (Minneapolis: University of Minnesota Press, 1983), 118.
74 Elizabeth Grosz, "A Thousand Tiny Sexes: Feminism and Rhizomatics," *Topoi* 12 (1993): 171.
75 Teresa de Lauretis, *The Practice of Love: Lesbian Sexuality and Perverse Desire* (Bloomington: Indiana University Press, 1994), xix.
76 Williams, *Autobiography*, 224.
77 Sandra Gilbert and Susan Gubar, *No Man's Land: The Place of the Woman Writer in the Twentieth Century* (New Haven, Conn.: Yale University Press, 1988), 1:48.
78 Cristina Giorcelli, "The King's Whore: Debasement and Transcendence of Woman in Williams' Late Poetry," in *The Rhetoric of Love in the Collected Poems of William Carlos Williams*, ed. Cristina Giorcelli and Maria Anita Stefanelli (Rome: Edizioni Associate, 1993), 262.
79 Ibid., 250, 260.
80 Luce Irigaray, *Speculum of the Other Woman*, trans. Gillian C. Gill (Ithaca, N.Y.: Cornell University Press, 1994), 22.
81 Luce Irigaray, *This Sex Which Is Not One*, trans. Catherine Porter with Carolyn Burke (Ithaca, N.Y.: Cornell University Press, 1985), 176.
82 In an essay titled "Woman as Operator," Williams writes, "The swooning voluptuousness of woman that she enjoys at the apex of yielding comes out in the end, for her, as a celebration of philosophic reality—whereas for man it turns up as a confession of philosophic nonentity." William Carlos Williams, "Woman as Operator," in *Women: A Collection of Artists and Writers* (New York: Samuel M. Koontz

Editions, 1948), unpaginated. Here we have a good example of that orgasmic "summatization" in which Williams imagines a sex-economic resynthesis of the social totality, but one that is denied to phallic sexuality and is available only to woman, who is the "universal solvent" (ibid.)—an indispensable function for a poet obsessed with libidinal-economic blockages.

83 Once again, Williams deflates or, in Kurt Heinzelman's term, "devalues" the image of Pound's generative imagination. In *The Economics of the Imagination* (Amherst: University of Massachusetts Press, 1980), Heinzelman argues, "To devalue Pound was, like the analogous process in money markets, to strip the currency of its artificially asserted value, to destandardize it as a measure of value, and to allow it to float and circulate in an unregulated market" (250). This helps explain the connection between the dissolution of the poet's phallic pretensions above and the dissolution of Williams's desires for a strong, enlightened regulator of the multitude's means of exchange.

84 See Jerome Mazzaro, *William Carlos Williams: The Later Poems* (Ithaca, N.Y.: Cornell University Press, 1973), 122, 124.

85 Laura (Riding) Jackson, *The Telling* (New York: Harper & Row, 1972), 88.

86 Wallace Stevens, *Letters*, ed. Holly Stevens (Berkeley: University of California Press, 1996), 351.

87 Of the modernist works he addresses, Brown writes: "Utopia no longer takes its positive, potentially totalitarian form—the mystical City of God, the ideal of the Harmonious Man, the impossible, totalitarian solution of a world of conflicts, which would only be, at best, an idealization of our own world anyhow.... Instead, utopia is understood here, in keeping with Hegel's critique of Plato's *Republic*, precisely as something negative, nothing other than a lack or contradiction in the actually existing social totality whose presence hints at an as yet unimaginable future." Nicholas Brown, *Utopian Generations: The Political Horizon of Twentieth-Century Literature* (Princeton, N.J.: Princeton University Press, 2005), 22.

2. Wyndham Lewis, Constituent Power, and Collective Life

1 Wyndham Lewis, *Time and Western Man*, ed. Paul Edwards (Santa Rosa, Calif.: Black Sparrow Press, 1993), 132.

2 Ibid., 298.

3 Vincent Sherry, *Ezra Pound, Wyndham Lewis, and Radical Modernism* (New York: Oxford University Press, 1993), 94.

4 This is the argument of Hal Foster, for example, who observes that Lewis erects the "armored ego" as a defense against "the masses ... the unconscious, the drives, sexuality." This leads to what Foster describes as a continual "binding of stimulus-shock into a protective shield, the conversion of energy into ego." Hal Foster, "Prosthetic Gods," *Modernism/Modernity* 4, no. 2 (1997): 21, 19, 20. Ella Zohar Ophir also carefully tracks this aspect of Lewis's thought, interpreting his forms of artistic abstraction in terms of his desire for "singular detachment from the general confusion." Ella Zohar Ophir, "Toward a Pitiless Fiction: Abstraction, Comedy, and Modernist Antihumanism," *Modern Fiction Studies* 52, no. 1 (Spring 2006): 96.

5. Wyndham Lewis, *Creatures of Habit and Creatures of Change: Essays on Art, Literature, and Society, 1914–1956*, ed. Paul Edwards (Santa Rosa, Calif.: Black Sparrow Press, 1989), 174.
6. Ibid., 120.
7. Wyndham Lewis, *Collected Poems and Plays*, ed. Alan Munton (Manchester: Carcenet, 1979), 197–98.
8. Lewis, *Time and Western Man*, 296. As E. W. F. Tomlin indicates, this model of spontaneity is based primarily on the philosophy of Henri Bergson, specifically, on Bergson's idea of *durée* as "an interpenetrative process ... responsible for that 'destruction of things of the intellect'... which might be detected in so much modern 'thought.'" E. W. F. Tomlin, "The Philosophical Influences," in *Wyndham Lewis: A Revaluation*, ed. Jeffrey Meyers (London: Athlone Press, 1980), 34. Lewis bases his critique of this interpenetrative process primarily on Bergson's *Creative Evolution*, whose élan vital Lewis describes as a "general fund of aimless power" that is presumed to determine the course of world-historical events according to its "blind, powerful, restless and unconscious" impulses; *Time and Western Man*, 308, 312. Though the élan vital is completely apolitical in the pages of *Creative Evolution*, Lewis fuses it with the "spontaneity philosophies" of Schopenhauer and Georges Sorel to create a vision of cosmic political mechanism and violence that is primarily of his own invention. In this context, Bergson's "general fund of aimless power" is recast as the "irresponsible Power" of "loan-capital [which] must come to a crash ... *unless it had within itself some intelligent principle of adaptation*, which it hasn't, [since] *it is without heart or intelligence, like a huge senseless insect*." Wyndham Lewis, *Count Your Dead: They Are Alive! Or, A New War in the Making* (London: Lovat Dickson, 1937), 230, my emphasis. The entomological metaphors of this passage, and its notion of biological adaptation, are both lifted from Bergson. But the idea, which Lewis continually reiterates in his criticism of "spontaneity philosophy," that Bergson somehow favored a condition of mechanism or automaticity is a pure philosophical fiction. As SueEllen Campbell correctly notes in *The Enemy Opposite: The Outlaw Criticism of Wyndham Lewis* (Athens: Ohio University Press, 1988), both Bergson and Lewis "see themselves as opposing the sterility of nineteenth-century mechanism" (113), and Bergson spent the majority of his philosophical career defining human will as a power of hesitation or self-suspension, which interrupts the circuit of stimulus and response. Indeed, this Bergsonian model of will as a detachment-in-immersion clearly shaped Lewis's positive model of spontaneity in ways he consistently refused to admit. On this point, see Jeffrey Meyers's analysis of the essential Bergsonism of the image of the Vortex as a combination of stillness and energy in *The Enemy* (London: Routledge & Kegan Paul, 1980) and Mary Ann Gillies's discussion of the still point of Lewis's Vortex as an embodiment of Bergsonian *durée*, where "stillness is a part of the overall dynamism of life" in *Henri Bergson and British Modernism* (Montreal: McGill-Queens University Press, 1996), 51.
9. Lewis, *Time and Western Man*, 307.
10. Ibid., 416.

11 Ever since Hugh Kenner's important author study *Wyndham Lewis* (London: Methuen, 1954), Lewis's sensitivity to ideological conditioning has occasioned a good deal of critical attention. Kenner notes how in Lewis "every appetite of life is invisibly organized to serve the ends of power" (70). This observation has led to widely varying critical responses. Geoffrey Wagner, for example, in *Wyndham Lewis: A Portrait of the Artist as the Enemy* (New Haven, Conn.: Yale University Press, 1957), sees individuality as a refuge from these forms of mass regulation. In his account, the proletariat may be "coerced by the environment or culture group," but the "'person' is the true individual, opposed to the social stereotype, free of the group or class 'rhythms'" (38–39). Tyrus Miller, on the other hand, in *Late Modernism: Politics, Fiction, and the Arts between the World Wars* (Berkeley: University of California Press, 1999), stresses the duress visited upon Lewis's models of heroic individuality. He argues that Lewis's sensitivity to ideological regulation is so profound that it places him in a subtradition of "late modernism," in which the pervasiveness of mass culture has begun to undermine modernism's faith in the socially redemptive value of its aesthetic practices and the forms of artistic subjectivity that supposedly secured it its autonomy. Finally, in his remarkable afterword to *Time and Western Man*, Paul Edwards claims that Lewis asks the following question: How can the artist "be anything more than a reflection of... 'contaminating' alien realities," since "ideologies... now, almost unnoticed, saturate the world" and saturate the artist too? For Edwards, Lewis's answer does not lie in an isolated and well-fortified ego—indeed, he rightly notes Lewis's emphasis on the artist's role as a "sacred prostitute" and the "necessary traffic" he or she must conduct "with the world." Instead, according to Edwards, Lewis hopes to promote a form of "ideological awareness" that will allow "human beings to detach themselves sufficiently from the ideologies of their time and to project... an ideal and values that could lead to a fuller and more meaningful life for their society." Edwards's sensitivity to this utopian element in Lewis is commendable—it is one whose ambivalences and contradictions I too attempt to document. Paul Edwards, "Afterword," in *Time and Western Man*, ed. Paul Edwards (Santa Rosa, Calif.: Black Sparrow Press, 1993), 462, 461, 463, 465.

12 Lewis, *Time and Western Man*, 177. This sense that objectivity is to be located outside the ego, in a collective material world, is amplified in Lewis's *Count Your Dead*, where he writes, "All 'subjective' means is what your ego *wishes*, and dreams it has, rather than what *is*. 'Objective' is the opposite of that. It is what is common to all men—seen, smelt, touched by all men" (267).

13 Lewis, *Time and Western Man*, 297.

14 Ibid., 8.

15 Wyndham Lewis, *The Art of Being Ruled*, ed. Reed Way Dasenbrock (Santa Rosa, Calif.: Black Sparrow Press, 1989), 227–28, 232.

16 Lewis, *Time and Western Man*, 377.

17 Ibid., 173.

18 Lewis, *The Art of Being Ruled*, 227.

19 Michael Levenson, *Modernism and the Fate of Individuality: Character and Novelistic Form from Conrad to Woolf* (New York: Cambridge University Press, 1991), 126.
20 Ibid., 127.
21 Jessica Burstein is another critic who focuses on the ways in which bodily wholeness unfastens in Lewis. According to her fascinating reading, Lewis reveals the fascist body to be a "forgery" and a stand-in for "that of the people." For her, therefore, Lewis's "subsumption of individual integrity into a landscape of supplements" is of more central importance than his paranoiac retreats into individual egos. As we shall see, her reading of the politics of supplementation and projection in Lewis anticipates much of what I have to say about Arghol as a self-exposing, self-undermining political agent in *Enemy of the Stars*. Jessica Burstein, "Waspish Segments: Lewis, Prosthesis, Fascism," *Modernism/Modernity* 4, no. 2 (1997): 139, 149.
22 Paul Peppis, *Literature, Politics, and the English Avant-Garde: Nation and Empire, 1901–1918* (New York: Cambridge University Press, 2000), 146.
23 Ibid., 149.
24 Wyndham Lewis, *"The Ideal Giant"; "The Code of a Herdsman"; "Cantleman's Spring-Mate"* (London: Shield & Spring, 1917; privately printed), 32.
25 Peppis, *Literature, Politics*, 151.
26 Lewis, *"The Ideal Giant,"* 32, 36.
27 Wyndham Lewis, *Blasting and Bombardiering* (London: Eyre & Spottiswoode, 1937), 85.
28 Ibid., 85, 84.
29 Ibid., 86, 85.
30 Wyndham Lewis, "The Objective of Art in Our Time," in *Wyndham Lewis the Artist: From 'BLAST' to Burlington House* (London: Laidlaw & Laidlaw, 1939), 331. In *A Pluralistic Universe*, William James repeatedly credits Henri Bergson as the intellectual force that enabled him to imagine the relationship of matter and mind Lewis describes here—another reason to reconsider Lewis's relationship to Bergson and the forms of spontaneity he comes to stand for in Lewis's writings. Indeed, for Bergson, mind's relationship to matter is best described as one of self-mediating spontaneity, *not* primal unity: "Thought which is only thought" is a simple *nothing;* thought becomes productive only when it is "spectator and actor alike, at once spontaneous and reflective." See Henri Bergson, "Life and Consciousness," in *Mind-Energy*, trans. H. Wildon Carr (Henry Holt, 1920), 28; and Henri Bergson, *The Creative Mind*, trans. Mabelle L. Andison (New York: Philosophical Library, 1946), 12.
31 Lewis, *Time and Western Man*, 132.
32 As Douglas Mao perspicaciously notes in *Solid Objects: Modernism and the Test of Production* (Princeton, N.J.: Princeton University Press, 1998), Lewis's early work often embodies Lewis's desire that the artist should enter "the vital game of changing our common life" (91). But in his work of the late 1920s and 1930s, Lewis rejects, even as an ideal, the notion of art "as an intersubjective mediator or as a subjectivity's achieved objectification" (ibid., 136). This does not mean that he has abandoned his investment in strong artistic subjectivity, but, according to Mao,

it does mean that he has renounced the idea that the common life can or should be repatterned after a forceful subjectivity's sense of form. During this period of Lewis's career, the division between subject and object must be maintained at all costs, because "any putative reconciliations between the two would merely disguise some further domination" (ibid., 101). The role of art now is to testify to the object's separation from the subject, as something that is ultimately external to all of the subject's projections. Mao is right to note this split in Lewis's career—that Lewis's late work exhibits a profound suspicion of individuals' attempts aggressively to transform collective life. And yet, even during this later period, Lewis continues to stage various subjects' excursions into the common life. My argument is that Lewis does this to stage a confrontation between two conflicting ideas he continues to entertain in the late 1920s and 1930s: the idea that the common life should learn to transform *itself* in the absence of central, authoritarian wills and the suspicion that such large-scale transformation may not be possible without some kind of centralized power structure.

33 As Nicholas Brown lucidly explains in *Utopian Generations: The Political Horizon of Twentieth-Century Literature* (Princeton, N.J.: Princeton University Press, 2005), Lewis's attraction to fascism is rooted in his "status quo anti-capitalism"—Nicolas Poulantzas's term for the politics of the "petty bourgeoisie in revolt" (132). This political position is defined by, among other things, "an antagonistic relationship to both the bourgeoisie and the proletariat that nonetheless sometimes requires strategic cooperation with one or another against its opponent" (132). This involves a slippery relationship to the proletariat that leads, in Fredric Jameson's account, to Lewis's simultaneous fascination and disgust with collective processes. Sometimes, Lewis appears mesmerized with "transindividual libidinal apparatus[es], in which characters are little more than the bearers, or vehicles, of great collective and ideological forces." Fredric Jameson, *Fables of Aggression: Wyndham Lewis, the Modernist as Fascist* (Berkeley: University of California Press, 1981), 16. At other times, Jameson notes, Lewis identifies with "the essentially placeless observer/satirist," a move that echoes the petty bourgeoisie's tendency to project the state, "in its own image, as an arbiter above the social classes" (16, 17). In this account, the fascist state provides a seemingly non-class-based but nevertheless populist, oppositional, and antiparliamentary solution to the petty bourgeois' political stalemate. That this "solution" could never be the populist gemeinschaft it promises to be is the suspicion that causes Lewis to interrupt its symbolic hegemony in *Enemy of the Stars*, as well as in his critical work.

34 I focus on Lewis's 1932 revision of *Enemy of the Stars* instead of the original, 1914, version, for several reasons. The original play was published in the 1914 number of *BLAST* and reflects a very different political and aesthetic perspective than the later version of the play. In his second autobiography, Lewis writes: "My literary contemporaries I looked upon as too bookish and not keeping pace with the visual revolution. A kind of play, 'The Enemy of the Stars' (greatly changed later and published in book form) was my attempt to show them the way. It became evident to me at once, however, when I started to write a novel, that words and syntax were

not susceptible of transformation into abstract terms, to which process the visual arts lent themselves quite readily." Wyndham Lewis, *Rude Assignment: An Intellectual Autobiography*, ed. Toby Foshay (Santa Barbara, Calif.: Black Sparrow Press, 1984), 139. This sense of *Enemy of the Stars* as a stark, hard-edged "abstractist" depiction of conflicting forces is greatly diminished in Lewis's 1932 revision of the play. Gone are the jarring parataxis, the two-dimensional characters, and that peculiar device Reed Way Dasenbrock describes as the "character-zone"; see Dasenbrock's *The Literary Vorticism of Ezra Pound and Wyndham Lewis: Towards the Condition of Painting* (Baltimore: Johns Hopkins University Press, 1985). These are replaced with lengthy, discursive expositions, character-idiolects, more conventional indices of speakers, and expository asides provided by an omniscient narrator. Also, Arghol's shifting relationship to the stars is brought into even clearer focus; Lewis goes out of his way to illustrate the transformation Arghol undergoes with respect to the stars' "cadaverous, beaming force" (148). In other words, the 1932 *Enemy of the Stars* seems intent on enacting a drama and providing its exposition at the same time. This marks a political shift as well as an aesthetic one. Characters are no longer exhibited as in an impersonal, asocial formal agon. Instead, Arghol's exposure of himself as a deceitful and unbenevolent "master" takes center stage. This is part and parcel of the highly ambivalent attitude Lewis cultivates toward fascist models of political agency during this period. The 1932 *Enemy of the Stars* is thus of a piece with this later political development and overlaps richly with the texts Lewis published in the late 1920s and 1930s.

35 Because of Lewis's richly deserved reputation for authoritarian political sentiment, his interest in forms of collective spontaneity is rarely discussed. Philip Head is an exception to this rule; he notes Lewis's proclamation "I believe the soviet system to be the best ... it looks to the East, which is spiritually so much greater and intellectually so much finer than Europe" (*The Art of Being Ruled*, 320) and suggests that what Lewis had in mind here was "not the highly-centralised Council of People's Commissars that by then effectively ruled the Soviet Union, but the semispontaneous, semi-syndicalist 'soviets' of workers, peasants and soldiers that had been instrumental in the successful 1917 revolution." Philip Head, "Lewis and 'the Political,'" *Wyndham Lewis Annual* 12 (2005): 31. Similarly, Nicholas Brown detects a utopian impulse in Lewis's "confidence that 'human nature' right down to the sensory apparatus is radically mutable along with the social forms in which it finds itself." Brown, *Utopian Generations*, 133–34. Finally, Douglas Mao cuts against the grain by claiming that "Lewis locates the genuine highbrow's claim to authority in a capacity to think *against* authority" — a disposition that Mao aligns with the political tradition of liberalism. Counterintuitive as this may be, Mao dexterously argues that Lewis's rants against institutional liberalism are rants against its willingness to use education and the press to destroy liberalism itself, which is predicated on the ideal of informed, critical thought. In this context, the ideal of a responsible, independent social body, accustomed to "principled dissent," is the collective vision against which institutional liberalism is condemned. Douglas Mao, "A Shaman in Common: Lewis, Auden, and the Queerness of Liberalism,"

in *Bad Modernisms*, ed. Douglas Mao and Rebecca L. Walkowitz (Durham, N.C.: Duke University Press, 2006), 214, 228.

36 Giorgio Agamben, *Homo Sacer: Sovereign Power and Bare Life*, trans. Daniel Heller-Roazen (Stanford, Calif.: Stanford University Press, 1998), 39.
37 Ibid., 42.
38 Alain Badiou, *Metapolitics*, trans. Jason Barker (London: Verso, 2005), 70.
39 Agamben, *Homo Sacer*, 44.
40 Badiou, *Metapolitics*, 72.
41 Antonio Negri, *Insurgencies: Constituent Power and the Modern State*, trans. Maurizia Boscagli (Minneapolis: University of Minnesota Press, 1999), 313.
42 Ibid., 322.
43 Michael Hardt and Antonio Negri, *Commonwealth* (Cambridge, Mass.: Harvard University Press, 2009), 374, 355.
44 Georges Sorel, *Reflections on Violence*, ed. Jeremy Jennings (New York: Cambridge University Press, 1999), 7.
45 Lewis, *Collected Poems and Plays*, 195.
46 Ibid., 198. It may difficult to believe one's ears when hearing Lewis recommend despoilment of the individual ego and unselfish sacrifice of oneself on behalf of the multitude. David Graver, however, is one critic alive to Lewis's very real ethics of self-despoilment. He describes the Not-Self as characterized by its "ability to understand and identify with others and the world in general." He continues in this vein: "Whereas the intellect is interested in truth and is willing to sacrifice itself to it, the ego is interested only in power, in the sphere of its own influence." David Graver, "Vorticist Performance and Aesthetic Turbulence in *Enemy of the Stars*," *PMLA* 107, no. 3 (May 1992): 490.
47 According to my analysis, this state of doubleness is meant to represent the tension between the spontaneous, collective impulses of the social world and the detached activity of the individual intellect. As David Ayers correctly observes in *Wyndham Lewis and Western Man* (New York: St. Martin's Press, 1992), *Enemy of the Stars* is structured around a set of such oppositions: "the opposition of the self to the material world; of the self to others . . . of the inner self to the social self" (58). Similarly, Toby Foshay understands Arghol to represent the self; Hanp, by contrast, represents the "sensuous man" and the "headless mob." But Foshay stresses even more firmly that the self's separateness from the external world is, for Lewis, a "precarious fiction." In his interpretation, when Arghol flings Max Stirner's *The Ego and His Own* out of his apartment window, he symbolically rejects Stirner's solipsist philosophy of the "absolute, uncategorizable uniqueness of the individual self." Toby Foshay, *Wyndham Lewis and the Avant-Garde: The Politics of the Intellect* (Montreal: McGill-Queens University Press, 1992), 27, 28.
48 Reed Way Dasenbrock comments on this ideal of detachment-in-immersion in Lewis in a way that demonstrates its centrality to Lewis's aesthetic and social imagination. He writes that for Lewis, "detachment does not mean finding a refuge from the world, a private or privileged space, as no such space exists. . . . It means opposing and interrogating the world and its values." Dasenbrock, *The Literary*

Vorticism, 60–61. This suggests that "the aesthetic of detachment ... does not necessitate a conservative approach to social and political matters," and Dasenbrock quotes Trotsky to this effect: "For art to be able to transform as well as to reflect, there must be a great distance between the artist and life, just as there is between the revolutionist and political reality." Leon Trotsky, *Literature and Revolution*, trans. Rose Strunsky (New York: International Publishers, 1925), 139. I would add that in *Enemy of the Stars* it is precisely the dangers of too great a distance and too small a distance between "the revolutionist" and "political reality" that define the problematic of "detachment" for Lewis.

49 Theodor W. Adorno, *Negative Dialectics*, trans. E. B. Ashton (New York: Continuum, 1973), 323.

50 Theodor Adorno, *Minima Moralia: Reflections from Damaged Life*, trans. E. F. N. Jephcott (London: Verso, 2000), 231.

51 In her *Rituals of Spontaneity: Sentiment and Secularism from Free Prayer to Wordsworth* (Waco, Tex.: Baylor University Press, 2006), Lori Branch introduces a similar idea of spontaneous practice, tracking its manifestations from "free prayer" to "dissenting and philosophic forms of self-scrutiny in the quest for natural responses, and the behaviors associated with sensibility, including effusions of joy, weeping, or poetic inspiration" (6). Her focus on the institutions and ideologies that frame these spontaneous demonstrations is what brings it closest to my own analysis. However, I would argue that the centrality of the tension between collective political spontaneity and individual artistic spontaneity differentiates the modernist spontaneities I analyze from the rich array of spontaneities she analyzes.

52 As I explain in the introduction to this book, Adorno is the most exact expositor of this modernist idea of spontaneity. In "On Lyric Poetry," he writes: "In every lyric poem the historical relationship of the subject to objectivity, of the individual to society, must have found its precipitate in the medium of a subjective spirit thrown back upon itself." However, "the less the work thematizes the relationship of 'I' and society, the more spontaneously it crystallizes of its own accord in the poem, the more complete this process of precipitation will be." Theodor Adorno, *Notes to Literature*, trans. Shierry Weber-Nicholsen (New York: Columbia University Press, 1991), 1:42. In other words, the spontaneity of artists consists in their surrendering themselves to their materials. In doing so, they allow a second-order spontaneity to occur, one in which the social content of their expressions is announced "behind the author's back" (43).

53 This accords nicely with SueEllen Campbell's definition of the Not-Self as a balancing term between subjective life and social objectivity; she describes it as an "intellectual force" that is "public, altruistic, and intellectual." Campbell, *The Enemy Opposite*, 61, 62.

54 Alain Badiou, *Theory of the Subject*, trans. Bruno Bosteels (London: Continuum, 2009), 9.

55 Lewis, *Creatures of Habit*, 124.

56 Lewis, *Collected Poems and Plays*, 160

57 Lewis, *Creatures of Habit*, 124.

58 Wyndham Lewis, *Hitler* (London: Chatto & Windus, 1931), 31.
59 Gilles Deleuze, *The Logic of Sense*, trans. Mark Lester (New York: Columbia University Press, 1990), 137–38.
60 In his 1937 *Count Your Dead: They Are Alive!*, Lewis describes this process of ideological enchantment. He refers to an "almost . . . clinical 'treatment' " that insulates the English citizenry from "psychological contamination with the truth" and that withdraws it from "contact with external reality" (26, 25): "The patient is cured of the ravages of truth, or truth is held at bay, by psychological manipulation. A highly *subjective* condition is induced. Subjectivity—the British brand—is praised to the skies. And all that is objective, that is to say all that is *not-self,* is never admitted to his consciousness until it has been neutralized, and stated in terms of his private mind. That a window should be thrown open somewhere, and a few currents of fresh air allowed to penetrate this stuffy atmosphere, appears to me obvious. For so much subjectivity is suffocating" (26).
61 Jameson, *Fables of Aggression*, 15.
62 Charles Sumner eloquently articulates the paradoxes that attend this act of political pedagogy. He argues that in exhorting individuals to resist social administration, Lewis himself "necessarily becomes a sort of social administrator," and that "in order to protect himself from this administrative function, Lewis adopted the Enemy persona, critiquing not only the agents of political and cultural administration, but also his own critical prescriptions." Charles Sumner, "Wyndham Lewis' Theory of Mass Culture," *The Space Between: Literature and Culture 1914–1945* 3, no. 1 (2007): 43.
63 Alain Badiou, *The Communist Hypothesis*, trans. David Macey and Steve Corcoran (London: Verso, 2010), 20, 21–22.
64 Ibid., 222, 245.
65 Wendy Stallard Flory explains Arghol's willingness to be battered by the boot of the universe in the following way: he "believes that it is necessary to resist what he considers to be the dishonest and egocentric desire to discover 'among the stars' evidence for the workings of a divine power well-disposed toward humanity—to rid himself of this particular kind of 'evaporation and lightness.' " Wendy Stallard Flory, "*Enemy of the Stars*," in Meyers, *Wyndham Lewis*, 96. In other words, Arghol's beatings are part of a process of disillusionment that reminds him that the universe has no beneficent intentions toward humankind. Flory develops this observation in an existentialist direction, but the notion that Arghol is resisting the idea that worldly existence is arranged from on high and for the benefit of all is one that fits with my political reading as well. The idea is that Arghol ritualistically purges himself of any emotional identification with forces that seek to tame and manipulate him.
66 Alain Badiou, *Deleuze: The Clamor of Being*, trans. Louise Burchill (Minneapolis: University of Minnesota Press, 2000), 12.
67 Andrew Hewitt's reading of Haroun al Raschid's masquerade as a form of drag performance involving "a ruler disguised as the ruled, a man disguised as a woman," lends support to this point. According to Hewitt, "The transvestite is the emblem

of modern Western democratism" because "politics exists in the public realm as the manipulation of signs of power," which is a principal characteristic of transvestism. According to this definition, Nazism is a form of transvestism as well, but one "freed from all belief in gender as/or essence" as a consequence of Germany's loss of a collective ground of national identity. Lewis's ambivalence toward the masquerades of the political leader in the late 1920s and 1930s, thus, in my reading, signals an early critical ambivalence about fascism, even as Lewis simultaneously held out hope for an altruistic, "love-awakening" form of political transvestism. See Andrew Hewitt, *Political Inversions: Homosexuality, Fascism, and the Modernist Imaginary* (Stanford, Calif.: Stanford University Press, 1996), 188, 187, 182.

68 Lewis, *Creatures of Habit*, 137.
69 In his analysis of *Enemy of the Stars*, Scott Klein also registers how crucial it is that Arghol "becomes an extension of the world rather than its opposite." According to Klein, this turn of events "results logically from [Arghol's] programmatic rejection of the other" and his refusal "to recognize the contradictions implicit in the cult of selfhood." Klein's analysis of the *Enemy of the Stars* thus foregrounds a point that is essential to my argument—that the play actively subverts many of Lewis's more familiar proclamations about the virtues of the "powerful self." Scott Klein, "The Experiment of Vorticist Drama: Wyndham Lewis and 'Enemy of the Stars,'" *Twentieth Century Literature* 37, no. 2 (Summer 1991): 229, 231, 228.
70 Wyndham Lewis, *The Lion and the Fox: The Rôle of the Hero in the Plays of Shakespeare* (London: Methuen, 1966), 23, 24. See Anne Quéma, *The Agon of Modernism: Wyndham Lewis's Allegories, Aesthetic, and Politics* (Lewisburg, Pa.: Bucknell University Press, 1999), 25.
71 This analogy is made even clearer in *Rude Assignment* when Lewis indicates that the subject of *The Lion and the Fox* is "the Patriot King" (179). Lewis continues: "His interests are identified with those of the People—he stands between them and the rapacity and pride of the oligarchy, the *ottimati*. And so it may be: may be *if* the king is not a blackguard or a fool, and is really a patriot" (179). This language of patriotism makes clear the contemporary associations Lewis was attempting to evoke in his analysis of the king, as does his suggestion in this connection that "for one benevolent ruler you might get nine who were bad," for example, "Hitler," who "revealed himself as a homicidal lunatic" (179).
72 Lewis consistently rejected the illusion that Jews were the controlling hand of this financial directorate. Nevertheless, as Moishe Postone points out, the tendency to personify Jews as embodiments of exchange value, as opposed to an organic community defined by Aryan workers and industrialists, would become a master trope of Nazi ideology. See Moishe Postone, "The Holocaust and the Trajectory of the Twentieth Century," in *Catastrophe and Meaning: The Holocaust and the Twentieth Century*, ed. Moishe Postone and Eric Santner (Chicago: University of Chicago Press, 2003).
73 Robert Harry Lowie, *Primitive Society* (New York: Boni & Liveright, 1920), 372, cited in Lewis, *The Lion and the Fox*, 131.

74 Lewis, *The Art of Being Ruled*, 47. This suggests Lewis's profound ambivalence about "cultural revolution," which, according to Tyrus Miller's definition, designates "the convergence of art and the state in a new, total aesthetico-political unity." According to Miller, the cultural revolutionist believes that art "is consummated in its becoming the most concentrated expression of a unitary power that is itself not more than the generalized form of art's power to impose meaningful order on material chaos." In the character of Arghol, Lewis flirts with such a model of comprehensive, unitary power. But in my analysis, his alignment with political fraud and opportunism also suggests Lewis's antipathy to the idea of art as "the co-substantial essence of dictatorial power." Tyrus Miller, "No Man's Land: Wyndham Lewis and Cultural Revolution," *Wyndham Lewis Annual* 12 (2005): 15, 13.

75 Ernest Renan, *Caliban: Suite de La Tempête* (Manchester: Manchester University Press, 1954), 62.

76 In his 1932 revision of *Enemy of the Stars*, Lewis suggests that Arghol deliberately provokes the split that eventually culminates in his murder. This is the moment in the play where Arghol most clearly embodies both the masquerade of the ruler and Lewis's mandate that all such masquerades be exposed and vituperated. Arghol verbally abuses Hanp to such an extent that Hanp is forced to terminate his discipleship and "*become[ ] at once another person*" (176). Then: "*At the sound of Hanp's voice, no longer borrowed, an expression of relief comes into the face of Arghol. The experiment is at an end . . . the strain of the mock-life at this particular point has been considerable, upon the underworld of energy of the rebellious muscles*" (177). In other words, Arghol seems to have deliberately involved himself in a *simulation* of the ruler's duplicity, so that Hanp could learn to recognize, within the realm of "mock-life," the forms of deception he will encounter in the harsher territory of political supersystems.

77 Negri, *Insurgencies*, 11.

78 Badiou, *The Communist Hypothesis*, 227.

79 Laura (Riding) Jackson, *The Telling* (New York: Harper & Row, 1972), 25.

80 Ibid., 134.

3. "An Instantaneous Sympathy of Communication"

1 Indeed, this is precisely what Sharon Stockton argues about the ritualistic sacrifice of the artist and king in Lewis's *The Lion and the Fox*—that in being sacrificed, "the powerful individual not only chooses but is forced by the mob to some other place of divine presence; after his 'death' the tragic hero's power becomes even stronger by virtue of mythic accrual." Sharon Stockton, "Aesthetics, Politics, and the Staging of the World: Wyndham Lewis and the Renaissance," *Twentieth Century Literature* 42, no. 4 (Winter 1996): 509.

2 See Laura Riding, *The World and Ourselves* (London: Chatto & Windus, 1938), 187.

3 This image of modernists as involved in the public world, attempting to discover new collective forms of affect, is an important theme in some of the best recent scholarly studies of modernism, including Justus Nieland's *Feeling Modern: The*

Eccentricities of Public Life (Urbana: University of Illinois Press, 2008); Jonathan Flatley's *Affective Mapping: Melancholia and the Politics of Modernism* (Cambridge, Mass.: Harvard University Press, 2008); Charles Altieri's *The Particulars of Rapture: An Aesthetic of the Affects* (Ithaca, N.Y.: Cornell University Press, 2003); and Jessica Berman's *Modernist Fiction, Cosmopolitanism, and the Politics of Community* (New York: Cambridge University Press, 2001). Riding provides one of the first critical studies of this tendency in modernism—a study whose *critique* of modernism's desire to repattern public affect still needs more scholarly attention.

4 Riding, *The World and Ourselves*, 287.
5 See Laura (Riding) Jackson, *The Telling* (New York: Harper & Row, 1972), 107.
6 Michael Hardt and Antonio Negri, *Multitude: War and Democracy in the Age of Empire* (New York: Penguin Press, 2004), 110.
7 Michael Hardt, "Affective Labor," *boundary 2* 26, no. 2 (1999): 89.
8 Patricia Ticineto Clough, "Introduction," *The Affective Turn: Theorizing the Social*, ed. Patricia Ticineto Clough with Jean Halley (Durham, N.C.: Duke University Press, 2007), 2.
9 Brian Massumi, *Parables for the Virtual: Affect, Movement, Sensation* (Durham, N.C.: Duke University Press, 2002), 15.
10 See David Staples, "Women's Work and the Ambivalent Gift of Entropy," in Clough, *The Affective Turn*, 11; Patricia Ticineto Clough et al., "Notes towards a Theory of Affect-Itself" *ephemera* 7, no. 1 (2007): 62; and Peng Cheah, "Nondialectical Materialism," *Diacritics* 38, nos. 1–2 (Spring–Summer 2008): 149.
11 Antonio Negri, "Value and Affect," *boundary 2* 26, no. 2 (1999): 85.
12 Anton Pannekoek, *Workers' Councils* (Oakland, Calif.: AK Press, 2003), 47.
13 (Riding) Jackson, *The Telling*, 65.
14 Carla Billitteri, "A Form of Tidiness: Laura (Riding) Jackson and the Work of Poetry-Writing," *Textual Practice* 22, no. 2 (2008): 324.
15 Ella Zohar Ophir, "The Laura Riding Question: Modernism, Poetry, and Truth," *Modern Language Quarterly* 66, no. 1 (2005): 93.
16 Billitteri, "A Form of Tidiness," 329.
17 Ophir, "The Laura Riding Question," 93.
18 Ibid.
19 Billitteri, "A Form of Tidiness," 320.
20 Ophir, "The Laura Riding Question," 112–13. Ophir sees this "move toward inclusiveness" as a break from the values that informed Riding's poetry (112). In this chapter, however, I will try to show that Riding was deeply concerned with the "authority-imposing devices" of poetry (*The Telling*, 66), even while she was continuing to write it.
21 Riding, *The World and Ourselves*, 503.
22 Luke Carson, "'This Is Something Unlosable': Laura Riding's 'Compacting Sense,'" *Texas Studies in Literature and Language* 37, no. 4 (Winter 1995): 417–18.
23 Jerome J. McGann, "Laura (Riding) Jackson and the Literal Truth," *Critical Inquiry* 18, no. 3 (Spring 1992): 463, 464. "Human life in the whole" is Riding's term

for what poetry should reflect in its processes. Laura (Riding) Jackson, "Excerpts from the Preface to *Selected Poems: In Five Sets*, 1970," in *The Poems of Laura Riding* (New York: Persea Books, 1980), 416, cited in McGann, "Laura (Riding) Jackson," 463.

24. Lisa Samuels, "Creating Criticism: An Introduction to *Anarchism Is Not Enough*," in Laura Riding, *Anarchism Is Not Enough*, ed. Lisa Samuels (Berkeley: University of California Press, 2001), xxix.
25. Riding, *The World and Ourselves*, 505.
26. (Riding) Jackson, *The Telling*, 136, 125.
27. Laura Riding, *Contemporaries and Snobs* (Garden City, N.Y.: Doubleday Doran, 1928), 14.
28. Riding, *The World and Ourselves*, 287.
29. In conformity with the wishes of the late Laura (Riding) Jackson, her Board of Literary Management asks us to record that, in 1941, Laura (Riding) Jackson renounced, on the grounds of linguistic principle, the writing of poetry; she had come to hold that "poetry obstructs general attainment to something better in our linguistic way-of-life than we have."
30. McGann, "Laura (Riding) Jackson," 459.
31. Michael A. Masopust, "Laura Riding's Quarrel with Poetry," *South Central Review* 2, no. 1 (Spring 1985): 51.
32. Laura Riding, "I Am," in *The Poems of Laura Riding*, 209.
33. (Riding) Jackson, *The Telling*, 6.
34. Antonio Negri, *Political Descartes: Reason, Ideology, and the Bourgeois Project*, trans. Matteo Mandarini and Alberto Toscano (London: Verso, 2007), 323.
35. Ibid.
36. Jane Malcolm, "'That Breeding Silence She': Laura Riding's Gendered Ethics and the Limits of the Word 'Woman,'" *Arizona Quarterly* 65, no. 3 (Autumn 2009): 67.
37. Susan M. Schultz, *A Poetics of Impasse in Modern and Contemporary American Poetry* (Tuscaloosa: University of Alabama Press, 2005), 66.
38. Ibid.
39. Ibid., 77.
40. Malcolm, "'That Breeding Silence She,'" 75.
41. Carson, "'This Is Something Unlosable,'" 414.
42. Laura (Riding) Jackson, "The Word 'Woman,'" in *The Word "Woman," and Other Related Writings*, ed. Elizabeth Friedmann and Alan J. Clark (New York: Persea Books, 1993), 74.
43. (Riding) Jackson, *The Telling*, 67.
44. Michael Hardt and Antonio Negri, *Empire* (Cambridge, Mass.: Harvard University Press, 2000), 293.
45. Dorothy E. Smith, *The Everyday World as Problematic* (Boston: Northeastern University Press, 1987), 83, 81.
46. Ibid., 83.
47. Nancy Hartsock, *Money, Sex, and Power: Toward a Feminist Historical Materialism* (New York: Longman, 1983), 234–35.

48 Susanne Schultz, "Dissolved Boundaries and 'Affective Labor': On the Disappearance of Reproductive Labor and Feminist Critique in *Empire*," trans. Frederick Peters, *Capitalism Nature Socialism* 17, no. 1 (March 2006): 79.
49 Kathi Weeks, "Life within and against Work: Affective Labor, Feminist Critique, and Post Fordist Politics," *ephemera* 7, no. 1 (2007): 234.
50 Rita Felski, *The Gender of Modernity* (Cambridge, Mass.: Harvard University Press, 1995), 18.
51 See Seyla Benhabib, *Critique, Norm, and Utopia: A Study of the Foundations of Critical Theory* (New York: Columbia University Press, 1986), 341.
52 This is exactly the process that Carla Billitteri analyzes under the gendered rubric of "tidiness," that is, the "mental or intellectual capacity for exerting a form of centralized control over the world of things, an ordering force of integration that keeps society together." Billitteri, "A Form of Tidiness," 321.
53 Michael Hardt and Antonio Negri, *Commonwealth* (Cambridge, Mass.: Harvard University Press, 2009), 355, viii.
54 Rudolf Rocker, *Anarcho-Syndicalism* (London: Phoenix Press, 1988), 53, 63.
55 Masopust, "Laura Riding's Quarrel," 50.
56 Carla Billitteri, "Stories, Not History: Laura Riding's Progress of Truth," *Arizona Quarterly* 65, no. 1 (Spring 2009): 90.
57 Pannekoek, *Workers' Councils*, 45.
58 Rocker, *Anarcho-Syndicalism*, 54.
59 Negri, "Value and Affect," 85.
60 See Marcel Mauss, *The Gift: The Form and Reason for Exchange in Archaic Societies*, trans. W. D. Hall (London: Routledge, 2000); and Jacques Derrida, *Given Time: I. Counterfeit Money*, trans. Peggy Kamuf (Chicago: University of Chicago Press, 1992). Riding is closest to Georges Bataille in her view of the gift as an expenditure of energy that does not develop society's productive forces but rather dissipates potentially explosive accumulations of surplus energy. Bataille's image of fortune, however, as "at the mercy of a need for limitless loss" evinces a catastrophism that is utterly remote from Riding's thought. Georges Bataille, *Visions of Excess: Selected Writings, 1927–1939*, trans. Allan Stoekl (Minneapolis: University of Minnesota Press, 1985), 123. Like all the modernists I consider here, Riding is drawn to the idea of a social system capable of resorbing and reciprocally organizing the productive energies of its members, not of discharging them in a spectacular "squandering of profits." Georges Bataille, *The Accursed Share: An Essay on General Economy*, trans. Robert Hurley (New York: Zone Books, 1988), 1:22.
61 Benhabib, *Critique, Norm, and Utopia*, 341.
62 Iris Young, "Impartiality and the Civic Public: Some Implications of the Feminist Critiques of Moral and Political Theory," in *Feminism as Critique: On the Politics of Gender*, ed. Seyla Benhabib and Drucilla Cornell (Minneapolis: University of Minnesota Press, 1987), 59.
63 Warren Montag, "The Pressure of the Street: Habermas's Fear of the Masses," in *Masses, Classes, and the Public Sphere*, ed. Mike Hill and Warren Montag (London: Verso, 2000), 139.

64 Ted Stolze, "A Displaced Transition: Habermas on the Public Sphere," in Hill and Montag, *Masses, Classes, and the Public Sphere*, 149.
65 Ibid.
66 Hardt and Negri, *Empire*, 328.
67 Michael Hardt and Antonio Negri, *Labor of Dionysus: A Critique of the State-Form* (Minneapolis: University of Minnesota Press, 1994), 142.
68 Christopher C. Norris, "Laura Riding's *The Telling:* Language, Poetry, and Neutral Style," *Language and Style* 11, no. 3 (Summer 1978): 139. Norris is deploying Kathleen Nott's idea of the "moral real"—that is, truths that we incorporate into "the orientation and practice of our lives." He cites Katherine Nott, "Further on Poetry," *Chelsea* 14 (1964): 44 (139).
69 Daniela M. Ciani, "Laura Riding's Truthfulness to the Word and to the Self," *Revue française d'études américaines* 61, no. 17 (August 1994): 302.
70 Mark Jacobs, "Preface to the Collected Poems," in *The Poems of Laura Riding*, xxiv.
71 Laura Riding, "Disclaimer of the Person," in *The Poems of Laura Riding*, 252.
72 Hardt and Negri, *Empire*, 293.
73 Hardt and Negri, *Commonwealth*, 180, 189.
74 Ibid., 195, 196.
75 Antonio Negri, *Time for Revolution*, trans. Matteo Mandarini (New York: Continuum, 2003), 251.
76 Hardt and Negri, *Commonwealth*, 198–99.
77 Negri, *Time for Revolution*, 228.

4. Rhapsodies of Change

1 Wallace Stevens, *The Necessary Angel: Essays on Reality and the Imagination* (New York: Vintage, 1951), 60.
2 See Gina Masucci Mackenzie and Daniel T. O'Hara, "Reading Stevens with Lacan on the Real: Toward a Poetics of Destitution," *Wallace Stevens Journal* 29, no. 1 (Spring 2005): 72–80.
3 William W. Bevis, *Mind of Winter: Wallace Stevens, Meditation, and Literature* (Pittsburgh: University of Pittsburgh Press, 1988), 12.
4 J. Hillis Miller, "Wallace Stevens' Poetry of Being," in *The Act of the Mind: Essays on the Poetry of Wallace Stevens*, ed. Roy Harvey Pearce and J. Hillis Miller (Baltimore: Johns Hopkins University Press, 1965), 150.
5 J. S. Leonard and C. E. Wharton, *The Fluent Mundo: Wallace Stevens and the Structure of Reality* (Athens: University of Georgia Press, 1988), 31, 12.
6 Michael Hardt and Antonio Negri, *Empire* (Cambridge, Mass.: Harvard University Press, 2000), 62.
7 Antonio Negri, *The Savage Anomaly: The Power of Spinoza's Metaphysics and Politics*, trans. Michael Hardt (Minneapolis: University of Minnesota Press, 1991), 213.
8 Hardt and Negri, *Empire*, 357.
9 Jacques Rancière, *Dissensus: On Politics and Aesthetics*, trans. Steven Corcoran (New York: Continuum International, 2010), 87, 85.
10 Ibid., 86.

11 Ibid., 86, 90.
12 Antonio Negri, *Subversive Spinoza*, trans. Timothy S. Murphy et al. (Manchester: Manchester University Press, 2004), 83.
13 Douglas Mao, *Solid Objects: Modernism and the Test of Production* (Princeton, N.J.: Princeton University Press, 1998), 215.
14 Ibid., 216.
15 Ibid., 225, 239.
16 As this statement implies, I read many of the seemingly apolitical paradoxes and aporias of much of Stevens's later work as refractions of the political dilemmas he confronted in the 1930s. According to my account, Stevens was still attempting to resolve these political conflicts, at the level of the imagination, in poems that seem quite remote from the world of the multitude. I will make a case for this position in my meditation on Stevensian spontaneity in the next section.
17 Frank Doggett, "Stevens on the Genesis of a Poem," *Contemporary Literature* 16, no. 4 (Autumn 1975): 467.
18 Wallace Stevens, *The Collected Poems of Wallace Stevens* (New York: Vintage Books, 1990), 58, cited in Doggett, "Stevens on the Genesis of a Poem," 473.
19 Wallace Stevens, *The Letters of Wallace Stevens*, ed. Holly Stevens (Berkeley: University of California Press, 1996), 136, cited in Doggett, "Stevens on the Genesis of a Poem," 468–69.
20 Stevens, *The Necessary Angel*, 115; Stevens, *The Collected Poems*, 301, 299.
21 Antonio Negri, *Reflections on "Empire,"* trans. Ed Emery (Cambridge: Polity Press, 2008), 115.
22 Ibid., 115, 118.
23 Stevens, *The Collected Poems*, 256, 254.
24 Ibid., 335–36.
25 Stevens, *Letters*, 370.
26 Joseph Riddell, *The Clairvoyant Eye: The Poetry and Poetics of Wallace Stevens* (Baton Rouge: Louisiana State University Press, 1965), 134, 122.
27 Angus Cleghorn, *Wallace Stevens' Poetics: The Neglected Rhetoric* (New York: Palgrave, 2000), 106.
28 Ibid., 101.
29 Stevens, *Letters*, 368.
30 Wallace Stevens, *Opus Posthumous*, ed. Milton J. Bates (New York: Vintage Books, 1989), 226, 225.
31 Stevens, *Letters*, 368.
32 Stevens, *The Necessary Angel*, 5, 4.
33 Stevens, *Letters*, 311, 366.
34 Cleghorn, *Wallace Stevens' Poetics*, 64.
35 Stevens, "Owl's Clover," in *Opus Posthumous*, 76.
36 Cleghorn, *Wallace Stevens' Poetics*, 68.
37 Ella Ophir, "'The Mode of Common Dreams': 'Owl's Clover' and the Social Imagination," *Wallace Stevens Journal* 24, no. 1 (Spring 2000): 43.
38 Stevens, *The Collected Poems*, 9, 465.

39 Stevens, *Letters*, 366.
40 Stevens, *Opus Posthumous*, 224.
41 Ibid., 272.
42 Henri Bergson, *Matter and Memory*, trans. N. M. Paul and W. S. Palmer (New York: Zone Books, 1990), 103.
43 Henri Bergson, *The Two Sources of Morality and Religion*, trans. R. Ashley Audra and Cloudesley Brereton (New York: Henry Holt, 1935), 90, 191.
44 Stevens, *The Necessary Angel*, 49.
45 Fredric Jameson, *The Modernist Papers* (London: Verso, 2007), 3.
46 Jameson seems to suggest something along precisely these lines when he claims, parenthetically, that the hubris of modernism's will to aesthetic success parallels the attitude of "middle-class groups driven into innovation by forces beyond their control and intent"—specifically, by those "forces" that drive "the most productive moments of revolutionary praxis." Ibid., 4.
47 Stevens, *Letters*, 367.
48 Frank Lentriccia, *Modernist Quartet* (New York: Cambridge University Press, 1994), 126.
49 Stevens, *The Necessary Angel*, 5.
50 Stevens, *Opus Posthumous*, 76.
51 Stevens, *Letters*, 366.
52 Helen Vendler, *On Extended Wings: Wallace Stevens' Longer Poems* (Cambridge, Mass.: Harvard University Press, 1969), 80, 81.
53 Stevens, *Letters*, 367.
54 In a letter to Hi Simons, Stevens defines "foppery" as that which resists "the evolution of what ought to be." Ibid., 366.
55 Rajeev Patke, *The Long Poems of Wallace Stevens: An Interpretive Study* (New York: Cambridge University Press, 1985), 54.
56 James Longenbach, *Wallace Stevens: The Plain Sense of Things* (New York: Oxford University Press, 1991), 170. Alan Filreis as well sees the "Marxist rhetoric" on display in this passage as salubriously transformed by the paramours' "hymn of reconciliation." Alan Filreis, *Modernism from Right to Left: Wallace Stevens, the Thirties, and Literary Radicalism* (New York: Cambridge University Press, 1994), 232. However, in his account, the paramours' hymn succeeds in "mediating communist and modernist" only at the cost of forecasting the "failure of the revolution . . . by revising the concept of 'change' sufficiently so that . . . it will be recognizable even to the muses" (233). Nevertheless, Filreis and I are fundamentally in agreement that the confrontation between the paramours and the statue involves a confrontation between the poet and some emerging revolutionary collective—one that is not ironized by Stevens but rather is woven into the poem's most weighty political hopes and anxieties. Indeed, Stevens's gloss on the passage contains no hint of irony; in order to adapt, the paramours must look to the future, and, Stevens writes of the passage, "apparently it is to be a future of the mass." Stevens, *Letters*, 366.

57 Milton Bates is one of the critics who notes that the "poem applauds the Marxist insistence on change, revolution, and the future of man." Milton Bates, *Wallace Stevens: A Mythology of Self* (Berkeley: University of California Press, 1985), 176. "Collective self" (177) is the term he uses to describe the composite, internationalist agency of the workers of "Owl's Clover."
58 Stevens, *Letters*, 371, 372.
59 Stevens, *Opus Posthumous*, 224.
60 Stevens, *Letters*, 372.
61 Antonio Negri, *Marx beyond Marx: Lessons on the "Grundrisse,"* trans. Harry Cleaver et al. (Brooklyn: Autonomedia, 1991), 99.
62 Antonio Negri, *Books for Burning: Between Civil War and Democracy in 1970s Italy*, trans. Arianna Bove et al. (London: Verso, 2005), 53.
63 Ibid.
64 Rancière, *Dissensus*, 86.
65 Ernesto Laclau and Chantal Mouffe, *Hegemony and Socialist Strategy: Towards a Radical Democratic Politics* (London: Verso, 2001), 93.
66 Ernesto Laclau, "Can Immanence Explain Social Struggles?" *Diacritics* 31, no. 4 (2001): 8.
67 Stevens, *The Necessary Angel*, 142.
68 Ibid.
69 Fredric Jameson, "Wallace Stevens," *New Orleans Review* 11, no. 1 (Spring 1984): 12, 13, 15, 11.
70 Brogan's attention to Stevens's wish to believe in "a new generational and collective 'hero,'" and his concomitant tendency to ironize or otherwise estrange this wish, is especially relevant in the context of my own analysis. See Jacqueline Vaught Brogan, *The Violence Within / The Violence Without: Wallace Stevens and the Emergence of a Revolutionary Poetics* (Athens: University of Georgia Press, 2003), 63. See also Leon Surette, *The Modern Dilemma: Wallace Stevens, T. S. Eliot, and Humanism* (Montreal: McGill-Queen's University Press, 2008); Alan Filreis, *Wallace Stevens and the Actual World* (Princeton, N.J.: Princeton University Press, 1991); Filreis, *Modernism from Right to Left;* and Mark Halliday, *Stevens and the Interpersonal* (Princeton, N.J.: Princeton University Press, 1991).
71 Justin Quinn, *Gathered beneath the Storm: Wallace Stevens, Nature, and Community* (Dublin: University College Dublin Press, 2002), 83.
72 Stevens, *Letters*, 373.
73 Critics have repeatedly testified to the radical and unique nature of this "remembrance" passage. Robert Emmett Monroe, for example, notes that in the passage "what is posited as the substratum in the problem of poetic figuration turns out to be identical to the human basis of material production." Robert Emmett Monroe, "Figuration and Society in 'Owl's Clover,'" *Wallace Stevens Journal* 13, no. 2 (1989): 141. Harvey Teres stresses the active aspect of this dynamic when he refers to the "unconscious" of "Owl's Clover" as "a source of emancipatory change." Harvey Teres, "Notes toward the Supreme Soviet: Stevens and Doctrinaire Marxism,"

Wallace Stevens Journal 13, no. 2 (1989): 162. Angus Cleghorn, in *Wallace Stevens' Poetics*, captures the collective quality of this unconscious agency in his suggestion that Stevens "turns away from the autonomous artist" and implies "the dreaming mass will be the agents exposing the old lies in their collective night music" (101).

74 In Hegel's *Science of Logic*, Erinnerung denotes the process of re-collection or "inwardizing" whereby social agents cease being inert, self-contained beings and begin to realize themselves in a self-mediating relational movement: "*pure being, the negation* of everything finite, presupposes an *internalization*, a *recollection [Erinnerung]* and movement which has purified immediate, determinate being to pure being." G. W. F. Hegel, *Science of Logic*, trans. A. V. Miller (Amherst: Humanity Books, 1999), 389. "Essence" is Hegel's name for this pure, or self-relating, movement of being. The key, however, is that "the determinatenesses of being are sublated in [essence]; they are contained in essence *in principle [an sich]* but are not *posited in it*" (390). In other words, this "purity" is not a complete evacuation of the personal and social realities that these agents embodied before they began their self-relating movement. It is not a Bergsonian self-annihilation but an unfolding of unexpressed possibilities of being. Similarly, for Stevens it is only through the continuous in-gathering and externalizing movement of re-collection that what is implicit in social being emerges.

75 I am thinking, in particular, of Theodor Adorno's conception of "the humane," which he defines specifically in opposition to praxis. Theodor Adorno, "Marginalia to Theory and Praxis," in *Critical Models: Interventions and Catchwords*, trans. Henry W. Pickford (New York: Columbia University Press, 1998), 262.

76 Jean Hyppolite, *Genesis and Structure of Hegel's "Phenomenology of Spirit,"* trans. Samuel Cherniak and John Heckman (Evanston, Ill.: Northwestern University Press, 1979), 314.

77 Charles Altieri, *Painterly Abstraction in Modernist American Poetry* (University Park: Pennsylvania State University Press, 1989), 356.

78 Ibid., 354.

79 Charles Altieri, "Stevens's Ideas of Feeling: Toward an Exponential Poetics," *Centennial Review* 36, no. 1 (1992): 145.

80 Herbert Marcuse, *Eros and Civilization: A Philosophical Inquiry into Freud* (Boston: Beacon Press, 1966), 143, 142.

81 Ibid., 213.

82 Stevens, *Letters*, 289.

83 Teres, "Notes toward the Supreme Soviet," 151.

84 Antonio Gramsci, *The Prison Notebooks*, trans. Quintin Hoare and Geoffrey Nowell Smith (New York: International Publishers, 1999), 152.

85 Ibid., 340.

Conclusion

1 Jean Baudrillard, *Simulacra and Simulation*, trans. Sheila Faria Glaser (Ann Arbor: University of Michigan Press, 1994), 1.

2 Jean-François Lyotard, *Des dispositifs pulsionnels* (Paris: Éditions Galilée, 1994), 31. Translation mine.
3 Jean-François Lyotard, *Libidinal Economy*, trans. Iain Hamilton Grant (Bloomington: Indiana University Press, 1993), 228.
4 Costas Douzinas and Slavoj Žižek, eds., *The Idea of Communism* (London: Verso, 2010), 146, 207.
5 Slavoj Žižek, *In Defense of Lost Causes* (London: Verso, 2008), 376.
6 Ibid., 378.
7 Douzinas and Žižek, *The Idea of Communism*, 202.
8 Ibid., 173.
9 Jacques Rancière, *La leçon d'Althusser* (Paris: Éditions Gallimard, 1974), 39.

INDEX

Aaron, Daniel, 20
Adorno, Theodor, 24–27, 29–31, 34–36, 238n21, 251n52; on false spontaneity, 50–51; and "the humane," 262n75; on ideology, 108–9; on spontaneity as an individual power, 80; on surrealism, 232n76
Aesthetic Dimension, The (Marcuse), 27
Aesthetic Theory (Adorno), 24–27, 30–31, 55–56
affect, 39, 136, 162–63; as exchange process, 157–58; as a force of mediation, 161; as prediscursive, 41; in the work of Laura Riding, 39, 134–37, 149, 157–58, 161–63; in the work of Wallace Stevens, 200, 215
affective labor. *See* labor: affective
Agamben, Giorgio, 97–99, 221
anarchism, 99, 137, 221; individualist, 140
Anarchism Is Not Enough (Riding): on the cooperative unity of the many, 16; critique of modernism in, 139–43
anarcho-syndicalism. *See* syndicalism
anti-art, 27–28
Ardis, Ann L., 43
Art of Being Ruled, The (Lewis), 120; ideology in, 109; intersubjectivity in, 93; theory of revolution in, 122–23
Autobiography (Williams), 84
automatic writing, 24–25, 27

Autonomia Operaia, 8, 32; collapse of, 14–15
Ayers, David, 250n47

Badiou, Alain, 98–99, 114–15, 119–20, 131, 221
Balibar, Étienne, 33, 233n94
Ball, Hugo, 21
"Basis of Faith in Art, The" (Williams), 34
Bataille, Georges, 257n60
Bates, Milton, 261n57
Baudelaire, Charles, 21
Beck, John, 240n44
Beckett, Samuel, 221
Belgrad, Daniel, 2
Bell, Edward, 240n39
Benhabib, Seyla, 154, 163
Bergson, Henri, 195, 205, 210, 212–13, 245n8, 247n30
Berman, Jessica, 40
Bernstein, Michael André, 240n41
Bevis, William W., 181
Billitteri, Carla, 137–38, 158, 242n65
Blasting and Bombardiering (Lewis): and mixing with the crowd, 21, 95
Bolshevik Party, 22, 124, 157
Bonefeld, Werner, 77
Books for Burning (Negri), 68
Branch, Lori, 251n51
Bremen, Brian A., 240n40, 243n70

Brennan, Timothy, 7
Breton, André, 21, 24
Brogan, Jacqueline Vaught, 208, 261n70
Brown, Nicholas, 41–42, 90, 244n87, 248n33, 249n35
Burke, Kenneth, 81–82

Caliban (Renan), 128–30
Callinicos, Alex, 7
Cameron, Sharon, 229n30
Campbell, SueEllen, 245n8, 251n53
capitalism, 163, 197, 206; as coterminous with the multitude, 230n35; and crisis, 32, 70, 76, 207, 215; equilibration of, 48–9, 63–65, 67–69, 71–74, 78–79, 220–21; as the object of literary representation, 41
Carson, Luke, 138, 151
centralization, 13, 19, 44, 73, 168; Proudhon's hostility toward, 102
Césaire, Aimé, 21
"Chocorua to Its Neighbor" (Stevens), 186–87
civil society, 165, 214
Cleghorn, Angus, 190, 192, 262n73
Clough, Patricia Ticineto, 135
"Collect of Philosophy, A" (Stevens), 195
common, the, 6
Commonwealth (Hardt and Negri), 78, 102
communism, 39, 90, 214, 221; left, 222–23
constituent power, 9, 38, 97–99, 110, 230n35; as collective functionality, 101; as the motor of revolution, 131; as preinstitutional, 103, 115; and the "self-abolishing" party, 114; and self-managed workers' associations, 100; in the work of Wyndham Lewis, 38, 100–105, 131
Counterrevolution and Revolt (Marcuse), 28
crisis. *See* capitalism: and crisis
Cunard, Nancy, 84

Dasenbrock, Reed Way, 37, 249n34, 250–51n48
decentralization, 44
Deficits and Desires (Tratner), 59
de Lauretis, Teresa, 86
Deleuze, Gilles, 85, 111–12, 119–20
depersonalization, 3–6, 12, 18–19, 34, 214, 229–30n32
Derrida, Jacques, 162
Descartes, René, 148, 171
Desnos, Robert, 24
Dickens, Charles, 91
"Disclaimer of the Person" (Riding), 35, 167–76
Doggett, Frank, 186
Douglas, C. H., 59, 66, 72, 239n38, 240n42; as an influence on Williams, 69
Douzinas, Costas, 221
Duffey, Bernard, 240n41

Edwards, Paul, 246n11
ego: as defense against involuntariness, 91
Empire (Hardt and Negri), 9, 152, 228n12
Empire and Beyond (Negri), 230n35
Enemy of the Stars (Lewis), 37–38, 113–24; and constituent power, 38, 131; images of the multitude in, 35, 121–23; models of spontaneity in, 97, 107–10, 116–23
Esteve, Mary, 44
"Extracts from Addresses to the Academy of Fine Ideas" (Stevens), 188

Fables of Aggression (Jameson), 229n32
fascism, 20, 90, 95–97, 112–13, 116, 125–26, 216, 253n67; in the work of Wyndham Lewis, 37–38, 95–98, 112–13, 116–19, 118–19, 125–26, 133
Feeling Modern (Nieland), 41–42, 227n12
Felski, Rita, 153–54
feminism, 86, 135, 150; critique of Negri to be found in the theoretical tradition of, 153

Filreis, Alan, 208, 260n56
Flory, Wendy Stallard, 252n65
Foley, Barbara, 20
Foshay, Toby, 250n47
Foster, Hal, 224n4, 228n13
"Foxes' Case, The" (Lewis), 3
French Communist Party. *See* Parti communiste français
Freud, Sigmund, 19, 83
Futurism, Russian, 22

general intellect, 7, 10, 59, 214
Gesell, Silvio, 81, 240n42, 241n45; and capitalist equilibration, 48, 71; on credit, 66; as an influence on Williams, 69–70, 78; on surplus value, 239n38
Gilbert, Sandra, 86
Gillies, Mary Ann, 245
Giorcelli, Cristina, 86
Grammar of the Multitude, A (Virno), 7
Gramsci, Antonio, 17–19, 26, 36, 103, 185, 203, 214
Graver, David, 250n46
Green, Jesse D., 237n17
Grosz, Elizabeth, 85
Grundrisse (Marx), 10, 69–70
Guattari, Félix, 85
Gubar, Susan, 86

Habermas, Jürgen, 163
Halliday, Mark, 208
Hamilton, Alexander, 72
Hardt, Michael, 6; contra Adorno, 30; on affective labor, 152–53, 176–77; on biopolitics, 135; contra bureaucratic ossification, 157; on civil society, 165; on constituent governance, 102–3; critiqued by feminist theorists, 153; on the crowd, 43; phobia of the negative of, 176–77, 182–84; on self-valorization, 50
Hartsock, Nancy, 153
Head, Philip, 249n35

Hegel, G. W. F., 30–32, 141, 195, 208, 211, 244n87; the concept of *Erinnerung* in the work of, 262n74
Heinzelman, Kurt, 244n83
Hewitt, Andrew, 252–53n67
Hitler, Adolph, 111
Holbo, Christine, 238n19
Huehls, Mitchum, 237–38n18
Huyssen, Andreas, 43

"I Am" (Riding), 143–48; images of the multitude in, 35
Industrial Workers of the World, 49, 236n8
Insurgencies (Negri), 14, 230n35, 233n94
Irigaray, Luce, 87–88
"Irrational Element in Poetry, The" (Stevens), 105–6
Italian Communist Party. *See* Partito Comunista Italiano

Jackson, Laura (Riding). *See* Riding, Laura
James, William, 95, 247n30
Jameson, Frederic, 18, 197, 208, 248n33, 260n46; on depersonalization, 5–6, 229–30n32; on the party, 235n127; on *Paterson*, 58, 240n41; on proto-fascism, 112
Jaurès, Jean, 100
Johnson, Bob, 239n38
Joswick, Thomas P., 238n18
Joyce, James, 40, 139
Jung, Carl, 209

Kenner, Hugh, 239n38, 246n11
Keynes, John Maynard, 68
Khalip, Jacques, 229n30
Klein, Scott, 253
Kora in Hell (Williams), 51–58; images of the multitude in, 47–48, 51–57, 89–90; as an improvisatory work, 47; models of spontaneity in, 51–57
Kropotkin, Pieter, 15, 49, 89, 236–37n9

labor: abstract, 9, 15, 78–79; affective, 135, 149, 152–53, 158, 176–77; associative, 9; gendered division of, 151; immaterial, 7; living, 13, 135; socialization of, 10, 15, 78

Labor of Dionysus (Hardt and Negri), 78

Laclau, Ernesto, 7, 208–9, 235–36n127

Lafargue, Paul, 100

Latimer, Ronald Lane, 201

left communism. *See* communism: left

Lenin, V. I., 13, 235n127, 236n9

Leninism, 10, 14–15, 102, 235n127

Leonard J. S., 181

Levenson, Michael, 94, 228n18

Lewis, Pericles, 39

Lewis, Wyndham: as an advocate of the stable ego, 91; ambivalence about the multitude in the works of, 16; as anti-egoist, 91–92; and constituent power, 38, 100–105; on creative production, 2; critiqued by Laura Riding, 133–34, 139–43; and fascism, 37–38, 95–98, 112–13, 116–19, 125–26, 133; on ideological conditioning, 1–2; images of the multitude in the works of, 35, 104, 121–23, 128–32; models of spontaneity in the work of, 92–98, 105–14, 116–23, 125, 128–32; on the passivity of the multitude, 3; on syndicalism, 100–102, 105

Lion and the Fox, The (Lewis): the role of the proletariat in, 124–27

Liu, Alan, 229n30

Loewinsohn, Ron, 237n14

Longenbach, James, 202

Lukács, Georg, 13, 103, 185, 238n18

Luxemburg, Rosa, 13, 28, 236n9

Lyotard, Jean-François, 219–20

Machiavelli, Niccolò, 33, 233n94

Mackenzie, Gina Masucci, 181

Malcolm, Jane, 150

"Man with the Blue Guitar, The" (Stevens), 209–10

Mao, Douglas, 42, 184–85, 229n27, 247–48n32, 249n35

Marcuse, Herbert, 27–29, 35, 103, 213

Marinetti, F. T., 20

Marx, Karl, 10, 59, 69–71, 100, 104

Marx beyond Marx (Negri), 69, 207

Marxism, 100, 104, 194; in "Owl's Clover," 202, 214–16; Stevens on, 201

Masopust, Michael A., 143, 158

masses, the: as irrational, 8; versus "the multitude," 8–9, 137–38

Massumi, Brian, 135–36

mass worker. *See* worker: mass

Mattick, Paul, 137

Mauss, Marcel, 162

McCann, Sean, 39

McGann, Jerome J., 138, 143

Meyers, Jeffrey, 245

Micro-Politics of Capital, The (Read), 77

Miller, J. Hillis, 181

Miller, Tyrus, 43, 246n11

Minima Moralia (Adorno), 50–51

modernism: conceptualizations of the proletariat, of, 9; figurations of collective life in, 219; importance of the multitude to, 44–45, 90; as a narrative about political spontaneity, 44–45; as regarding sociality as an elsewhere, 151; rhetoric of, used in contemporary theory, 221–22; Riding's critique of, 133–35, 139–43, 149–51, 156, 173; and self-organization, 31, 44–45; suspicions about spontaneity of, 1

Modernist Papers, The (Jameson), 58, 197, 208

Monroe, Robert Emmett, 261n73

Montag, Warren, 164

Mouffe, Chantal, 208–9

multitude, the: as agent, 48, 89–90; as alienated, 60–63, 65–66, 72–73; and biopolitics, 135; as a conflation of intellectual and manual workers, 11–12, 187–88; as coterminous with capitalism, 230n35; versus "the crowd," 43–44; as a directive force, 40, 131, 185, 221; as hypnotically responsive, 35, 143–48; importance of, to modernism, 44–45, 90; as an ineffable "beyond," 47; versus "the masses" and "the people," 8, 137–38; as mute, 191–93; as mutually embedded singularities, 137–38; and negativity, 182–84, 194; as potentiality, 6–7; as proletariat, 7; as self-regulating, 83–86, 88–89, 176–78, 209–16, 222; as spontaneous, 129, 203–8; in the work of Wyndham Lewis, 3, 16, 35, 104, 121–23, 128–32; in the work of Laura Riding, 16, 35, 137–38, 143–48, 176–78; in the work of Wallace Stevens, 184–85, 187–88, 191–93, 203–16; in the work of William Carlos Williams, 34, 47–48, 51–58, 60–63, 65–66, 71–74, 81–90, 220–21

Nancy, Jean-Luc, 221
Natural Economic Order, The (Gesell), 70, 239n38, 240n42, 241n45
negativity, 39, 145–46, 176–79, 181–86; as an attribute of the multitude, 182–84, 194; phobia of, 176–77, 182–84, 207–8; in the work of Wallace Stevens, 39, 181–86, 192, 194, 214, 224
Negri, Antonio, 6; contra Adorno, 30; on affect, 39, 136, 162; on affective labor, 152–53, 176–77; ambivalence about spontaneity of, 14–15; and autonomism, 8, 32; on biopolitics, 135; contra bureaucratic ossification, 157; on civil society, 165; on constituent governance, 101–2; on constituent power, 98–99, 131; critiqued by feminist theorists, 153; on Descartes, 148; contra Hegel, 32; on "the masses" and "the people," 9; phobia of the negative of, 176–77, 182–84, 207–8; and self-organization, 17; on self-valorization, 50; on the "socialized worker," 10; on Spinoza, 31–34

Nekola, Charlotte, 20, 231n64
New Modernist studies, 42
Nieland, Justus, 41–42, 227–28n12
"Noble Rider and the Sound of Words, The" (Stevens), 191, 195
"Notes toward a Supreme Fiction" (Stevens), 187–88
Not-Self, the, 115–16, 105–6; as deception, 109–11; as an emotional mimetic, 103–4; as a figure of political agency, 3, 224; as a form of spontaneity, 107–8, 125; as a social organ, 91
Nott, Kathleen, 258n68

O'Hara, Daniel T., 181
operaismo, 10
Ophir, Ella Zohar, 137–38, 244n4, 255n20
"Owl's Clover" (Stevens): affect in, 200, 215; analysis of, 190–216; communism in, 39, 214; epistemological binarisms in, 190–91; Marxism in, 202, 214–15; the multitude in, 184, 191–93, 203–8, 209–16; and negativity, 39, 192, 214, 224; and the proletariat, 11; and self-organization, 204–8, 224; socialist organizer in, 20; as staging a confrontation between the imagination and the multitude, 184

Pannekoek, Anton, 137, 161
Parti communiste français, 22
Partito Comunista Italiano, 22, 32
party, the, 18, 222–23, 235n127; as constituted power, 99; Leninist, 10; as self-abolishing, 114, 214; as transcendent structure, 183; as vanguard, 8, 13–14, 22, 40
Paterson (Williams): and capitalist equilibration, 48–49, 71–74, 220–21; as an epic focused on systemic forces, 58; images of the multitude in, 47–51, 58, 60–63, 65–66, 71–74, 81–90, 220–21;

Paterson (Williams) *(continued):* models of spontaneity in, 58, 60–63, 80–89; primitive accumulation in, 71, 73, 77–78; self-valorization in, 37, 67, 79–80, 90; and Social Credit, 20, 37, 48–49, 64–67

Patke, Rajeev, 202

people, the: as corollary of the state, 8–9; versus "the multitude," 8

Peppis, Paul, 914, 228n18

"Physics of the Not-Self, The" (Lewis), 3, 91, 105–10, 111–12, 116; models of spontaneity in, 106–10

Political Unconscious, The (Jameson), 230n32

Politics of Subversion, The, (Negri), 14

Post-Marxism, 44

Postone, Moishe, 253n72

potentiality, 19, 78–79, 206; as a capacity for recombination, 209

Poulantzas, Nicolas, 248n33

Pound, Ezra, 20–21, 155; conflation of employer and employee in, 241n45; on credit, 66, 219, 240n42; and leadership, 59, 67

primitive accumulation, 71, 73; permanence of, 77–78, 241n53

Prison Notebooks, The (Gramsci), 18

private sphere, the, 134, 151–52, 154, 163–65, 175; as gendered female, 131; as related to industrialization, 154; as the source of spontaneous organization, 156–57

proletariat, 10, 11, 221; modernist conceptualizations of, 9; as spontaneous agent, 14–15; in the work of Wyndham Lewis, 124–27; in the work of Wallace Stevens, 11

Proudhon, Pierre-Joseph, 69, 78, 99–102; on equilibration, 71

public, the, 3, 227–28n12

public sphere, the, 134, 148, 159, 175; as characterized by abstract reciprocity, 163–65; as commercialized, 138

Quéma, Anne, 124
Quinn, Justin, 209

Rabinowitz, Paula, 20
Rancière, Jacques, 207, 223; on the negativity of political subjects, 182–83
Rashid, Haroun al, 120, 252n67
Read, Jason, 77, 241n53
Reich, Wilhelm, 81, 85
Renan, Ernest, 128
Rhodes, Shane, 243n70
Richards, I. A., 141
Riddell, Joseph, 190
Riding, Laura: and affect, 39, 134–37, 149, 157–58, 161–63; ambivalence about the multitude in the work of, 16; on creative production, 2; as a critic of Wyndham Lewis, 133–34, 139–43; critique of modernism in the work of, 133–35, 139–43, 149–51, 156, 173; depersonalization in the work of, 4; on ideological conditioning, 1; images of the multitude in the works of, 35, 137–38, 143–48, 176–78; models of spontaneity in the work of, 38–39, 133–35, 139–48, 149–51, 158–59, 165, 167, 169, 171–78; the private and the public in the works of, 131, 134–35, 138, 148, 151–52, 154, 156–57, 159, 163–65, 175; and self-organization, 39; vision of self-government in the work of, 158–67
Rilke, Rainer Maria, 43
Rimbaud, Arthur, 21
Rocker, Rudolph, 137, 157, 161
Rodgers, Audrey T., 237n15
Romains, Jules, 21–22
Rousseau, Jean-Jacques, 101
Russian Revolution, 15, 33
Russian Revolution, The (Luxemburg), 13
Rustin, Michael, 11

Samuels, Lisa, 138
Schnapp, Jeffrey T., 43

Schopenhauer, Arthur, 245n8
Schultz, Susan M., 150
Schultz, Susanne, 153
self-extinction. *See* depersonalization
self-organization, 17, 222; as employed by Habermas, 164–65; and modernism, 31, 44–45; as opposed to the party and the state, 9; as opposed to vanguardism, 14; and the "socialized worker," 10; in the work of Laura Riding, 39; in the work of Wallace Stevens, 39, 204–8, 224
self-valorization, 9, 49, 50; versus bureaucracy, 159; as a limit to capital, 69; as the reproduction of the multitude's own capacities, 50; as simultaneously inside and outside of capital, 67–69; in the work of William Carlos Williams, 37, 50, 67, 79–80, 90
Shakespeare, William, 91, 124, 128
Shelley, Percy Bysshe, 199
Sherry, Vincent, 91, 228n13
Sieburth, Richard, 239n38, 241n45
Simons, Hi, 209, 215
"Sketch of the Ultimate Politician" (Stevens), 188–89
slavery, 75–76, 77
Smith, Dorothy E., 153
Social Credit, 20, 37, 59–60, 63–67, 72–74, 81, 90, 216; and capitalist equilibration, 48–49, 63–65, 71, 220; metaphorics of, 66–67; as reformist, 239n38, 240n44; as similar to economic models in the work of Lyotard, 220; in the work of William Carlos Williams, 37, 48–49, 63–67, 69, 78, 240n40
socialization. *See* labor: socialization of
socialized worker. *See* worker: socialized
Socrates: as a man among the multitude, 108, 111–12, 122
Sorel, Georges, 99–102, 104, 124, 245n8
Soupault, Philippe, 24
Spengler, Oswald, 139, 142

Spinoza, Baruch, 31–34, 135, 182, 233n94
spontaneity: as acting on impulse, 92–92; artistic production and, 2, 12, 15–16, 24–27, 47–48, 110, 184, 189–90, 193–94; as automaticity, 139; versus automaticity, 25; as collective self-regulation, 83, 89, 97, 129, 130, 158–59, 165, 177–78, 209–16; as collective unconscious memory, 186; as deception, 110, 113–14, 130, 133, 143–48; and depersonalization, 4; as experimentation, 134, 141–43; as gendered female, 151; as gendered male, 141–43, 151; as ideological reflex, 1, 29, 106, 108–9, 181; as immanent self-valorization, 49–50; as an individual power, 51–52, 80, 197–201; as intersubjective, 134, 149–50, 169, 174–76, 202–8; as involving negativity, 181–84; as "irrationalism," 24; as mass action occurring outside institutional channels, 17, 49; mediated, 27–29, 95–96, 103, 105; of the Not-Self, 107–8, 125; as preaccomplished, 167, 171; and the private sphere, 156–57; as public, 3; as a spiritual discipline, 108–9; as systemic recalibration, 50; as walking abroad in a common world, 93, 172–73; in the work of Wyndham Lewis, 92–98, 105–14, 116–23, 125, 128–32; in the work of Antonio Negri, 14–15; in the work of Laura Riding, 38–39, 139–48, 133–35, 149–51, 158–59, 165, 167, 169, 171–78; in the work of Wallace Stevens, 39, 186, 189–90, 193–94, 197–201, 202–16; in the work of Williams Carlos Williams, 48–58, 60–63, 80–90
"Spontaneity of the Masses and the Activity of the Party, The" (Lukács), 13
"Spontaneity of the Masses and the Consciousness of the Social-Democrats, The" (Lenin), 13

state, the, 223; as based personal anonymity, 159; as constituted power, 99; as corollary of "the people," 8–9; as transcendent structure, 183; as unable to represent the mass movement, 98

Stein, Gertrude, 24, 139, 141

Stevens, Wallace: and affect, 200, 215; and communism, 39, 214; on creative production, 2; depersonalization in, 4; images of the multitude in, 35, 185, 187–88, 191–93, 203–16; on Marxism, 201; models of spontaneity in the work of, 39, 186, 189–90, 193–94, 197–201, 202–16; and negativity, 39, 181–86, 192, 194, 214, 224; and self-organization, 39, 204–8, 224

Stirner, Max, 94, 250n47

Stockton, Sharon, 254n1

Stolze, Ted, 164

Sumner, Charles, 252

Surette, Leon, 208

surplus value, 70, 87, 89, 239n38

surrealism, 232n76

syndicalism, 99–101, 105, 137, 161, 162, 222, 249n35; opposed to bureaucratic ossification, 157–8; as opposed to individualist anarchism, 140; in the work of Wyndham Lewis, 100–102, 105

Szalay, Michael, 43

Teres, Harvey, 214, 261n73

Time and Western Man (Lewis): critique of pantheistic merger in, 93

Tomlin, E. W. F., 245n8

Toscano, Alberto, 223

Tratner, Michael, 40, 59

Trotsky, Leon, 15, 251n48

Ulysses (Joyce), 40

Utopian Generations (Brown), 42

Vattimo, Gianni, 221

Vendler, Helen, 199

Virno, Paolo, 7, 59

virtuality, 3, 45, 227–28n12

Wagner, Geoffrey, 246n11

Wald, Alan, 20

Walkowitz, Rebecca, 40, 42

Warner, Michael, 227n12

Washington, George, 75

"Was Weiter" (Luxemburg), 13

Welge, Jobst, 43

Wharton, C. E., 181

Williams, William Carlos: ambivalence about the multitude in the works of, 16; and capitalist equilibration, 48–49, 71–74; on creative production, 2; on credit, 219–20; depersonalization in the work of, 3–4; on ideological conditioning, 1; images of the multitude in the work of, 34, 47–48, 51–58, 60–63, 65–66, 71–74, 81–90, 220–21; images of self-valorization in the work of, 37, 50, 67, 79–80, 90; models of spontaneity in the work of, 48–58, 60–63, 80–90; and primitive accumulation, 71, 73, 77–78; and Social Credit, 37, 48–49, 63–67, 69, 78, 240n40

Wood, Ellen Minkins, 11

Woolf, Virginia, 139, 141

worker: mass, 10; socialized, 10, 33

workers' councils, 14–15, 98–99, 161, 221–22, 249n35

working class. *See* proletariat

World and Ourselves, The (Riding), 39, 154–67; against the multitude as a subject of knowledge, 16; importance of overproduction to, 154–55; vision of self-government in, 158–67

Young, Iris, 163

Zabriskie, George, 67

Žižek, Slavoj, 221–23, 235–36n127

JOEL NICKELS is assistant professor of English at the University of Miami.

www.ingramcontent.com/pod-product-compliance
Lightning Source LLC
Chambersburg PA
CBHW031802220426
43662CB00007B/495